MW00761256

AT DEATH HE WAS 25 YEARS OLD

Background and Biographies of
20th Century Service Casualties
in Small Town America –

Ridgewood, New Jersey
1894 to 2004

Based on the award winning series
"Recalling First Line News"
As published in *The Ridgewood News*,
Ridgewood, N.J.

Christopher C. Stout
Published by King of Spain Press LLC
Ridgewood, NJ

For the
Garcia family —
Thanks for keeping the
memory of Ronnie Helms
alive —

C Smit
08/05/2009

Published by
King of Spain Press LLC
P.O. Box 221
Hohokus, NJ 07423
kospress@aol.com
ISBN 1583968490

Printed in the United States of America by
Long Dash Publishing
368 Stratford Road
Brooklyn, NY 11218
718-940-0450
longdash@gmail.com

3rd Edition

Acknowledgements

This book could not have been possible without the support and encouragement of the Ridgewood Public Library, in particular local historians Peggy Norris and Joe Suplicki, the Ridgewood Village Council, the Superintendent of Ridgewood Schools and the many friends who encouraged me in my research. Later editions became necessary as new information became available.

Thanks also to the many friends and relatives of our martyrs who cooperated by providing information, photos and anecdotes. I am especially grateful for the patience and understanding of my wife and daughter who must have thought I would never finish or do anything else through many months of work.

I wish to dedicate this book to the youth of Ridgewood, of Bergen County, NJ and of America in memory of all young people of all times who died in the service of their country.

Please don't forget to say thank you.

"It is, in a way, an odd thing
to honor those who died in defense
of our country in wars far away.
The imagination plays a trick.

"We see these soldiers in our mind
as old and wise. We see them as
something like the founding fathers,
grave and gray-haired.

"But most of them were boys when
they died. They gave up two lives:
the one they were living and
the one they would have lived.

"When they died, they gave up their
chance to be husbands and fathers
and grandfathers. They gave up
their chance to be revered old men.
They gave up everything for
their country. For us.

"All we can do is remember."

President Ronald W. Regan
Arlington National Cemetery
November 11, 1985

CONTENTS

2LT. Leonard Cowherd, 22, who died in May 2004 in Iraq, wrote in his last letter to his wife, Sarah "Some of these guys out here, Sarah, they are just kids. If you saw them walking down the street, you would think they belong in the arcade at a movie theater, hanging out with their friends, getting in trouble, doing stuff kids do – not putting their lives on the line, every second of every day."

All wars are boyish,
and are fought by boys.

Herman Melville
"The March into Virginia"
Battlepieces and Aspects
of the War (1866)

Preface

One evening I was tuned in to the History Channel when my young teenaged daughter came in and asked what I was watching. When I told her it was a documentary film from World War II she said "oh! They had cameras in those days?" Her reaction made me realize that, to her and her generation, any historical event that pre-dated her cognizant life was ancient history and anyone who served in Vietnam, Korea, World War II or World War I could just as easily have fought for George Patton, George Washington, King George or Saint George. I decided to try to teach her generation, and to remind older generations, that the history of war is not a blur of overlapping events and dates. There are carefully defined timelines inside of which is one constant feature - the participants. They are generally young.

Industrial-strength foolishness sets in
in males, at least –
at about the age of 18.
This is why the military prefers males in the 18 – 25
year old range
when there's combat to be done.
Russell Baker, The New York Times 4/1/94

In order to bring this reality closer to home, I researched the lives of all the casualties listed on the memorial plaques in my hometown of Ridgewood, New Jersey and found that these people were talented and comfortable young men and women, just like you and me, who were suddenly uprooted and thrown into the alien atmosphere of combat to preserve their heritage and to assure the future of that heritage.

When I first looked at Ridgewood's memorial plaques, I realized that for me, and perhaps many others, these casualties had become nothing more than a list of anonymous names - once unforgettable, now forgotten. On the premise that a

1

man is not dead until he is forgotten, I decided to find out who they were and to create a permanent archive so that these people will never be forgotten and can therefore live forever. This book is the fruit of that research, the foundation of which was the list of names on Ridgewood's memorial plaques. The result of the research is that, with the discovery of one additional casualty, what for many years had been Ridgewood's 112 Honored Dead became Ridgewood's 113 Honored Dead.

Because of this research, the memorial plaque at the war monument in Van Neste Square in Ridgewood, NJ was changed and rededicated on Memorial Day May 31, 2004 to reflect the corrected spellings of 17 names. To avoid any confusion, the corrected plaque indicates the names of the casualties as they are inscribed on the person's burial marker. The $2,500 cost of the new plaque, which was furnished by Memorial Arts of Ridgewood, was more than 50% financed by private donations, with the Village of Ridgewood covering the balance.

In my mind, the value of doing and documenting this sort of research is to allow subsequent generations to see and appreciate the personal sacrifices – the supreme sacrifices – made by young people just like you and me but at another time. To this end, I have tried to show how these people lived as well as how they died.

Actuarial tables say that at age 25 a person is barely one third of the way through their normal life span. They have half a century of life, career, family and happiness ahead of them. By the time a person reaches the age of 25 years old, many have finished several years of school, "retired" from amateur careers as athletes, musicians or artists and left their parents to start a life on their own. They have begun a career, begun a family. And if they came from Bergen County, New Jersey they have benefited from strong school systems and municipal infrastructures, good churches and a generally pleasant social and cultural life style. It is therefore difficult in this day and age to imagine how a young person coming from such a protected environment can be transformed from the passivity of urban life to the chaos of combat; how a kid just like yours or mine who once would help a wounded bird only a few months later would willingly kill another human being. The book includes the contradiction of festive send-offs of new draftees early in WWII to distraught parents trying to get information on their dead sons long after the fighting had stopped.

In this age of flavored floss and scented toilette paper, it is difficult to imagine sitting outside, unprotected and drenched in constant monsoon rains, living outside in a sub-freezing winter with constantly drenched feet, frequent diarrhea, rare food and no personal hygiene. In this age of crisp clean shirts every day it is difficult to image not changing clothes for days or weeks at a time. In an age of bungee jumpers, it is out of the question to jump out of an airplane at 25,000 feet in the dead of winter. None of us would ever think of going off to war with the sole purpose of killing OURSELVES! Can anybody appreciate the irony of a decorated serviceman who celebrated victory in combat only to die in a non-combat accident? Do you know what it is like to see a whole generation of our youth, including your own 18 year-old son, go off to unknown places to kill other human beings? For most of us all this is an unreal world. Some people can imagine all of this because they remember it, because they lived it. But over half a million Americans don't remember because they died for it. To those of you who were surprised to learn that there were movie cameras in WWII, I hope you will never go through the experiences described in this book.

It was different when America was at war. In this book I share with you what I have learned about a dozen dozen men and women who called

3

Bergen County, New Jersey home and whose average age at death while performing military duty was just 25 years old – thus the title of the book.

A representative microcosm of all the young Americans who went to war, these young people were raised and lived within a few miles of each other but died thousands of miles from each other, sometimes as a result of ironic turns of fortune. They looked like you and me, thought like you and me; they were the teacher's pet, their grandmother's favorite, the kid next door.

"Yet this corporate being,
though so insubstantial to our senses,
binds a man to his country with ties which,
though light as air,
are as strong as links of iron.
That is why young men die in battle for their country
and why old men plant trees
they will never sit under."
Walter Lippmann

There have been many 20th century retrospectives, some covering the whole century and some covering specific events, several about men and women who served their country in time of war. They were the answer to their country's immediate needs and the promise for their country's future, people who went on to make a variety of contributions to their community and to America in many different endeavors.

This book is the flip side of that scenario - about young people from New Jersey, from Bergen County and most specifically from Ridgewood who served their country in 20th century conflicts, beginning with the deflowering of Ridgewood in 1918 when news came of our first war casualty and brought with it the realization that no city, town or village is immune.

4

They too were the answer to their country's needs and the promise of their country's future. But these people did not have the opportunity to make contributions after the war. They meant to build the future of their country but instead they laid the foundation. Their contribution was immediate and everlasting - it was the ultimate sacrifice, made with the hope that others could "laugh and be well", to quote one of them. Unrealized promises that would have been, could have been, should have been. The promise of their lives was their sacrifice; their sacrifice was made for our future. They gave their today for our tomorrow.

The prolific author, Anonymous, wrote this Eulogy for a Veteran:

> *Do not stand at my grave and weep.*
> *I am not there, I do not sleep.*
> *I am a thousand winds that blow.*
> *I am the diamond glints on snow.*
> *I am the sunlight on ripened grain.*
> *I am the Gentle autumn rain.*
> *When you awaken in the morning's hush,*
> *I am the swift uplifting rush*
> *of quiet birds in circled flight,*
> *I am the soft stars that shine at night.*
> *Do not stand at my grave and cry,*
> *I am not there, I did not die.*

PART I

Memorial Day, originally called Decoration Day, is a day of remembrance for those who have died in our nation's service. Memorial Day was first officially proclaimed on May 5, 1868 by General John Logan and was first observed on May 30, 1868 when flowers were placed on the graves of Union and Confederate soldiers at Arlington National Cemetery. That was a long time ago.

I remember as a child, during many years after WWII, decorating my bike so I could participate in the Memorial Day Parade, riding with all the other kids behind the high school band and the veterans as they proudly marched in uniform. That too was a long time ago.

Now there are no more big parades and only relatives and the American Legion go to the cemetery. The last vestige of any such public manifestation in Ridgewood, New Jersey is the Memorial Day service at the war memorial in Van Neste Square.

Van Neste Square sits in the heart of Ridgewood. It is what many would refer to as the town-square and is used for a variety of local manifestations - from Easter egg hunts to car shows. Centered on the west side of the square is a memorial park, the centerpiece of which is a monument to Ridgewood's 20th century war casualties - what American Legion Post 53 calls Ridgewood's 113 Honored Dead. The 113 names are listed along with a reference to all others who died in the service, although their names are not listed. Perhaps they should be. Just because they did not die in an official "period of service" in no way diminishes their contributions to their country. Their deaths are as great a loss to their families and community as any other premature death.

The monument is a classic revival memorial column which was designed by Henry Bacon, architect of the Lincoln Memorial in Washington,

6

D.C. Made of Georgia marble, it weighs 183 tons and stands 34' high. The cost to village was $18,000. Despite a cold wind and snow flurries, the memorial was dedicated in the afternoon of Sunday November 9, 1924 in the presence of 5,000 people. After letters to Mayor Garber from President Coolidge and General Pershing were read, the mother of Jesse Douglass, a World War I casualty, unveiled the monument. It is now the backdrop for annual Memorial Day ceremonies honoring Ridgewood's war dead.

At the dedication in 1924, Oliver Surpless, Chairman of the Memorial Committee, called upon the citizens to " foster every effort to bring the leading races of the world closer to one another in the arts of peace so that our children will be spared disaster, suffering and a sacrifice, compared to which we have experienced but a pale preliminary." As these words were spoken, an imprisoned veteran of the defeated Kaiser's army sat in a cell and penned *Mein Kampf.*

On November 16, 1930 a plaque listing the 14 WWI casualties was placed on the monument and on Armistice Day 1931 an individual plaque honoring each World War I casualty was attached to ash trees planted in Graydon Park, many of which can still be seen. In 1964 the names if Ridgewood's WWII and Korean casualties were added. Plaques honoring casualties from Vietnam were later added to the monument. Two additional casualties from WWII and two additional casualties from Vietnam were added in 1989. Six additional WWII casualties were added in 1991. The 113th casualty was added in 2004. The average age of all these martyrs was 25 years old.

Abraham Lincoln spoke of "the silent artillery of time" which will accomplish what all our enemies have not accomplished as the survivors of the same battles that took our martyrs are slowly swept away. Think of that next Memorial Day and thank a veteran.

War Memorial Monument,
Van Neste Square
Ridgewood, NJ

"Madam, I took away your son,
but I give you back the memory of a hero.
Each year we will celebrate together
his immortal passing."

A. A. Milne

8

The monument faces west and, in 2008, there was discussion about rotating the monument 180° to face into the park. Since its initial installation, the Opera House has been replaced by a bus station and parking lot, separated from Van Neste Memorial Park by Oak Street. Guests and speakers sit on Oak Street during Veterans' Day and Memorial Day ceremonies, facing the monument, as they did in 1924.

The question was asked if it was significant that the eagle on the war memorial faces west. It was pointed out that at the time the war memorial was dedicated the expression "gone west" had a clear meaning. In reading articles about our WWI casualties, the expression often appears as meaning death, or dying. At that time, British soldiers in France developed a terminology that was plain to them, albeit confusing to civilians. They spoke of "Blighty," and of "Gone West." Blighty meant home for rest and recuperation. "Gone West" meant gone from the east with its conflict to the refuge of death, where peace waits in the glory of sunset.

GOING WEST
"West to the hills, the long, long trail that strikes
Straight and away into the sunset's glow,
Ribbed by the narrow barriers of Death--
Dark are the waters that beside it flow.
The red flowers fade upon the fields of France.
The soaring larks are fallen to their nest.
The glare of battle soothes a little space....
As they go west.... "

Hugh Pendexter, in *Adventure Magazine*, says "going west," used to mean death, is of American origin. The Karok Indians of California believed the spirit of the good Karok went to the "happy western land." The Cherokee myths picture the west as the "ghost country," the twilight land where the dead go. The Shawnee tell of the boy who "traveled west"

9

to find his sister in the spirit land. The Chippewa believes the spirit "followed a wide, beaten path toward the west". The spirit world of the Fox Indians is at the setting of the sun.

Further, North American pilots also use the expression "gone west". Meetings of pilots often start with a toast to those who have "gone west". The pilots face the west and drink to those who have died. West, in this case, refers to the place the sun sets or is extinguished. Also, *Wings & Airpower* Magazine's obituaries are listed under the heading "Gone West".

However, no memorial protocol has been found which requires that monuments face west and the monument, as of this writing, has not been rotated.

PART II

Ridgewood's 113 Honored Dead
- 112 Men, 1 Woman

World War I

The Office of the Actuary at the Department of Veterans Affairs in Washington gives April 6, 1917 to November 11, 1918 as the dates for Periods of Service in World War I.

In 1918 Ridgewood was a much smaller village than it is today – a more intimate place where everybody knew everybody else, where people had almost an insular attitude toward the outside world. Nonetheless, as reported in the *Ridgewood Herald News* of the time, on Tuesday March 20, 1917 the Ridgewood Village Council met in front of a record crowd who came to hear "what was proposed for home defense" for the village and its neighbors from Glen Rock, Midland Park and Hohokus. The police force was appointed as the nucleus of the Home Guard with the assistance of 30 firemen and their deputies. Functions included "watching any resident who might by his past record or actions in the Village cause him to be looked upon with suspicion" and enlisting citizens who had firearms to arrange for the training of the Home Guard. Owners of automobiles were asked to volunteer their services for transportation of men, the YMCA offered its facilities and staff for the physical training of the Home Guard and "older" men were asked to do clerical duties and lend financial and moral support. Citizens were encouraged to use their gardens for the production of vegetables.

Suddenly, in February 1918, the village was rocked by the news that one of its favorite sons had died in the service. Reading reports from the time, one gets the impression that Ridgewooders felt that nothing like this could happen to them. Reality struck home hard.

A month later, Ridgewood adopted the tradition of placing a Golden Star on the Village Service Flag. Families who lost a loved one in the service became known as gold star families, more specifically gold star mothers. Subsequently, 13 more gold stars were added to Ridgewood's Service Flag in WWI. The tradition has lasted to today.

If Ridgewood was shocked by the news of its first casualty in February, the village read of nothing else later in the year. Of the 14 village casualties of WWI, 11 died in the 3-month period from August 27 to November 14, 1918. 6 of the 14 died within 9 days of each other as the war wound down in deadly fashion.

Thomas Milton Boyd	USA 10/2/18
John A. Cadmus	France 9/29/18
Thomas W. Connor	France 9/29/18
Leonard De Brown	France 10/25/18
George R. Denie	France 2/1/19
Jesse E. Douglass	France 9/30/18
Lindley De Garmo	England 2/16/18
William Kruskopf	France 9/24/18
Frank M. Patterson, Jr.	USA 8/27/18
Floyd A. Stevens	France 6/12/18
Ulmont A. White	USA 9/28/18
Charles Wolfhegel	France 11/14/18
Daniel S. Yeomans	France 10/8/18
Jacob A. Yeomans	France 10/27/18

Often forgotten is the fact that more people died in 1918 of illness than of war. In a few early autumn weeks in 1918 an epidemic of Spanish Influenza ravaged the United States. It was called the Spanish Flu because it was believed to have been carried to the USA on a Coast Guard Cutter from Spain. You would be working with someone one day, they would go home because they didn't feel well and within days they were gone. Remote Eskimo villages in inaccessible Alaskan regions were completely wiped out. The flu began with a high fever and aching bones. After about four days, many cases developed pneumonia. The lungs of the victims would fill with fluid, causing death. Highly contagious, "open face sneezing" in public was subject to fines and imprisonment. The death toll around the world was 21 million of which 548,452 were in the USA – five times more than the 116,700 American lives lost in WWI. The Spanish Flu killed its millions and then mysteriously disappeared.

It also circulated in the military, striking first at Fort Riley, Kansas in March 1918 but remaining relatively dormant until the fall. Eventually a call-up of 140,000 draftees was canceled because camp hospitals were full. Two of Ridgewood's 113 Honored Dead died within a week or each other, victims of the flu. Two additional victims are among Ridgewood High School's honored service dead.

Ridgewood's first victim of Spanish Influenza was Ulmont White who went to Lafayette College in Easton, Pa. to join the Lafayette Student's Army Training Corps but immediately developed a severe cold and died of Spanish Influenza.

Another victim of the flu was Thomas Boyd who joined a Medical Detachment in the Sanitary Corps. only to die a month later of septic pneumonia developed from Spanish influenza.

The third victim of the flu was Arthur Warren Travell whose family moved to New York after he graduated from RHS in 1916. He too died of Spanish Influenza, while at Cornell.

Another RHS graduate who succumbed to the flu was James Hubbard of Allendale who graduated from Ridgewood High School in the class of 1914 and died aboard the USS *Arizona* December 23, 1918 of Spanish Meningitis.

4.7 million Americans enrolled for WWI of which 424 were from Ridgewood. 116,708 died, including 14 from Ridgewood. Ridgewood's first

13

World War I casualty was Lindley De Garmo who died February 16, 1918 in an air crash outside London.

Subsequent research shows he was not Ridgewood's first casualty of the 20th century. The January 18, 1901 issue of the *Ridgewood Herald* announces that George H. Rae, whose family lived in Ridgewood, was killed in Luzon, Philippines December 30, 1900 while serving with the Engineer Corps during the Philippine Insurrection.

World War II
The Office of the Actuary at the Department of Veterans Affairs in Washington gives December 7, 1941 to December 31, 1946 as the official dates for Periods of Service for World War II.

The 1940 census of Ridgewood gave the population as just under 15,000 and the village advertised itself as "The Garden Spot of the Garden State". But if WWI had brought the shock of the human cost of war to provincial Ridgewood, by the time the USA entered WWII warning flags were up all over as dictatorship had taken root in Europe. André Gide wrote in his Journals September 13, 1938 "It is easier to lead men into combat and to stir up their passions than to temper them and urge them to the patient labors of peace." A month later, on October 26, Franklin D. Roosevelt, in a Radio Address, said "You cannot organize civilization around the core of militarism and at the same time expect reason to control human destinies."

Events like Jesse Owens' victory over the "Super Race" in the Berlin Olympics in 1936, Joe Louis' knock out of the symbol of "Aryan superiority" Max Schmeling in 1938 and Don Budge's Davis Cup victory at Wimbledon over Baron von Cramm in 1939 had the free world - and Ridgewood - more than geared up to fight Hitler.

Regardless, the US was ill prepared. In 1939 the US Army/Air Force ranked 17th in the world with a headcount of 615,256 compared to Turkey with 710,000, Rumania with 1,800,000, Japan with 6,271,000, Germany with 7,188,000 and Italy with 7,633,000. And then Pearl Harbor was attacked.

Unlike World War I, Korea or Vietnam, the quest for revenge after Pearl Harbor was such that many young Americans voluntarily left school or quit their jobs to enlist. They volunteered until the draft made that decision for them. The Selective Service Training Act was signed in September 1940 requiring all men between 21and 36 to register for the draft.

Ridgewood's local draft board, District No. 3, which covered Ridgewood, Paramus, Glen Rock and Midland Park, met for the first time October 16, 1940. President Roosevelt pulled the name of the first man to be drafted on October 26. By December 7, 1941 many Ridgewood men had sensed the threat of war and had already volunteered or been drafted into military service. Shortly after Pearl Harbor the age window was opened for men aged 18 to 64 with men aged 20 to 45 most eligible for immediate call-up.

Everybody had to register for the draft, although initially it was anticipated that 65% would be excused from service for one reason or another. Ridgewood's first draft registration counted only 1,265 men. Others registered near where they worked. To prepare them for being called up, there were monthly "Off-to-Camp Information Meetings" at the Ridgewood YMCA for "new selectees" where they could learn the ways of the military and prepare for their new life in the service.

Initially, enlistment standards were high but, as manpower needs increased, many who were initially classified 4-F (including convicted felons) suddenly were re-classified as 1-A. Standards were relaxed to the point that it was said that if you could pass the physical there was a good chance you would be accepted in a cadet program. There was a joke going around that if two medical officers, one looking up your rear end and the other down your throat didn't see each other, you were in. One-third of all inductees failed their physicals. Some who failed did so because of the eye test; many promptly memorized the eye chart, took the exam again and passed. The draft did not apply to women, all of whom served in WWII as volunteers.

The village also anticipated the conflict: on that same fateful December 7th day, the headline of the Ridgewood *Sunday News* announced that between 150 and 200 air raid wardens would be appointed to head up air raid protection in Ridgewood. Immediately after the attack on Pearl Harbor, Ridgewood's Red Cross War Fund was begun with a target of $20,000.

Draftees left from the Beech Street School; in the early days of the war there was music, a prayer and a speech before the draftees were loaded on a bus for Fort Dix. But soon it was decided that going off to kill other humans should not be a happy occasion so the festivities were toned down and the ceremonies were limited to a short talk by the mayor and a roll call by the Secretary of the draft board. The Defense Service Council's U.S.O. committee gave each draftee a sewing kit - and then they got on the bus.

The next year, school children submitted to regular air raid warnings, ration boards were established to govern the use (or lack of use) of sugar, rubber and eventually gasoline and fuel oil. Nonetheless, the July 4th parade was maintained, including the fireworks. In no other war was the participation in the war effort of the civilian population as evident and widespread as it was in WWII.

It was in 1943 that the village, and the rest of the country, truly began to feel the cost of the war as the names of more and more local boys were listed among the casualties. On the home front, the war's insatiable need for fuel to power the military machine and rubber for its tires resulted in the

16

imposition of restrictions. The lack of young men curtailed the distribution of newspapers and magazines; home delivery of groceries was halted. Other items rationed included firewood, typewriters, bicycles, coffee, processed food, soft cheese and finally sugar. Americans were urged to eat a meatless diet on Tuesdays.

Vacation travel was severely restricted because of the lack of gasoline and tires. The Ridgewood Country Club had to lock up their supply of pre-war golf balls in a bank vault and strictly ration their sale to club members only. The Victory Book Campaign gathered used books for distribution to troops overseas. Housewives saved the fat from cooking for use in munitions. The story has it that collection points would post signs saying "Ladies, please do not bring your fat cans in here on Thursdays". Slogans on war posters included "A careless word ... another cross", "Save your cans ... help pass the ammunition", "Salvage Victory – throw your scrap into the fight:" "enemy ears are listening". A 5% Victory Tax was imposed on incomes over $624 a year and Victory Bonds went on sale. Children would buy war savings stamps at school. When their savings stamp book was full they would pay $18.75 for a War Savings Bond that would be worth $25 in 10 years.

Ridgewoodites adapted by switching from fuel oil to coal and by planting their own "victory gardens" at home. Victory Gardens were the suggestion of the Secretary of Agriculture who said American farmers would be too busy producing food for servicemen so civilians should grow their own food. Over 20 million victory gardens were planted – in back yards and on rooftops. Frozen food lockers could be rented to preserve the produce of these gardens. Graydon Pool opened on schedule, concerts went on as usual and, with an eye to the future, the concept of a hospital in Ridgewood became a reality as contracts were signed for the purchase of land on the corner of

Van Dien and Linwood Avenues. Nonetheless, business was not entirely as usual, particularly for the following:

Wm. L. de Forest Anderson	Pacific 7/11/42
Thomas E. Ashton, Jr.	Pacific 3/15/43
William G. Bavin	Holland 9/18/44
Robert O. Bennett	Mediterranean 11/27/43
Robert W. Berkhofer	Germany 4/13/45
Lester Richard Bessell, Jr.	Mediterranean 9/11/43
Robert Armstrong Black, Jr.	Pacific 8/19/44
Joseph A. Bowen	Germany 11/23/44
John James Brickell	Germany 2/20/45
Charles Elmer Brooks	Italy 12/24/43
William R. Burnett	Hawaii 4/13/44
Eugene J. Busteed	Philippines 3/6/45
William Todd Campbell	Bougainville 1/8/44
Thomas J. Carroll, Jr.	Germany 3/16/45
Alan R. Clarke	N. Atlantic 3/2/43
Thomas Anthony Cobb	France 12/25/44
Richard H. Condo	Italy 4/14/45
Charles D. Connolly	USA 6/17/44
Gordon E. Dempsey	France 7/31/44
John R. de Richemonde, Jr.	Nova Scotia 4/24/45
Davis H. Dunn	Pacific 6/18/44
Richard A. Dwenger	Mediterranean 10/9/43
William Stratton Easterly	Germany 4/11/44
John Faas	Germany 7/7/44
Howard Holmes Ford, Jr.	France 7/11/44
Walter J. Freund, Jr.	Belgium 1/7/45
Herman G. Garritsen	N. Atlantic 11/4/42
James H. Gilson	Italy 4/10/45
Donald Jacob Goris	USA 2/13/43
Lindol French Graham	Germany 3/18/44
Donald C. Haldane	USA 7/3/44
Mandeville E. Hall	France 10/7/44
Frank Hamilton	Germany 11/30/44
Philip W. Harris	India 8/18/44
Elwood H. Hearne	Philippines 4/28/45

Ronald W. Helps	Germany 11/20/44
David Ellsworth Himadi	Japan 8/20/44
Robert A. Hird	Germany 1/1/45
Arthur Morris Hughes, Jr.	Australia 10/14/42
Walter Jackson	USA 7/8/43
Paul Jordan	France 12/4/44
Charles J. Kartz	USA 12/12/44
Donald B. Koukol	Italy 4/22/43
Richard S. Lane	Japan 8/7/45
Arthur W. Lanigan	Pacific 3/1/42
Charles Upham Leonard	England 11/18/44
Walter F. Livingston, III	Pacific 7/21/44
Joseph Charles Mallory	Italy 4/3/44
John Mansfield Mason	Burma 8/15/45
Thomas B. McGuire, Jr.	Philippines 1/7/45
Charles E. McDermott	Holland 7/28/43
Albert Montick	England 12/29/44
Robert La Roy Morris	Italy 10/8/44
Walter Jacob Neske	Belgium 9/13/44
Milton Ness	USA 4/23/44
Harold B. Parks	Okinawa 4/29/45
William Robert Petsche	France 9/19/44
Charles Derek Redgrave	Germany 1/2/44
Joanne Redyke	USA 11/23/45
Richard K. Robb	France 10/8/44
Theodore D. Robb, III	Italy 8/31/44
Steven K. Roos	S. Pacific 10/12/43
Donald Hector Rose	Germany 4/8/45
Louis Seaton Sailer	France 11/24/44
Karl L. Sandmann	Pacific 2/11/43
Chester Sawicki	France 8/27/44
Howard A. Smith	Italy 11/1/43
William Smyser	Germany 12/19/43
Arthur W. Stanley	USA 2/22/44
George T. Starck	S. Pacific 9/23/43
Robert D. Stockbower	USA 11/18/43
Max F. Stoessel	Belgium 12/17/44
Richard C. Stowell	Atlantic 9/14/42
Edwin Alven Taylor	Germany 2/7/45

George Alexander Tatosian	USA 11/19/43
Edward Leonard Vanderbeck	Pacific 5/14/44
Kenneth M. Walter	Germany 13/3/44
Sydney R. Windham	Pacific 6/17/44
Paul Wines	Pacific 11/26/44
John R. Wohlrab	Pacific 2/26/45

16,353,700 Americans enrolled for WW II of which 2,314 were from Ridgewood. 407,316 died, including 80 from Ridgewood. Karl Sandman was the first World War II casualty, going down in the submarine *Shark* on February 11, 1942. As of this writing, the United States still has over 80,000 troops stationed in Europe and over 34,000 stationed in Japan.

Korea

The Office of the Actuary at the Department of Veterans Affairs in Washington gives June 27, 1950 to January 31, 1955 as the dates for Periods of Service for the Korean War.

The Korean War is now often called the forgotten war. Even during that conflict, enthusiasm was minimal. In 1950 a war-weary America couldn't see the need to undertake a new war and people in Ridgewood were more upset by the gas war going on at home than by the military war halfway around the world. Even a year later the local population simply yawned when asked about the war in Korea. Although air raid procedures were again in effect, one Saturday afternoon a local reporter watched in dismay as, during an air raid alert, local citizens continued upon their way unphased in Ridgewood's central business district as the air raid siren wailed.

Howard Raymond Carlough	USA 4/24/53
Harry J. Coyne, Jr.	USA 9/12/52
Theodore A. Deakyne	USA 8/20/51

20

William R. Estell	USA 5/17/53
LeWayne N. Felts	USA 4/22/54
Thaddeus Kulpinski	USA 4/9/52
Allan Vanderyerk	USA 12/16/51

5,754,100 Americans enrolled for the Korean War and 33,651 died, including 7 from Ridgewood. Combat spared Ridgewood: of the casualties listed on Ridgewood's plaques for the Korean War, none of them died in Korea and only two of them ever set foot there. Together they had more combat experience in WWII than in Korea. As of this writing, the United States still has over 39,000 troops stationed in Korea.

Vietnam

The Office of the Actuary at the Department of Veterans Affairs in Washington gives August 5, 1964 to May 7, 1975 as the dates for Periods of Service for the Vietnam War. But there is as much dissent about the official dates for the Vietnam War as there was about the conflict itself. Mr. Frank R. Shirer, Archivist U.S. Army Center of Military History in Washington states "Prior to the enactment of 38 US Code, Section 4212, Federal agencies differed in their views on the inclusive dates for the Vietnam conflict, and there is a lack of uniformity even within the Department of the Army. Various dates used are:
1. Office, Chief of Public Affairs, Department of the Army: 1 Jan 1961 - 28 Jan 1973;
2. Military Awards Branch, Military Personnel Center, Department of the Army: 1 July 1958 - 29 Mar 1973;
3. Center of Military History, Department of the Army: 11 Dec 1961 - 29 Mar 1973 (Dates are from the assignment of first Army unit to Vietnam to the withdrawal of the last Army unit from Vietnam);
4. Veterans Administration: 5 Aug 1964 - 7 May 1975*. Title 38 US Code, Section 101 (29) set

21

the dates of the Vietnam era as 5 Aug 1964 - 7 May 1975; however, based upon current Veteran's preferences in force in the U.S. Government, the dates have apparently been changed to 28 February 1961 - 7 May 1975.
* Under Title 38 US Code, Section 4212, a "veteran of the Vietnam era" means a veteran of the U.S. military, any part of whose service was during the period August 5, 1964 through May 7, 1975, who (1) served on active duty for a period of more than 180 days and was discharged or released with other than a dishonorable discharge, or (2) was discharged or released from active duty because of a service-connected disability. "Vietnam era veteran" also includes any veteran of the U.S. military who served in the Republic of Vietnam between February 28, 1961 and May 7, 1975." Mr. Shirer concludes "Unfortunately I have not found a significance for declaring 28 February 1961 as the beginning of the Vietnam War other than as a start point for receiving veteran benefits established by Congress."

Edwin S. Brague, Jr.	Vietnam 1/7/67
John F. Crikelair	Vietnam 8/6/69
Michel André R. de Magnin	Vietnam 11/1/69
Bruce Carlton Fryar	Laos 1/2/70
David J. Gunster	Vietnam 6/6/68
Jon H. Holley	Germany 8/4/68
Stephen Sherwood MacVean	Vietnam 10/29/69
William W. Nichols, Jr.	Vietnam 10/4/65
Jay Julius Schmid	Vietnam 12/7/68
Clement O. Stevenson, Jr.	Vietnam 6/17/66
John C. Williams	Mediterranean Sea 12/27/62

8,744,000 Americans enrolled for the Vietnam War and 58,168 died, including 11 from Ridgewood.

Mother's Day

Sometimes we concentrate on the men in combat only to overlook their families. Among the stories of valor on the battlefield are untold stories of how families managed. One local mother proved that often the responsibility of being a mother is as dangerous and adventurous as being a father in time of war.

On Mother's Day we celebrate our own lives by giving thanks to the person who gave us life. Most of us were brought in to this world and weaned in a very traditional manner. Our early years were comfortable thanks to the security and love of our parents, starting with mom. But not everybody enjoyed this luxury. Many mothers lost children; some mothers exhibited extraordinary strength in protecting their children.

There are many remarkable stories of how our young men made the transition from a pleasant peacetime life in the suburbs as we all know it to the chaos of the world war battlefield as few of us know it. But there are very few stories of our women during time of war. Of the towns involved in my research, there are only two women casualties listed on the memorial plaques and both of them died after the fighting had stopped.

As we show mom (at least once a year) how much we love her on Mother's Day, listen to the incredible story of a mother's love for her children as experienced by a local woman whose plight, flight and survival from the Japanese invasion and conquest of Singapore in early 1942 are stunning. It underscores the question, when the best option is the lesser of two evils, what do you do?

Mary Carol Brown of 191 Harding Road, Glen Rock was born in 1918, went to Glen Rock elementary schools and graduated from Ridgewood High School in the class of 1935. She was a tall and hardy young woman, vivacious and very bright. While in high school she was active in the riding

23

club, the German club, girl's club, was secretary of the Biology club, worked on the *Spectator* and sang in the glee club, mixed chorus and the A Cappella choir.

Known to most simply as Carol, she went on to study at Bradford Junior College and then Stanford University where she met Donald Purdie, a chemistry graduate research student from Swaffham, Norfolk, England. They were married on Palm Sunday 1939 at the Community Church in Glen Rock and sailed for England on the *Queen Mary* to live in Cambridge where he was a fellow at Kings' College.

It wasn't long before German bombs were raining down on England and the Purdies had several close calls at their home. Donald had an offer to teach in Singapore and the couple decided it would be safer there than in England which was in the middle of the Blitz. Despite pleas from her parents to come home, they soon sailed around the Cape with their infant son Robin (Rob) who was born in February 1940, arriving in Singapore in early 1941 where Donald was to teach chemistry at Raffles College, benefiting from all the advantages of an expatriate – big house near the Botanical Gardens, housekeeper, nanny etc. It was in this atmosphere that, a year later, on January 26, 1942, their second child Diana was born, just as the Japanese siege of Singapore was raging.

Japan's attack on Singapore was coordinated with the attack on Pearl Harbor as their Southern Army attacked Thailand and Malaya on December 8, 1941 and the Philippines on December 10. On February 8, 1942, 23,000 Japanese soldiers attacked Singapore. The fall of Singapore to the Japanese on February 15, 1942 is considered as one of the worst defeats in the history of the British Army which had considered Singapore an impregnable fortress, calling it the Gibraltar of the Far East. Singapore was connected to the Malaya mainland by a causeway across the

24

Straits of Jahore. Their 15" guns faced only toward the sea and had limited range and only armor-piercing shells; the northern approach was not properly protected and there were no air raid shelters.

Japanese troops were ordered to take no prisoners because that would slow up their advance. They were told "When you encounter the enemy after landing, think of yourself as an avenger coming face to face at last with his father's murderer. Here is a man whose death will lighten your heart." Captured wounded Allied soldiers were often killed and those who had surrendered often also were murdered. Some Australian troops were doused with gasoline and burned to death. Locals who had helped the Allies were tortured before being murdered. Japanese soldiers murdered patients in a Military Hospital. Additionally, the fall of Singapore presented numbers too great and ushered in three years of inexcusable treatment of the 120,000 POWs taken in Singapore.

Professor Donald Purdie PhD, who had joined the Straits Settlements Volunteer Force as a Private, was taken prisoner. Mary Carol was given two hours notice before being evacuated in the darkness of night February 6 with her infant son and new-born daughter on one of the last Allied ships to leave Singapore, the SS *Felix Russell* - a crowded, old and barely sea-worthy vessel with no facilities. She literally left with nothing more than the shirt on her back and the basics for the children. There were three ships with evacuees that left Singapore that night, escorted by British navy destroyers. When leaving the harbor, the *Felix Russell* was bombed by the Japanese. Its water tank was hit and the ship was without fresh water for the rest of the trip. The Japanese continually bombed the ships and the other two were hit and sunk. Despite unhygienic conditions and the close attention Japanese bombers paid to ships laden with evacuated civilians, the *Felix Russell* safely reached Bombay just over three weeks later, the first stop on Mary Carol's trip back to Glen Rock. While in Bombay, Carol's purse, containing all proof of her relationship to Diana, was stolen.

Her family then received news that she and the babies had successfully completed the voyage around the Cape and through the Panama Canal and had arrived in California where she was met by relatives. She and the babies completed their incredible trip home to Glen Rock on April 15, 1942.

Mary Carol subsequently received news from her husband in July 1943 saying he was still a prisoner in Singapore and was well. Nonetheless, not knowing what was happening to her husband created great stress. POW conditions then were not nearly as bad as they would become when he and the other prisoners were moved to Thailand to work on the Burma-Siam railway (see "*Bridge over the River Kwai*"). She later received a printed prisoner of war card confirming that he was in a prisoner of war camp in Thailand.

Donald's brother Ian, a Major, was also a prisoner in the same camp and in October 1944 informed his parents that Donald had died of malnutrition and amoebic dysentery on May 27, 1943 after long hours working on the railway. The news was quickly transmitted to his widow in Glen Rock who was devastated. Private Donald Purdie's remains were eventually buried in plot 8.J.55 in Kanchanaburi War Cemetery, 129 kilometers northwest of Bangkok, with other casualties of the Burma-Siam railway. During its construction, approximately 13,000 prisoners of war died and were buried along the railway. An estimated 80,000 to 100,000 civilians also died while working on the railway, mainly forced labor from Malaya, the Dutch East Indies, Siam (Thailand) and Burma.

Rob, Mary Carol & Daina & safe in Glen Rock

Life goes on. Three years later young Diana's nationality was challenged and, because such proof had been stolen in Bombay, she was deported to Canada where she spent two weeks before returning to Glen Rock with a British passport. Mary Carol Brown Purdie was remarried in 1946 to Robert Rice, a long-time friend who had been an usher at her wedding in 1939. They moved with the children to LaJolla, California where she worked for a time in the San Diego Zoo. They divorced and she eventually moved to Hawaii where she died in 1972. Her ashes were scattered. Robert Rice and his new wife died in the crash of Egypt Air Flight 990 June 9, 1999.

To this day Rob and Diana remember and thank their mother for the extraordinary determination she showed in extricating them from disaster.

Oh, what a power is motherhood.
Possessing a potent spell.
All women alike
Fight fiercely for a child.

Euripides, *Iphigenia in Aulis*

A Study of 20th Century Service Casualties

My research has been fascinating, rewarding and shocking. The findings run the spectrum from the glory of a Congressional Medal of Honor winner to the shock of a Ridgewood boy being beaten to death by a fellow GI in their barracks. The casualties include a Ridgewood Country Club singles tennis champion and an NCAA champion. They include the second leading American air ace of WWII; they were Ridgewood High School class presidents, Student Council Presidents, star athletes and All State musicians. They were week-end warriors, a career serviceman on the eve of assignment to the Pentagon; they died on their father's birthday, they were lost on their own birthday; they died a day before their unit was withdrawn from the front, they died on VJ Day; they died on Route 17. Some died after the war was over. They were decorated combat pilots who died flying their buddies out on furlough; they died with war trophies in their pockets, they died disintegrated by a bomb-laden Kamikaze - never to be found; they died decapitated and butchered by the Japanese Military Police August 15, 1945 upon news of the Emperor's unconditional surrender. Two WWI casualties were cousins, three WWII casualties lived in the same two-family house on Ackerman, and two Korean casualties were brothers-in-law.

These casualties were men, women, white, black, Christian and Jew - people with all the promise any generation could offer the world. They include a Ridgewood Policeman and a local doctor; they worked at the Grand Union, the Warner Theater, AT&T, Schweinfurth Florist, Hillman Electric and Van Dyke's Ice Cream store. They delivered the *Ridgewood News* and worked for the water company. Ridgewood boys drove ambulances to the front in WWI, participated in the invasion of France, the invasion of Italy, the invasion of the Philippines and the invasion of Japan. They bombed oil fields in Rumania, landed on Omaha Beach June 6, 1944, fought and died in the Battle of the Bulge, died in front line combat, died as a result of Kamikaze attacks, died advising the Vietnamese; they went down in ships, went down in submarines, went down in airplanes. 35 of the 113 died of causes other than combat, 3 died after the fighting had stopped. The remains of 23 Ridgewood boys were never found or identified and are still missing. They were people very much like you and me. Many of them were teenagers, barely old enough to shave. All of them were off to the adventure of a lifetime – literally. As in every war, from the minutemen to today, they were common men, reluctant warriors. And they were all very young. The average age of these casualties was 25 years old in a range from 18 years old to 42.

Causes of Death

18 Died in Air Accidents

In WWI aviation was in its earliest stages. Pilots flew machines flimsier that most toys we allow our children to play with in the back yard. In WWII, more American pilots died in training accidents than in combat. Many of the following men were decorated airmen with many missions under their belt. Some survived the peril of combat only to die in accidents. Some served in two wars.

1) Theodore Deakyne
2) Lindley De Garmo
3) George Denie
4) William Estell
5) LeWayne Felts
6) Donald Haldane
7) Philip Harris
8) Arthur M. Hughes, Jr.
9) Charles Kartz
10) Thaddeus Kulpinski
11) John Mason
12) Albert Montick
13) Theodore Robb, III
14) Arthur Stanley
15) George Starck
16) Robert Stockbower
17) Allan Vanderyerk
18) John Williams

9 Died of Illness

1) Thomas Boyd
2) William Burnett
3) Charles Connolly
4) Harry Coyne, Jr.
5) Donald Goris
6) Walter Jackson
7) Joanne Redyke, the only woman on Ridgewood's plaques
8) George Tatosian
9) Ulmont White

4 Died in Misc. Events

1) Howard Carlough was killed in automobile accident on Route 17.
2) Jon Holley died of injuries sustained when assaulted in his barracks by a drunken GI.
3) Seaton Sailer died when hit by a truck during blackout in France.

4) Milton Ness died of a brain hemorrhage in basic training.

3 Died while Prisoners of War

Although the Geneva Convention governs the treatment of prisoners of war, it is not always respected. In WWII, less than 5% of American POWs held by the Germans died in captivity. The fatality rate for American POWs captured by the Japanese was 6 times that. Japanese troops were ordered to take no prisoners because that would slow up their advance. Captured wounded Allied soldiers were often killed and those who had surrendered often also were murdered. All three of Ridgewood's prisoner of war casualties died while a prisoner of the Japanese.

1) Robert Black   2) Richard Lane
3) Edward Vanderbeck

11 Died When Their Ship Sank

1) Lester Bessell aboard the *Rowan*
2) Alan Clarke aboard the *Meriwether Lewis*
3) Thomas Cobb aboard the *Leopoldville*
4) Jack de Richemond on the *Frederick C. Davis*
5) Richard Dwenger aboard the *Buck*
6) Herman Garritsen on the *William Clark*
7) Arthur Lannigan on the *Houston*
8) Harold Parks aboard the *Hazelwood*
9) Franklin Patterson on S*ub Chaser 209*
10) Richard Stowell aboard the *Daniel Morgan*
11) John Wohlrab while serving on a repair ship

6 Died in Submarine Service

An airman can bail out and a rifleman can run for cover but where does a submariner go? Unlike coal miners, they have no escape, no way out. It must be one of the most horrible ways to die - knowing you are facing imminent death but not being able to do anything about it as the waters rise around you.

1) L. de Forest Anderson aboard the *Runner*
2) Thomas Ashton aboard the *Triton*
3) Davis Dunn aboard the *Bonefish*
4) Karl Sandmann aboard the *Shark*
5) Charles Leonard aboard the *Shark II*
6) Paul Wines aboard the *Tang*

20 Died When Their Aircraft Was Shot Down

In WWII more airmen died than Marines. 71% of those hoping to complete the required number of missions died in the attempt.

1) William Bavin
2) Edwin Brague
3) William Campbell
4) Michel de Magnin
5) Gordon Dempsey
6) William Easterly
7) John Faas
8) Bruce Fryar
9) James Gilson
10) Lindol Graham
11) David Gunster
12) David Himadi
13) Robert Hird
14) Charles McDermott
15) Thomas McGuire
16) Charles Redgrave
17) Richard Robb
18) Steven Roos
19) William Smyser
20) C. O. Stevenson

42 Died in Combat on the Ground

If there could be any doubt about the role of Willie and Joe or Private Ryan, 35 of these casualties had the rank of Pfc. or under. Their average age was 22 years old. It is no surprise that they were called the "infant"ry.

1) Robert Bennett
2) Robert Berkhofer
3) Joseph Bowen
4) John Brickell

5) Charles Brooks
6) Eugene Busteed
7) John Cadmus
8) Thomas Carroll
9) Richard Condo
10) Thomas Connor
11) John Cricklear
12) Leonard de Brown
13) Jesse Douglass
14) Howard Ford
15) Walter Freund
16) Mandeville Hall
17) Frank Hamilton
18) Elwood Hearne
19) Ronald Helps
20) Paul Jordan
21) Donald Koukol
22) William Kruskop
23) Walter Livingston

24) Steven MacVean
25) Joseph Mallory
26) Robert Morris
27) Walter Neske
28) William Nichols
29) William Petsche
30) George Rae
31) Donald Rose
32) Charles Sawicki
33) Jay Schmidt
34) Howard Smith
35) Floyd Stevens
36) Max Stoessel
37) Edward Taylor
38) Kenneth Walter
39) Sydney Windham
40) Charles Wolfhegel
41) Daniel Yeomans
42) Jacob Yeomans

Among the 113, 24 are Missing in Action

*"Sometimes, when one person is missing,
the whole world seems depopulated"*
Lamartine
Premières Méditations Poétiques (1820)

When you left home this morning you probably said goodbye to your family, fully expecting to see them tonight. But think of what it would be like if, during the day, you received a phone call telling you that your child or spouse had disappeared. There have been some very visible cases of missing persons or kidnapped children in the news over the past years. And there has been no event in our recent lifetime that manifests more clearly the pain of missing persons as the terrorist attacks of September 11. As tragic as these stories are, the one common link found among the surviving families is the comfort of closure when a missing person's body is recovered -

the ultimate proof. Now imagine the pain of losing a loved one but never knowing where the remains lie - lost forever. Vietnam veterans have made a concerted and very visible effort to remember and locate their buddies who are POW/MIA. We see the black flag everywhere.

Hope springs eternal. As recently as February 2003 newspapers reported the return of recently found remains believed to be those of American servicemen recovered in Laos. As a reminder, there remain 1,889 MIAs from the Vietnam conflict. But over 2,000 casualties remain un-recovered from September 11. The American Battle Monuments Commission, which is responsible for operating and maintaining permanent American military burial grounds in foreign countries, talks of MIAs as well as "Americans who gave their lives in the service of their country but whose remains were never recovered or identified". On their "Tablets of the Missing", they list 4,452 names from WWI, 78,773 from WWII, and 8,100 from Korea. That makes a total of 93,214 American service personnel who never came home. They sleep in unknown graves. To put it in perspective, the seating capacity of Giants Stadium is 80,242.

In fact, the term "Missing in Action" is generally used out of context. For historians at the National Archives in College Park, Md. the key word seems to be "Action". Since Vietnam, the term MIA applies only to casualties resulting from hostile action but not to an active serviceman who was lost when his plane slipped off the side of an aircraft carrier or exploded in mid-air. The latter are listed as "non-hostile" casualties and are not included among the Vietnam MIAs. This distinction does not seem to apply to previous conflicts where service personnel not recovered are listed on the "Tablets of the Missing". Just ask a grieving family if they care about such an innocuous distinction. There is no closure - the key word therefore certainly is "Missing".

This position is confirmed by the Defense Prisoner of War/Missing Personnel Office at the Pentagon which states that their mission is "to account for American personnel missing from our nation's conflicts..." They report that "the respective service secretaries are legally responsible for making status determinations for their members.

"There are seven categories of a person declared to be missing in accordance with United States Code: beleaguered, besieged, captured, detained, interned, missing and missing in action. Although Americans who remain unaccounted for from the Vietnam War are routinely and popularly referred to as MIA, this is not their legal status. In the 1970s and 1980s the secretaries of each of the military services held formal status review boards that changed the missing status to killed in action/body not recovered. Likewise, though memorials and/or monuments may refer to them as such, no American serviceman is listed in an MIA status".

Bureaucrats be damned! The term "MIA" has taken on a magically enigmatic aura – reflecting perhaps the worst part of war. Regardless of how, when or why, if the remains of American service personnel are not recovered or identified, their sacrifice nonetheless weighs on all of us, above all their families and friends who will never know the answer to the question "what happened?" Knowing is better than not knowing.

There are in fact 27 men from Ridgewood, including 24 of Ridgewood's 113 Honored Dead, whose remains were never recovered or identified: 1 was lost in WWI, 22 in WWII, 1 in Southeast Asia and 1 in the Mediterranean Sea. The additional two lost servicemen died outside an official "period of service".

1) Lawrence de Forest Anderson (submarine sunk)
2) Thomas Ashton (submarine sunk)
3) Robert Bennett (ship sunk)
4) Lester Bessell (ship sunk)
5) Robert Black (died in captivity)
6) William Campbell (air craft shot down)
7) Alan Clarke (ship sunk)
8) Jack de Richemond (ship sunk)
9) Davis Dunn (submarine sunk)
10) Richard Dwenger (ship sunk)
11) Bruce Fryar (air craft shot down)
12) Herman Garritsen (ship sunk)
13) Richard Lane (killed while prisoner)
14) Arthur Lanigan (ship sunk)
15) Charles Leonard (submarine sunk)
16) Harold Parks (Kamikaze attack)
17) Frank Patterson (ship sunk)
18) Charles Redgrave (air craft shot down)
19) Steven Roos (air craft shot down)
20) Karl Sandmann (submarine sunk)
21) Clement Stevenson (air craft shot down)
22) Richard Stowell (ship sunk)
23) Paul Wines (submarine sunk)
24) John C. Williams (aircraft lost at sea)
25) Douglas C. MacKeachie (plane crash)
25) Frank Roehrenbeck (plane crash)
27) Gerald Ramsdell (plane crash)

If I knew
(Author Unknown)

*If I knew it would be the last time that I'd see you
fall asleep,
I would tuck you in more tightly, and pray the Lord
your soul to keep.*

*If I knew it would be the last time that I see you
walk out the door,
I would give you a hug and a kiss and call you back
for one more.*

*If I knew it would be the last time I'd hear your voice
lifted up in praise, I would videotape each action and
word so I could play them back, day after day.*

*If I knew it would be the last time I could spare an
extra minute or two to stop and say "I love you,"
instead of assuming you would KNOW I do.*

*If I knew it would be the last time I would be there to
share your day, well I'm sure you'll have so many
more, so I can let just this one slip away.*

*For surely there's always tomorrow to make up for
an oversight. We always get a second chance to
make everything right.
There will always be another day to say our "I love
you" and certainly there's another chance to say
"Anything I can do?"*

*But just in case I might be wrong, and today is all I
get, I'd like to say how much I love you, and I hope
we never forget.
Tomorrow is not promised to anyone, young or old
alike. Today may be the last chance you get to hold
your loved one tight.*

*So if you're waiting for tomorrow, why not do it
today. For if tomorrow never comes, you'll surely*

regret the day
That you didn't take that extra time for a smile, a
hug, or a kiss and you were too busy to grant
someone what turned out to be their one last wish.

So hold your loved ones close today, whisper in their
ear. Tell them how much you love them and that
you'll always hold them dear.
Take time to say "I'm sorry," "please forgive me,"
"thank you" or "it's okay." And if tomorrow never
comes, you'll have no regrets about today.

Blue Star Banners & Gold Star Banners
A blue star banner is symbolic of the sacrifices of
families who endure long periods of separation
during the deployment of their loved ones. The
banner has become the symbol of a loved one
serving in the armed forces during war.

The tradition of displaying a Blue Star
Banner during times of war dates to 1917 when
Army Capt. Robert L. Queissner of the 5th Ohio
Infantry, who had two sons serving on the front
lines, designed the first banner. It quickly became
the unofficial symbol of a relative in the service with
each blue star on the banner representing a family
member on active duty.

The Blue Star Banner symbolizes pride in
the commitment of our youth on the one hand and
concern for the seriousness of the war effort on the
other hand. By displaying the Blue Star Banner in
a window, American families demonstrate their
support and pride in those serving in the various
branches of the United States Military.

When a service person is killed, the blue
star banner is replaced by a gold star banner.
Ridgewood's first gold star banner went up in
March 1918 when we adopted the tradition of
placing a Golden Star on the Village Service Flag.
Families who lost a loved one in the service became
known as gold star families, more specifically gold
star mothers.

Repatriation

Starting with the Korean War, all war casualties have been repatriated to the United States. On the other hand, repeating a program instituted in the early 1920s for the repatriation of WWI casualties, in 1947 the Quartermaster General of the Army instituted a repatriation program addressed to the next of kin of war dead entitled "Disposition of World War II Armed Forces Dead" through which the bodies of American service personnel killed overseas could be brought back to the United States for re-interment. The remains of 60 of Ridgewood's Honored Dead are buried in the USA.

It was a cumbersome, bureaucratic and impersonal exercise. One anguished mother replied to government correspondence saying, "Please try not to write to other mothers as if a shipment of merchandise was involved." A frustrated father wrote "The government was very quick in taking our boys and sending them out to the combat zones with very little or no training, and the least they can do is to exert every effort to bring back the boys who gave their lives, instead of making arrangements to transport foreign war brides and permitting refugees to utilize space on ships for traveling and entering our country." In one case, a family waited over 7 years to learn the final fate of their loved one.

All the memorial services conducted upon receipt of the remains were closed casket, mainly because of the ravages of time but also because often there was not much in the casket. For example, the remains of Medal of Honor winner Tom McGuire weighed 10 pounds when repatriated; all that could be found of any remains of the 5-man crew in the crash that killed Ted Robb were ten fingers, five of which matched the prints of Lt. Robb.

Many of Ridgewood's Honored Dead are buried in the Ridgewood area. 15 are buried at

Valleau, 7 are buried in Maryrest Cemetery in Darlington, 2 are in Fair Lawn Cemetery, 2 are in Laurel Grove in Paterson, 2 are in Cedar Lawn in Paterson and 1 is buried in Hackensack Cemetery. Several are buried on Long Island, 5 are buried in Arlington and 41 are buried or lost overseas. 11 are buried in George Washington Memorial Park in Paramus, one of whom died over 20 years before the cemetery was opened. The remains of Jacob A. Yeomans were originally repatriated after WWI and buried in Paramus Plains Cemetery at the corner of South Pleasant and East Ridgewood Avenue in Ridgewood. When the cemetery was closed in the late 1940s in order to build the Somerville School, he was moved to George Washington Memorial Park. That makes him the only WWI casualty buried there.

In addition, several of the markers at Valleau memorialize a war casualty who is either buried overseas or lost, for example:

1) Walter Livingston's marker states that he is buried in National Memorial Cemetery of the Pacific, Honolulu;

2) William Campbell's marker states that he was lost. He is listed on the Tablets of the Missing at Manila American Cemetery.

3) John Cadmus is buried in Somme American Cemetery, Bony, France;

4) Richard Dwenger is listed on the Tablets of the Missing at Sicily-Rome American Cemetery, Nettuno, Italy;

5) William Kruskop is buried in St. Mihiel American Cemetery, Thiaucourt, France

6) Charles Leonard is listed on the Tablets of the Missing at Manila American Cemetery in the Philippines.

Every Memorial Day the entire list of Ridgewood's Honored Dead is read at Memorial Day services at Van Neste Square.

PART III

Until fire devastated the church on January 8, 2002, West Side Presbyterian Church in Ridgewood had a Roll of Honor, listing the 210 men and women from that congregation who served in the military in World War II. There are eight men on the list with stars beside their names. 210 served; 8 died.

"Greater love hath no man than this,
that a man lay down his life for his friends"
(John 15:13)

My interest in researching war casualties began in 1998 when I decided to find out about the eight members of the congregation of West Side Presbyterian Church who died in World War II. On Memorial Day 1999 the church used my research to dedicate a Supreme Roll of Honor which now contains 13 names.

But I was not satisfied with the cursory information I had found at that time and decided to develop full biographies on the eight West Side casualties from WWII. Actually, they ended up being autobiographies because I wrote them in the first person, as though the man were telling his own story. These eight WWII West Side martyrs were:

Robert Berkhofer	Arthur M. Hughes, Jr.
Elwood Hearne	John Mason
Ronald Helps	Harold Parks
Robert Hird	C. William Schlenz

Dr. Arthur M. Hughes was West Side's minister from 1933 to 1957. In November 1942, the "Service Supplement" to West Side's newsletter was begun and was circulated through Christmas 1945. Throughout the war, Dr. Hughes faithfully sent it to as many people as he could, peaking at 287 men

41

and women in the service plus 250 families in January 1945, all the while bearing the substantial burden of his own personal loss. The Service Supplement was begun the month after it was reported that his son, Arthur M. Hughes, Jr. "... went out with his plane, giving everything that he had of brains and brawn and nerve and faith for your freedom and mine." He was killed October 14, 1942 in Australia. The following Sunday his father's sermon was entitled "The Triumph of Life" and spoke to the good that must come from the evil of war. There was hardly a dry eye in the congregation.

Dr. Hughes once said, "Civilization is something that is continually at stake. It demands a daily plebiscite. We have got the think for it, live for it, fight for it and die for it, or else there is no continuing civilization." Dr. Hughes felt that "if you believe in the ideals that have been taught to you at home, at church, at school, in your community, you will realize that there are certain things in life that are more important than life itself'.

Dr. Hughes quoted the political philosopher Joseph de Maestro who once said that

"Patriotism is the love of one's country;
it is the sacred compact between the noble past,
the creative present and the future.
Everything that we hold dear in our lives today
has been bought at a tremendous price
by those who have gone before.
The challenge of today is
to see that those things are not lost."

Further research revealed one WWI casualty, one non-member whose parents were members, two Vietnam War casualties and one casualty from outside an official period of service.

Jacob Yeomans   Jon Holley   Albert Spickers
    C. O. Stevenson   Lansing Shield

PART IV

Ridgewood High School
Supreme Roll of Honor

An offspring of my research was a second project - the Ridgewood High School project. There is a great deal of overlap between the two projects but, because several neighboring towns at one time or another sent their students to Ridgewood High School, my research extended beyond the boundaries of Ridgewood to include casualties from Allendale, Radburn, Glen Rock, Hohokus, Midland Park and Wyckoff.

In 1999 Ridgewood's Superintendent of Schools Dr. Frederick Stokely learned of my research on local service casualties and asked that I prepare a memorial to the students of Ridgewood High School who died in wars. The first manifestation was the creation of a memorial to Bob Hird at the Ridge School. His family sold the land to the village on which the School stands.

The list as it currently stands includes 94 names and is probably not a final product. It is almost surely incomplete as it is difficult to finalize a list of RHS students who died in the service when one includes those who died in times other than an official "period of service" (viz. other than during WWI, WWII, Korea or Vietnam). Also, some casualties attended but did not graduate from the high school and not all RHS casualties lived in Ridgewood. At different times, various surrounding towns sent students to RHS so casualty lists from outside Ridgewood must be consulted as well. Even for RHS students who died during an official period of service, some had moved away and their deaths were not noted locally. Some went away to school or moved after graduation and enlisted or were drafted by boards outside New Jersey and therefore are not on the official lists of New Jersey casualties. Nonetheless, with a goal to memorialize all RHS students who gave their life in the service of our country, the list as it stands is an attempt to bring back to public awareness the sacrifice of these local martyrs.

War hit RHS students indiscriminately. It didn't matter if you were the most popular man on campus or some unnoticed kid. War gives special treatment to no one.

It is the soldier, not the poet, who gives us
freedom of speech.
It is the soldier, not the reporter, who gives us
freedom of the press.
It is the soldier, not the campus organizer, who gives
us freedom to protest.
It is the soldier who serves beneath the flag,
who salutes the flag,
and whose coffin is draped by the flag,
who gives the demonstrator the right
to burn the flag.

Fr. D. E. O'Brien

The school has a memorial plaque for WWI; however, their WWII plaque only starts with the class of 1939. So far 30 students from earlier classes who died in WWII have been identified. That memorial also includes students who did not graduate - either because they enlisted before graduating or, in some cases, transferred to other schools. There is no memorial in the school for the Korean or Vietnamese conflicts.

World War I - 10 names

The list of WWI casualties is based on a memorial plaque in the hallways of the high school with footnotes on three students who left Ridgewood before graduation and later died in the war:

Class

Allan G. Barton	moved
Oliver P. Jackson	moved
Lindley de Garmo	1908
Floyd A. Stevens	1910
Peter W. Ebbert	1913
James R. Hubbard	1914
Gustave Wil Nadler	1916
Arthur W. Travell	1916
Ulmont A. White	1917
Lionel G. Watkins	moved

1. Allan G. Barton lived on Murray Ave. and went to the high school early in the 20th century until his family moved to Brookline, Mass.
2. Oliver P. Jackson attended the high school but moved to Buffalo in 1904.
3. Lionel G. Watkins attended the high school but moved to Staten Island with his family.
4. Perhaps most intriguing is a photo found in the 1926 Yearbook of the Schools which lists Alfred N. Lee as a casualty with all the WWI casualties on the Honor Roll plaque now found at RHS. He is listed in the yearbook with the graduating class of 1918 but no biographical information on him has been found, nor is he listed among the WWI casualties from Ridgewood or any of the surrounding towns who sent their students to RHS. He is not even on government lists of WWI casualties. The only conclusion is that he survived and the 1926 Yearbook entry is an error.

World War II - 67 names

The WWII Roll of Honor plaque in the high school starts with the class of 1939. 31 RHS students from classes prior to 1939 who died in the service have since been identified. The school's oldest WWII casualty graduated in 1918.

There were several RHS memorials dedicated to WWII casualties:

1. Richard Condo, killed in Italy, was a star football player in the class of 1943 and is said to have punted a football 70 yards. Shortly after the war, with a grant from his parents, RHS created the Dick Condo Trophy, dedicated to good sportsmanship, to be awarded to the winner of three consecutive annual Thanksgiving Day football games against Fair Lawn. Ridgewood finally won three games in a row in 1961 but there is no mention of the trophy.

2. The Robb Football Trophy in memory of Richard Robb, RHS '41 who died in France, was created in 1983 by his friends at RHS and is still presented to the outstanding varsity lineman upon the player's graduation in June.

3. Although he did not graduate from the high school, RHS offers an annual memorial scholarship in memory of Ridgewood's only Medal of Honor casualty, Thomas McGuire for "academic achievement, service to the school and the potential to uphold the high ideals embraced by Major McGuire".

Several young Ridgewood men were able to temporarily continue their studies after having been drafted while still in college. The Army Specialized Training Program (ASTP) was established to pull college students into the service to bring divisions up to combat strength. These men had to be qualified through competitive tests and rigorous infantry basic training before being sent to colleges and universities around the country to study languages, medicine or engineering. 150,000 men benefited from the program but an urgent need for combat troops ended the ASTP on March 28, 1944.

73,000 of these "soldier students" were transferred to infantry units.

Ridgewood High School Roll of Honor

	Class
Douglas MacKeachie	1918
Warren C. M. Lessing	?
Stephen K. Roos	1924
George T. Starck	1925
Walter W. Jackson	1929
Joseph A. Bowen	1930
Howard Holmes Ford, Jr.	1930
Richard A. Dwenger	1931
Karl L. Sandmann	1932
William Todd Campbell	1934
Albert Montick	1935
Robert D. Stockbower	1935
David Ellsworth Himadi	1936
Arthur Morris Hughes, Jr.	1936
Howard Anthony Smith, Jr.	1936
Edward A. Taylor	1936
Edward Leonard Vanderbeck	1936
John E. Faas	1937
Ralph Hameetman	1937
Harold Parkinson Johnston	1937
Charles McDermott	1937
William M. Smyser	1937
Max Stoessel	1937
William G. Bavin	1938
Donald Goris	1938
Charles J. Haeberle	1938
Frank Hamilton	1938
Christopher Lambert	1938
Harley Benton Lewis, Jr.	1938
Theodore D. Robb, Jr.	1938
Paul T. Wines	1938
Lester R. Bessell	1939
Bruce H. Bode	1939
Roger Colby Lawn	1939
Walter Livingston, III	1939

Donald W. Maddox	1939
John Mansfield Mason	1939
Charles Victor McHenry	1939
George Cotton Munroe, Jr.	1939
Alan R. Clarke	1940
Davis H. Dunn	1940
Herman G. Garritsen	1940
Elwood H. Hearne	1940
Richard S. Lane	1940
George Alexander Tatosian	1940
Richard D. Drager	1941
Betty Jo Hicks	1941
Joseph Charles Mallory, Jr.	1941
Robert La Roy Morris	1941
Walter J. Neske	1941
Richard K. Robb	1941
William R. Burnett	1942
Charles D. Connolly	1942
John R. de Richemond, Jr.	1942
William Ralph Francis	1942
Donald C. Haldane	1942
Thomas L. Hawkins	1942
Ronald Helps	1942
Robert Ainsworth Hird	1942
Jeremy Leonard	1942
Harold Bacon Parks	1942
William P. Abbott	1943
John James Brickell	1943
Richard H. Condo	1943
Donald Hector Rose	1943
Charles Upham Leonard	1944
Donald B. Koukol	1944

Several students survived WWII only to die during the Korean Conflict or even many years later in Vietnam. The school had no memorial to casualties of the Korean Conflict or the Vietnam War until three new memorial plaques were dedicated in 2005 - one for the Korean War, one for the Vietnam War and one for the students who died during peace time.

Korea (3 names)

	Class
Theodore A. Deakyne	1939
William R. Estell	1942
Howard Raymond Carlough	1947

Vietnam (9 names)

	Class
David James Gunster	1944
William Ward Nichols, Jr.	1955
Peter Fransson Russell	1958
Jay Julius Schmid	1960
Edwin S. Brague, Jr.	1961
Stephan Sherwood MacVean	1961
Charles "Ken" Harvey	1962
Thomas E. Carnegie	1963
Jon Holley	1963

Peacetime (7 names)

This research includes all RHS students who died while in the service. None of the following casualties is listed on local memorial plaques.

	Class
William Sprague	1938
Frank J. Roehrenbeck, Jr.	1943
Lansing P. Shield	1947
Jack Neil Moore	1948
Charles Hall	1953
Gerald Ramsdell	1981
Heather O'Mara	1982

The High School's motto is "A Tradition of Excellence". There are different ways to measure excellence and excellence always requires sacrifice.

"... each man is preferred according to his virtue
or to the esteem in which he is held
for some special excellence."
Thucydides: History, Book II, Chapter 37

PART V

Errors & Omissions

One unexpected result of my research was that I discovered 17 misspelled names out of 98 names on the memorial plaque listing casualties from WWII, Korea and Vietnam. Believing that if a person gives their life for us, we should at least spell their name correctly, that plaque was replaced during the Memorial Day ceremony on May 31, 2004. These are the names that were misspelled:

1. Lester Richard Bessel, Jr. should be Lester Richard Bessell, Jr.;
2. Joseph E. Bowen should be Joseph A. Bowen;
3. Thomas J. Carrol, Jr. should be Thomas J. Carroll, Jr.;
4. Davis H. Dunne's name should be Dunn;
5. Herman Gerritsen should be spelled Garritsen;
6. Charles J. Kartz, Jr. should be Charles J. Kartz;
7. Walter Livingston, Jr. should be Walter Livingston, III;
8. Joseph Charles Mallory, Jr. should be Joseph Charles Mallory;
9. Robert Leroy Morris should be Robert La Roy Morris;
10. Derrick Redgrave should be Charles Derek Redgrave;
11. Johanna A. Redyke should be Joanne D. Redyke;
12. Stephen K. Ross should be Stephen K. Roos;
13. Max F. Stossel should be Max F. Stoessel;
14. Lewane Felts should be LeWayne N. Felts;

15. Stephen F. MacVean should be Stephen Sherwood MacVean;
16. Michael R. de Magnin should be Michel R. de Magnin;
17. William M. Nichols, Jr. should be William W. Nichols, Jr.

Further, there was some confusion about Edwin Stephen Brague, Jr. He is listed in different documents as Edwin Stephen and Edwin Steven Brague. His burial stone reads Edwin S. Brague, Jr. Max Stossel's name is misspelled on the memorial plaque at Bethlehem Lutheran Church.

Although all the men and woman listed on the memorial plaques are in one way or another linked to Ridgewood, some rarely if ever called Ridgewood home, among them:

1. George Rae never lived in Ridgewood but his family were residents when he was killed in the Philippines in 1900.
2. Robert Bennett was from Fort Lee but his brother, sister and mother moved to Ridgewood after he finished high school.
3. Eugene Busteed was from Midland Park. Although his mother eventually lived in Ridgewood, he is on Midland Park's plaques and has a street named after him there.
4. Thomas McGuire moved from Ridgewood at age 10 to live with his mother in Florida. His father remained in Ridgewood. However, when his body was found a few years after the war and returned to the USA amid great fanfare, it was his father in Ridgewood who was the main point of contact for the military and it was through Ridgewood that the convoy made its way to Arlington National Cemetery.
5. Kenneth Walter was from Newark but his sister lived in Ridgewood.
6. Arthur Lanigan lived in Waterville, Maine with his mother but his father lived in

Ridgewood.

7. Chester Sawicki was from upstate New York but his mother lived in Ridgewood.
8. Albert Montick was from Fair Lawn and is also listed among their war casualties.

Ridgewood is a beautiful village with beautiful people. Among our Honored Dead are several war casualties who were not from Ridgewood but discovered the wonders of our village – and its women.

1. Sydney Windham was from North Carolina; married Priscilla Stewart (RHS 38');
2. LeWayne Felts was from Ohio; married Ethel Sproul (RHS 40');
3. Thaddeus Kulpinski was from Pennsylvania; married Lois Deakyne (RHS 42');
4. Paul Jordan was from New York; married Angela Cavagnaro (RHS 36').

Not listed on our plaques, but meeting this latter criteria are:

1. Major George Putnam Moody, an Air Force pioneer, who died in an air crash near Wichita, Kansas May 5, 1941 – outside an official "period of service" His widow was the former Dorothy Perkins of 658 Hillcrest Road in Ridgewood;
2. Tech. Sgt. Garret T. Cooper of the 1838th Ordinance Company, Aviation died December 7, 1944. He was born in Patterson and married the former Irene Portsmore (RHS '39);
3. Capt. Arthur S. Cosgrove, 101st Infantry Regiment, 26th Infantry Division was from Minnesota. He married Betty Craig (RHS '36);
4. Major Dana Wesson Mitchell, from Lawton, OK. died in Vietnam September 17, 1969, was married Harriet Butler of Ridgewood (RHS '58);
5. Air Corps Major Robert J. Fitzgerald

married Alice Prevost, whose family lived on Beverly Road and later at 50 North Van Dien in Ridgewood;
6. Col. John Thomas Murtha, Jr. married Margaret Heathcock of Ridgewood;
7. Lt. Col. Edward E. B. Weber married Helen Bryant of Ridgewood.

Several other young Ridgewoodites died in the service but are not listed on our plaques because they did not die in an official period of service:

1. William Sprague died after an operation in Hackensack July 20, 1946 - within the official "period of service" for WWII - of injuries resulting from combat in France. He is not listed on our plaques whereas, although he too had just been discharged, one of Ridgewood's 113 Honored Dead died in 1946.
2. Lansing Shield died in an air crash November 1, 1948;
3. Jack Neil Moore (RHS '48) was a pilot in the Air Force when he died in a crash in Washington State May 28, 1954;
4. Frank J. Roehrenbeck, Jr. (RHS '43) died July 18, 1950 when the jet he was piloting slid off the side of an aircraft carrier;
5. Charles Hall (RHS '53) died in France in an automobile accident in 1959;
6. Gerald Ramsdell died in an air crash November 11, 1988;
7. Heather O'Mara was on active duty in the Army when she died in a commercial airline crash in 1989.

Several young men who once lived in Ridgewood and moved away are not listed on our memorial plaques but hopefully are listed on the memorial plaques in their new hometowns:

1. Alan Barton (WWI) moved to Brookline, MA.
2. Douglas MacKeachie moved to MA.
3. Oliver Jackson (WWI) moved to Buffalo, NY
4. Lionel Watkins (WWI) moved to Staten

Island, NY
5. Jeremy Leonard (WWII) moved to Montclair, NJ
6. Donald Maddox (WWII) moved to Holmdel, NJ
7. Frank Roehrenbeck (Korea) moved to Suffern, NY
8. Jack Neil Moore (Korea) moved to Oakland, CA.

Also not listed on Ridgewood's memorial plaques before 2004 is Ridgewood's first war casualty, George Rae, who died in Luzon in 1900 during the Philippine Insurrection. In 2004 Ridgewood's 112 Honored Dead became Ridgewood's 113 Honored Dead when his name was added to the plaque as a casualty from the Philippine Insurrection.

There are several other men linked to Ridgewood or Ridgewood High School who, although their families were not residents of the area when they died, gave their lives in the service and therefore should not be overlooked:

- **Captain Colin Purdie Kelly, Jr.,** America's first aviation hero of WWII, married Marian Wick of Hamilton Road in Ridgewood, whom he had met in 1936. She and her parents lived in Ridgewood for about four years before moving to Brooklyn.

With the wife and son living in Hawaii, he was assigned to Clark Field on the island of Luzon in the Philippines and in November 1941 he told his wife to take their child and go home. She and Colin III left on the last ship carrying dependents from Hawaii about a week prior to the attack on Pearl Harbor and returned to Brooklyn.

A month later, still reeling from the attack on Pearl Harbor, alone and far from friendly territory, Capt. Kelly attacked and damaged a heavily armed enemy ship, then sacrificed his own life to save his crew. His heroism inspired a nation in shock.

On the morning of December 10, 1941, Japanese aircraft based on Formosa attacked Clark

Field, trapping most of the American aircraft of the 19th Bomb Group on the ground while refueling. The only US aircraft to survive had been dispersed to a small strip at Del Monte Field, Mindanao where they had spent the night. They had no news of the war except that Japan had attacked Clark Field and other installations near Manila on Dec. 8, destroying most of the US B-17s and pursuit planes.

The surviving B-17s returned to Clark Field to load bombs; one of these planes was piloted by Captain Kelly, a former B-17 instructor and one of the most experienced and respected pilots of the 19th Bomb Group. Captain Kelly managed to get only three 600lb bombs aboard when the air raid alarm was sounded. He took off immediately to attack enemy shipping.

Captain Kelly and his crew flew alone without fighter escort into territory where the Japanese held total air superiority. As they flew north they passed over a large Japanese landing on the north coast of Luzon. Kelly decided to attack a cruiser and released his three bombs, two of which made a direct hit on the Ashigara.

As Kelly headed back for Clark Field, his B-17 was jumped by 10 Japanese Zero fighters led by Saburo Sakai, the highest scoring Japanese Ace to survive the war, attacking one by one from astern as they approached Clark Field. Kelly held the burning B-17 steady and remained at the controls as, one by one, his crew bailed out. Then the bomber exploded and crashed about five miles from Clark Field. Kelly's body was found with the remains of his aircraft.

Captain Kelly was awarded the Distinguished Service Cross and the Distinguished Flying Cross, posthumously. He was also inducted into the Air Force Hall of Fame. His bravery, success and sacrifice were a very positive shot in the arm for an American public still in shock from the devastation of Pearl Harbor. Captain Colin

Kelly's remains were repatriated and buried in the Oakridge Cemetery, Madison, Florida. At death, he was 26 years old.

- Lt. Col. **Edmund C. Buckley** was born in Brooklyn and moved to Ridgewood as a child. He was the nephew of Mrs. Edmund Corcoran and Mrs. James Crowley or 456 Heights Road in Ridgewood. His mother was Mrs. Theodore Shirley of Atlantic City, formerly of Ridgewood. He attended elementary school in Ridgewood before moving to Los Angeles where he graduated from Franklin High School. Both he and his wife were graduates of the University of Pennsylvania. They had two children. He took R.O.T.C. in high school and in college. He then worked for the American Paper Goods Company and was a reserve officer. He was called to the service in April 1941 and went overseas in November 1943. He died October 31, 1944 in France where he was commanding the 2nd Battalion, 28th Infantry. At death he was 35 years old.

- Cpl. **Jacob J. Cleenput** of Paramus was born September 8, 1921 and lived at 470 Paramus Road with his three brothers, three sisters and his parents. They attended Mount Carmel church. He attended Ridgewood High School but did not graduate, leaving to help his father with his dairy and farm. He went overseas in February 1944 and died November 29, 1944 in Germany while with the 10th Tank Battalion, 5th Armored Division. He is buried in the Ardennes American Cemetery. At death he was 23 years old.

- Tech. Sgt. **Garret T. Cooper** of the 1838th Ordinance Company, Aviation died December 7, 1944 of wounds received at Leyte the previous day. He was born in Patterson and married the former Irene Portsmore (RHS '39) of 51 Fairmount Road in Ridgewood. His father was a Councilman in Paramus. He graduated from the Midland School in Paramus, Cocoa High School in Cocoa, Fla., where his family lived for about 10 years. They were members of the First Baptist Church of Cocoa. He also attended the Brewster Parker Institute in Mount Vernon, Ga. His family returned to Bergen County in 1938 and he worked as a production engineer tester at the Paterson plant of the Wright Aeronautical Corp. Gary joined the service November 16, 1942, a month after his marriage. He went overseas in September 1943 and had seen action in New Britain, New Guinea, Dutch East Indies and Leyte where he was the chief armorer for the 1838th Ordinance Company, service and maintenance Aviation. He received two Bronze Stars for meritorious achievement in action. He is buried in Manila American Cemetery in the Philippines. At death he was 27 years old.

-       Capt. **Arthur S. Cosgrove**, 101st Infantry Regiment (Yankee Division), 26th Infantry Division was from Minnesota. He attended Stattuck Military School in Faribault, Minn., Clark School in Hanover, NH and the College of William and Mary where he was a member of Phi Kappa Tau. He worked for the Minnesota Valley Canning Company before entering the service in February 1942. He went overseas August 27, 1944, arrived in Cherbourg September 7 and moved to the front lines in October of that year. He married Betty Craig (RHS '36), whom he met in college and who was living with her parents at 335 Mountain Ave. when he died. He was awarded the Silver Star for "gallantry in action near Metz on 8 November, 1944. In the offensive against the enemy on 8 November Company G spearheaded the assault units of the 101st Infantry Regiment. Captain Cosgrove, Company Commanding Officer, led the company forward under fire over open ground offering no cover against strongly entrenched enemy positions. In the lead throughout, he was the first man to enter the town of Moyenvic and begin the mopping-up operations. On the second day of the progressive attack by our forces, Captain Cosgrove was mortally wounded by enemy mortar fire. His inspiring leadership and aggressiveness in action reflect the highest credit upon Captain Cosgrove and the armed forces of the United States." Capt. Cosgrove is buried in Lorraine American Cemetery, St. Avold, France. At death he was 27 years old.

\-   Lt. **Robert Evison** attended the Willard School and George Washington Junior High School while living with his aunt and uncle at 718 Hillcrest Road. He died in an air crash at Esler Field, La. July 31, 1944.

\-   Air Corps Major **Robert J. Fitzgerald**, whose mother lived in Pittsburgh, married Alice Prevost, whose family lived on Beverly Road in Ridgewood, and they lived 50 North Van Dien. They were married in 1942, two years after he joined the service, and had just purchased a home at 132 Waiku Road.

He was first heard from in February 1945 when he the radio broadcast entitled "Army Hour" announced that the next speaker was Major Robert Fitzgerald of Ridgewood, NJ, based in Saipan at a B-29 bomber base. Shortly thereafter, the *Ridgewood Herald* ran an article entitled "Who is Major Fitzgerald?" because nobody knew who he was. The paper received several reports from listeners. Representatives of the newspaper phoned the two Fitzgeralds in the telephone book to no avail so they published a plea to their readers for information on who this Major Fitzgerald was. His wife, who had not heard the broadcast, promptly replied saying that her husband had been in the Pacific area since November 4, 1944.

A graduate of the University of Pittsburgh, Major Fitzgerald got his wings at Maxwell Field and was promoted to Major in September 1944. He then went to the Pacific with the 21st Bomber Command as pilot of the lead ship in raids and took part in the first air raid over Tokyo on January 16 as he shepherded home a stricken B-29. The ship had had two engines shot out by Japanese fighters but nonetheless made the 1,500-mile trip from Japan on two engines. When the third engine went out Major Fitzgerald flew with the wing of his plane under the other plane giving it enough power to return to Saipan. He was lost on March 17 in a midnight raid over Kobe while piloting a B-29. He is buried in Arlington National Cemetery.

- **Ralph M. Hameetman** was an only child and lived with his parents at 296 South Maple Ave. in Glen Rock. He attended elementary and middle school in Glen Rock going on to Ridgewood High School but did not graduate because his family moved to Freedom, California in the early 1940s. He entered the U.S. Navy Aviation Corps as a turret gunner on a B-24, spending 3½ years of combat in the Pacific. He flew 56 missions and won 8 major battle stars while being shot down three times. He was awarded the Purple Heart for shrapnel wounds and a personal commendation from Admiral Nimitz. He was also an amateur photographer and had special permission from the Navy to take many battle shots. He was then sent to Miami for rest. He asked to be returned to combat and was sent to Oxnard, Ca. where he was killed in a mid-air collision September 4, 1945 when another plane dove out of the clouds and hit his plane. He is not listed on the memorial plaques in Glen Rock. At death he was 23 years old.

- Cpl. **Jeffrey Kay Hoagland** was born July 14, 1950 and lived in Ridgewood before moving to Falls Church, VA. He joined the Marines, went to Vietnam December 3, 1968 and died April 24, 1970 of small arms fire in combat near Quang Nam during his second tour. He is buried in Arlington National Cemetery. At death he was 19 years old.

- **2 Lt. Oliver Phelps Jackson, A.S.S.C.** lived in Ridgewood with his family, attended Ridgewood Grammar School and two years of High School when the family moved to Buffalo, NY in 1904. Before entering the service, he did government work in Puerto Rico. He received his commission in 1917 and died October 29, 1918 at the Air Service Flying School, Selfridge Field, Mt. Clemens, Mich. where he was an instructor. He is buried in Canandaigua, NY. At death he was 31 years old.

- **Capt. Warren Charles Miller Lessing,** 653rd Tech. Sch. Squadron, USAAF was born September 30, 1902 in New York City, he moved to Glen Rock with his parents, brother and two sisters when he was 15 years old. His father was in the restaurant business and was Glen Rock Police Commissioner and on the borough council in 1922. Although he is reported to have graduated from Ridgewood High School, his name does not appear on any graduation lists. He married Irene Hillman with whom he had a son. They moved to Saddle River in 1939 for a year and then to 97 Grand Boulevard in West Orange. His family eventually returned to this area to live in Hohokus. He managed the Newark branch of the Coastal Oil Company in Anchor Point, Newark. He was also Executive Officer of the Civilian Air Patrol and held a civilian pilot's license.

With his son and namesake already in the Navy, and because he was a specialist in oil, he resigned to join the service in June 1942 as an oil analyst. He worked in Washington as a light oil analyst, was commissioned on September 17, 1942 and died while on a special mission in an air crash off Botwood, Newfoundland three weeks later. On Saturday October 3 American Export Airlines' *Flying Ace*, a 27-ton Sikorsky S 44 flying boat, left Laguardia Field, New York on a regularly scheduled commercial flight with 26 passengers aboard (of which 8 were civilians), for a flight to Foynes, Ireland with a stop in Newfoundland. While in Botwood to refuel, the passengers were advised that they would have to make an emergency stop in Gander for repairs because the necessary facilities were not available in Botwood. As she took off from Botwood, Newfoundland at 6:45 p.m., the plane hit an air pocket and stalled in mid-air, bouncing in a "porpoise take-off". It went about 30 feet in the air and suddenly crashed in the water. The aircraft remained afloat while rescue boats picked up survivors and casualties. The plane was then towed to about one mile from shore where it sank. Six bodies were recovered from the plane. Five passengers and three of the crew were taken to the hospital. Two were not recovered, their bodies still in the sunken plane. Among the missing was Warren Lessing, who was traveling in civilian clothing. He is listed on the Tablets of the Missing at the East Coast Memorial in New York City. At death he was 40 years old.

- **Major Dana Wesson Mitchell** was born April 13, 1939 in Boston. He graduated from St. Lawrence University and received his commission upon graduation. He married Harriet Butler of Ridgewood (RHS '58) and they had two sons and a daughter. He joined the Army and went to Vietnam April 4, 1969 in the 2nd Battalion, 4th Field Artillery, 9th Infantry Division. Five months later he was killed, on September 17 in Long An Province in a helicopter accident. He was awarded the Bronze Star and a cluster to the Army Commendation Medal and is buried in Arlington National Cemetery. At death he was 30 years old.

- Lt. Colonel **Floyd A. Mitchell** of the 91st Coast Artillery Regiment, Philippine Scouts died December 15, 1944. A West Point graduate in the class of 1924, he got a Masters degree from MIT and taught at West Point before going to the Pacific in July 1941. His wife and 2 daughters lived for a year on Godwin Avenue in Ridgewood with her aunt Mrs. John Collins while he was in the service. Colonel Mitchell was captured at Corregidor in May 1942, put in a concentration camp in Manila and was being transported on the "Hell ship", the Japanese passenger ship Oryoku Maru which left Manila for Japan December 13, 1944 with 1,619 prisoners of war crammed into the three cargo holds. The ship was not marked to indicate that it was carrying prisoners of war. On December 15,

1944 U.S. Navy planes sank the ship off Olangapo Point in Subic Bay from the aircraft carrier USS *Hornet* who did not know of its cargo. They disabled the ship on December 14th and finished their job on December 15th. Less than half of POWs survived, only to be recaptured. He is listed on the Tables of the Missing at Manila American Cemetery. At death he was 43 years old.

- Murtha Field, San Jose on Mindoro, Philippines is named for Col. **John Thomas Murtha, Jr.** He married Margaret Heathcock of 242 Demarest Road, Ridgewood in 1929. They had one daughter. Born in New York City April 4, 1908, he attended Lasalle Military Academy and graduated from West Point in 1928. His father was a pilot in WW I and later owned his own plane. Col. Murtha was stationed in Argentina and England before WW II. He had been the Air Force officer in charge of the Munitions Building in Washington and later at the Pentagon building. He moved to the Pacific in April 1943 as an Air Officer with General MacArthur and participated in all of the main landings in the Pacific Theater. As on of the air force's leading heavy bombardment experts, he was the original commander of the Mindoro Air Task Forces and lost his life in a Japanese air raid December 14, 1944 in the Philippines while in command of the 310th Bomb Wing. He was awarded the Distinguished Flying Cross, Legion of Merit and the Air Medal and is buried in the Manila American Cemetery in the Philippines. At death he was 38 years old.

- Lt. Col. **Edward E. B. Weber** married Helen Bryant of Ridgewood whose family lived on Prospect Street. They had twin children. He was born in the Philippines, lived in Portland, Oregon and graduated from the U.S. Military Academy at West Point in 1943. He then attended the Infantry Command and General Staff schools at Fort Leavenworth, Kansas. Before going overseas January 2, 1942, Col. Weber was Assistant G-2 of the 6th Corps. Col. Weber was killed May 30, 1944 in Italy while commanding the 3rd Battalion, 179th Infantry Regiment, 45th Infantry Division. He was awarded the Silver Star and is buried in Sicily-Rome American Cemetery, Nettuno, Italy. At death he was 35 years old.

PART VI
September 11, 2001

That day I was walking across Times Square listening to "Imus in the Morning" when it was announced that an airplane had flown into the World Trade Center in downtown New York City. As the day progressed it quickly became clear that it was not an accident as a second plane hit in New York, one crashed in Pennsylvania and one hit the Pentagon. The United States had again been victim of a surprise attack. Ridgewood lost 12 of its citizens that day – all civilians.

Because we know the circumstances of their deaths, their biographies are not included in this book because they were not military service casualties. However, that in no way diminishes the tragedy of their loss. Individual biographies are available in the Ridgewood Public Library. These are their names:

Richard M. Blood, Jr.	Michael San Phillip
Michael T. Carroll	Bruce E. Simmons
Daniel F. McGinley, Jr.	Steven Frank Strobert
James D. Munhall	Gina Sztejnberg
Charlie Murphy	Jon C. Vanedvander
Steven Peterson	Christopher Wodenshek

PART VII

The Biographies

Based on the premise that a man is not dead until he is forgotten, I have written a biography on each of Ridgewood's 113 Honored Dead, plus those mentioned earlier who died outside an official "period of service" those who moved away or who were not from Ridgewood but who attended Ridgewood High School. To create the biographies, I used as a foundation the reports of service people published by the *Ridgewood News*, or its predecessor, under the banner "First Line News" during World War II, Korea and Vietnam. These stories are fully factual, based on their obituaries, but most of the nitty-gritty came from the men's families and friends, government documents available under the Freedom of Information Act, veteran associations' Internet web sites and eyewitness accounts.

Beginning in June 2001 these biographies were published, most often in the month of the person's death, over a period of nearly three-and-a-half years in the *Ridgewood News,* and the *Glen Rock Gazette* under the banner "Recalling First Line News" (sometimes mis-titled as "Recalling Front Line News"). The series of articles won an award from the New Jersey Society of Professional Journalists for weekly series writing and reporting in 2002. The series ended in November 2005 and was run for a second time in its entirety, ending in September 2008.

Each of the biographies is structured the same way: I tried to incorporate their civilian lives and personalities with their duties while in the service in order to show that all of these people were very much like you and me. They were ordinary people who were thrown in to a chaos beyond their imagination. My goal was to create a profile of each casualty as a person, not simply a soldier. And if you feel you are reading about your own children, you are. These were the children of Ridgewood. Each biography ends with the person's age, therefore the title to this work.

I was flattered and honored when Ridgewood resident Tim Dyas, poet Laureate of the 505th Regimental Combat Team, 82nd Airborne Division and a prisoner of the Germans for 23 months in WWII, was inspired by my research to write a poem entitled "So Young":

Why is it that in visiting veterans' cemeteries,
you are struck by the ages of the dead,
struck because they're so young!
Stopped at an age when
their blood flowed so vigorously within
and then
outward as they crumpled.
War demands that the young,
since time immemorial, be sacrificed.
If all nations said the ages be forty or more,
would there be any war?

Tim Dyas 29 Sep 03

Alphabetical Index to Biographies

Kulpinski, Thaddeus
Lambert, William
Lane, Richard
Lanigan, Arthur
Lawn, Roger
Leonard, Charles
Leonard, Jeremy
Lewis, Harley
Livingston, Walter
MacKeachie, Douglas
MacVean, Stephen
Maddox, Donald
Mallory, Joseph
Mason, John
Mc Henry, Victor
McDermott, Charles
McGuire, Thomas
Montick, Albert
Moore, Jack
Morris, Robert
Munroe, George C.
Nadler, Gustav
Neske, Walter
Ness, Milton
Nichols, William
O'Mara, Heather
Parks, Harold
Patterson, Frank
Petsche, William
Rae, George
Redgrave, Charles D.
Redyke, Joanne
Robb, Richard
Robb, Theodore
Roehrenbeck, Frank
Roos, Steven
Rose, Donald
Russell, Peter
Sailer, Seaton
Sandmann, Karl
Sawicki, Chester

Schmid, Jay
Shield, Lansing
Smith, Howard
Smyser, William
Sprague, Wm.
Stanley, Arthur
Starck, George
Stevens, Floyd
Stevenson, Clement
Stockbower, Robert
Stoessel, Max
Stowell, Richard
Tatosian, George
Taylor, Edwin
Travell, Arthur
Vanderbeck, Edward
Vanderyerk, Allan
Walter, Kenneth
White, Ulmont
Williams, John
Windham, Sydney
Wines, Paul
Wohlrab, John
Wolfhegel, Charles
Yeomans, Daniel
Yeomans, Jacob

Pvt. William Purcell Abbott
42001561
Company D
83rd Armored Reconnaissance Battalion Cavalry
3rd Armored Division

Billy was born December 19, 1924 in Paterson and moved with his parents and sister to live at 36 Van Allen Road in Glen Rock. They were members of All Saints Episcopal Church where he was an acolyte and a member of the Servers Guild at the church.

He attended elementary school in Glen Rock, was in Boy Scout Troop 17, went to Lawrenceville Academy and returned to graduate from Ridgewood High School in 1943. While there he participated in Hi-Y basketball and bowling, was on the senior play ticket committee, in the booster club and was home room president his senior year.

Upon graduation, he immediately entered service in July 1943 and was stationed at Fort Riley, Kn. and Fort Meade before going overseas in

February 1944 as part of the 83rd Armored Reconnaissance Battalion "Spearhead".

A "heavy" Armored Division consisted of 4 regiments and included an Armored Reconnaissance Battalion (ARB). In 1943 most armored divisions were converted to a "light" design except for the 2nd and 3rd Armored Divisions which remained "heavy". Cavalry groups were occasionally attached to divisions. The 82nd and 83rd ARBs did some reconnaissance work for the division but performed more special operations including acting as mobile reserve, protecting flanks, maintaining contact between units, controlling rear areas and operating as an army information service.

While the 83rd was attached to the 1st US Infantry Division "Big Red One", Abbott died of a gun shot wound in Rennes, France August 15, 1944 and is buried in Section G, Plot 142B, Grave 1 at George Washington Memorial Park in Paramus. All Saints dedicated a chancel rail together with lectern and pulpit in his memory. At death he was 19 years old.

Lt. jg Lawrence de Forest Anderson
0-120159
USS *RUNNER SS 275*

In WWII, of the 319 US submarines launched, 52 of them never returned. Of the nearly 14,750 submariners, over 3,500 remain on silent patrol. Among them is Lawrence de Forest Anderson of Ridgewood who grew up at 32 Garfield Place with his brother and parents. He attended elementary schools in Ridgewood but graduated from Solebury School in New Hope, Pa. in 1935 where he was captain of the football team. He went on to graduate from Yale in 1939, where he was a member of the senior society, Book and Snake.

Anderson joined the service during his last year at Yale Law School. After officers' training school at Northwestern University, he served as an executive officer on a PT boat in the South Atlantic and the Pacific. Then he joined the submarine service and was piped aboard the USS *Runner* SS-275, a Gato Class submarine. This bookish Ivy Leaguer was about to become an efficient hunter – and to die as the hunted.

71

The *Runner* sailed from New London in late 1942, arriving in Pearl Harbor via the Panama Canal on January 10, 1943. Her first patrol from January 18 to March 7 was between Midway and the Palau Islands during which she torpedoed five Japanese cargo ships while suffering damage from a bomb dropped from a patrol bomber which knocked out her sound gear and the power supply for both periscopes. After repairs, she started her second patrol, from April 1 to May 6. One freighter was torpedoed and she returned to Midway May 6, 1943.

USS *Runner SS 275*

She again left Midway May 28, 1943 on her third patrol, headed for the area south of Hokkaido and east of the northern tip of Honshu where she was to patrol from June 8 to July 4. She was expected back at Midway July 11 and should have reported in when about 500 miles from base but she failed to transmit. On July 20 *Runner* was reported presumed lost as of July 11 with 78 men aboard. Information obtained after the war about Japanese antisubmarine attacks contains no mention of an attack which would explain the loss of *Runner.* Thus her loss most likely can be attributed to an enemy minefield - there were at least four in the area the *Runner* was patrolling.

Anderson is listed on the Tablets of the Missing in Action at Honolulu Memorial. At death he was 26 years old.

Elect. M/3 Thomas Edward Ashton, Jr.
06464572
USS *TRITON* SS-201

The USS *Triton* is one of 52 World War II U.S. Navy submarines that remain on Eternal Patrol. Commissioned at the Navy shipyard in Portsmouth, New Hampshire in July 1940, she and her 74 officers and crewmen were on patrol off of Wake Island on Pearl Harbor Day December 7th, 1941. Three days later she torpedoed a Japanese destroyer gaining the distinction of being the first Navy submarine to sink a Japanese vessel. By September 1942 *Triton* had sunk 19 Japanese ships and damaged 7 more - more Japanese tonnage than all other Navy submarines operating out of Pearl Harbor at the time. On board was Tom Ashton of Ridgewood, NJ.

Tom lived at 45 Cathedral Avenue in Nutley with his family while he attended St. Mary's School in Nutley and later St. Mary's High School in Rutherford from which he graduated in 1939. Known to some as Huck, he was active in dramatics, football, basketball and baseball, was class treasurer his junior year and on student council his senior year. His family moved to Ridgewood to live at 642 East Glen and he attended St. Peters in Jersey City. He enlisted in the Naval Reserve immediately after Pearl Harbor and did his initial training in Rhode Island. He later trained in California and Australia before being assigned to the USS *Triton,* a Tambor Class submarine.

Ashton was lost aboard the *Triton* March 15, 1943 in the Caroline Basin, northwest of the Admiralty Islands and southwest of Rabaul. On March 16, 1943 the *Triton* was ordered to change her area slightly and to return to Brisbane on March 25, 1943. When she failed to make a routine report of position, she was ordered to do so. When no report was received she was reported overdue from patrol and presumed lost on April, 10, 1943, without a doubt sunk by enemy destroyers since the Japanese reported on that day seeing "a great quantity of oil, pieces of wood, corks and manufactured goods bearing the mark 'Made in U.S.A.'." His Shakespearean high school quote seems eerily appropriate: *"A scar nobly got is a good livery of honor".*

Tom Ashton is listed on the Tablets of the Missing at Manila American Cemetery, Manila. At death he was 21 years old.

USS Triton SS-201

Lt. William George Bavin
O-794611
9th Air Force Service Command
326th Ferrying Squadron
31st Air Transport Group

Bill, an only son, was born February 1, 1920 and lived with his parents at 24 East Side Ave. He graduated from Ridgewood High School in 1938 where, at 6', 160 lbs., he was co-captain of the football team his senior year. He also participated in intramural baseball, basketball and bowling and was President of the Acolyte Guild at Christ Church. He went on to graduate from Newark Academy in 1940.

He began his military career in December 1941 and received his commission at Maxwell Field, Alabama on January 22, 1943. He later was stationed at Lakeland, Fla., Bainbridge, Ga. and Columbus, Miss before going overseas on October 16, 1943 with the 9th Air Force Service Command to be based at Station # 472 Ascot, Berkshire, England. Later he was assigned to temporary duty with the 326th Ferrying Squadron, 31st Air Transport Group where he piloted a twin engine Douglas A-20B "Havoc" Marauder light bomber. 47' 11" long and weighing 16,993 lbs empty, it was 17' 7" high with a wingspan of 61' 4". Powered by two 1,600 hp Wright engines, it had a range of 945 miles, a maximum speed of 317 mph and a ceiling of 23,700'. It was armed with seven .50 caliber machine guns and could carry a bomb load of up to 4,000 lbs.

Douglas A-20B "Havoc"

Flying out of Greenham Commons, England just after noon on September 18, 1944, he was killed by an enemy artillery battery in the village of Groede in Zeeuws Vlaanderen, Holland while on a photographic mission carrying specially trained personnel who were to photograph the airborne invasion.

Airborne troops were being brought into Holland and dropped in the vicinity of Eindhoven, Arnhem and Nijmegen. These troops were to seize and hold important bridgeheads and road junctions ahead of the British Second Army which was turning the German flank in order to enter the flat plain of northwestern Germany. The air train bearing these troops was said to have been 285 miles long. Many of the enemy bunkers, some of which were camouflaged as houses, were built under the ground.

The plane piloted by Lt. Bavin was last seen in the target area at Westmole at 3:45 in the afternoon when it was hit in the left motor with antiaircraft fire from enemy Unit L-51998, causing it to crash with its 4-man crew. Only Lt. Bavin parachuted from the plane but he was shot by the Germans as he was falling before his parachute could open. Initially listed as missing, his family received an "official finding of death" a year later, indicating that the body had not been found. Shortly thereafter, four bodies were recovered from the crash site and Lt. Bavin was identified among them.

Lt. Bavin is buried in Plot B Row 29 Grave 12 at the Ardennes American Cemetery, Neupre, Belgium. Christ Church dedicated its St. Luke window in the Four Gospel Windows to him September 9, 1945. At death he was 24 years old.

Pfc. Robert Oliver Bennett
12182941
Company B
31st Signal Construction Battalion

The average age of Ridgewood's 112 Honored Dead is 25 years old. In general, sailors died at sea, soldiers died on the ground and airmen were shot down. Robert Bennett went counter to those three elements: he was not from Ridgewood, he was much younger than the average and he was an untested soldier who died at sea.

Born August 18, 1924, he did not grow up in Ridgewood. Nicknamed "Speed", he was 5' 6" tall, weighed 133 lbs. and had brown hair and brown eyes when he graduated from Fort Lee High School in 1942. While there he was on the Senior Council, Finance Committee and ran intramural track. His brother, sister and mother moved to Ridgewood after he finished high school and lived at 319 East Franklin Turnpike.

Bennett joined the service, trained at Fort Dix and Camp Attenbury, Indiana and was assigned to the 31st Signal Construction Battalion in November 1942.

A year later, on November 26, 1943, the day after Thanksgiving, he was one of 1,988 Army and Red Cross passengers aboard the British transport HMT *ROHNA* on its first day at sea sailing from Oran, Algeria. The ship, badly in disrepair, was part of Convoy KMF-26 en-route to Bombay transporting American troops and Red Cross workers to the China-Burma-India Theater of war. Shortly after 5:00 in the afternoon, and 15 miles north of Djidjelli, Algeria, the *Rhona* was hit in the engine room on the port side, just above the waterline by a missile launched from a German bomber. It marked the first successful hit by a remote-controlled rocket-boosted bomb, launched in the air from a German bomber, marking the start of the missile age.

H.M.T. Rhona

1½ hours later, after abandon ship had been given and the Indian crew had lowered two lifeboats for themselves and departed, the *Rhona* sank. The remaining davits were rusted and immovable; regardless, the GIs had not received any training in the use of the davits. Heavy seas generating 15 to 20 foot waves contributed to the disaster. Many of the initial survivors died of gradual exhaustion from the very effort of trying to preserve life by attempting to remain afloat in the 60° water. 1,015 American troops, 3 Red Cross workers and 120 ship's officers and crewmen perished. Bennett was among those reported missing November 27, 1943. Over eight hundred bodies were never recovered.

The event received little notice and the War Department immediately suppressed news of this catastrophe. No details were provided to the grieving families until much later. Bennett is listed on the Tablets of the Missing at North Africa American Cemetery, Carthage, Tunisia. At death he was 19 years old.

**Pfc. Robert William Berkhofer
42187047
Third Squad, Third Platoon
Company F, 290th Infantry
75th Infantry Division**

The 75th Infantry Division was originally nicknamed the "Diaper Division" because it was the youngest unit to enter the fighting in WWII. Activated April 15, 1943 at Fort Leonard Wood, Missouri they moved to England in November 1944 and shipped out to France on December 13, to participate in the Battle of the Bulge, later fighting in the Ardennees campaign, the Colmar and Alsace-Lorraine regions, as well as the Rhineland campaign, spending 94 consecutive days in contact with the enemy. The strain on manpower was great and replacements were constantly needed. The division lost 817 soldiers killed, 3,314 wounded and 111 who died of wounds. Among the young replacements who became one of those statistics was Robert Berkhofer of Ridgewood. In one year, this teenager went from the innocence of amateur photography in prep school to become a seasoned combat veteran on the front lines of the battlefields of Europe.

Bob, an only child, was born in Jersey City June 13, 1926. His family moved to Hasbrouck Heights where he got his elementary education and in 1937 they moved to Ridgewood to live at 51 North Hillside. He attended George Washington elementary and junior high school, attended West Side Presbyterian Church and was sent to Phillips Exeter Academy in New Hampshire where he became the photographic editor for the school paper the "*Exonian*" and was goalie on the lacrosse and hockey teams. The family summered in Brielle on the Jersey shore. He loved water sports and was a member of the Manasquan River Yacht Club. Upon graduation from Exeter in June 1944 he was accepted at Princeton pre-med.

Although he had indicated a preference for the Navy, he was drafted into the Army on September 1, 1944, doing his basic training at Camp Hood, Texas. He was sent to Tenby, Pembrokeshire in England in January 1945 and on February 20, 1945 he was assigned as a Rifleman in the 290th Infantry, one of many replacements assigned that day. He was promoted to PFC on March 16.

In April the 75th was attacking toward the Ruhr River, south of Witten, southwest of Dortmund, trying to finish clearing the Ruhr pocket. While being momentarily halted, an enemy sniper fired from the woods, hitting him and instantly killing him on Friday the 13th, his father's birthday. The following day, the 290th Infantry was relieved by elements of the 313th Infantry.

Robert Berkhofer was awarded the WWII Victory Medal, European-African-Middle Eastern Campaign Medal with one Bronze Service Star and a Purple Heart, all posthumously. He is buried in Greenwood Cemetery in Brielle, N.J. The Manasquan River Yacht Club now holds an annual Berkhofer Memorial Race for local junior sailors. At death, he was 18 years old.

Y S/2 Lester Richard Bessell, Jr.
07060419
USS *Rowan* (DD-405)

Born in 1920, "Bud" was an only child and lived most of his life with his parents in Ridgewood at 125 Hamilton Rd. Before graduating from Ridgewood High School in 1939, he was a bowler and played in the high school orchestra, including three years in the county orchestra. He was also active in the music program at the Methodist Church. A quiet, earnest youth and devoted son, he also was a patrol leader in Boy Scout Troop 7. He attended Rensselaer Polytechnic but left to work at Wright's Aeronautical.

He enlisted in July 1942, trained at Naval Training School in Newport and was assigned to the Benham-class destroyer USS *Rowan*. On board there were lots of books and motion pictures shown nightly, except when going through enemy submarine waters. Meals were fine with chicken every Sunday. Nonetheless, he got seasick each time he went back aboard ship after shore leave.

The *Rowan* escorted transatlantic merchant marine convoys in the face of the Luftwaffe, shooting down attackers but nonetheless losing several Liberty ships. She participated in Operation Torch, the invasion of North Africa, patrolled off Casablanca conducting anti submarine warfare patrols and escorted convoys along the North African coast

USS *Rowan* (DD-405)

On September 9, 1943 the *Rowan* entered the Gulf of Salerno in the screen of the Southern Attack Force in Operation Avalanche, the invasion of Italy at Salerno. She screened the transports and freighters for two days as the assault force and supplies were landed at Paestum. Late on the night of the 10th, she headed back to Oran with the emptied ships. Shortly after midnight, German motor torpedo boats from the 3rd Motor Torpedo Boat Flotilla attacked. The *Rowan* pursued them and fired. As the enemy pulled away, she ceased firing and changed course to rejoin the convoy. Within 5 minutes a new contact was made, less than 3,000 yards away. Again she changed course to avoid torpedoes and bring her guns into position. As the range decreased to 2,000 yards, the *Rowan* was hit by a torpedo and sank in less than a minute. Of the 273 officers and enlisted men on board, Bessell was one of the 202 killed or missing September 11, 1943. Bessell's parents heard the news of the *Rowan*'s sinking on the radio the day before they were advised by the Navy of the loss of their son.

Saint Elizabeth Episcopalian Church, where he had been a member of the Acolytes Guild, dedicated an Episcopal Church Flag to him. He is listed on the Tablets of the Missing at Sicily-Rome American Cemetery, Nettuno, Italy. At death he was 23 years old.

Qm/1 Robert Armstrong Black, Jr.
08114404
UDT 10
USS *Burrfish SS-312*

In May 1943 the Navy Combat Demolition Training program was created at the Amphibious Training Base at Fort Pierce, Florida to train Navy sailors as members of small units whose mission would be to locate and demolish enemy beach obstacles. They were known as swimming scouts, the naked warriors but are best known now as frogmen or SEALS. They were all volunteers and their existence at the time was unknown to the public. Robert Black of Ridgewood was one of the 10 original 1943 Navy Combat Demolition Unit volunteers. By mid-July five officers and 35 enlisted men, mostly ex-Seabees were ready and in December six officers and 120 Army enlisted men from the 299th Combat Engineer Battalion underwent combat demolition training. They first participated in a full-scale test of beach obstacle clearance techniques in February 1944.

Bob was born in Jersey City January 13, 1911 and eventually lived with his parents and two sisters at 15 Fairview Ave. in Glen Rock before moving to 249 Van Emburgh Ave. in Ridgewood. He graduated from Jersey City High School and traveled abroad working for the Ocean Leather Company of Newark. He married Ada Wilma Maar of Glen Rock in New York March 7, 1942, had a son and enlisted in the in the Navy Reserve on July 16, 1943 through a Recruitment Program sponsored by Ridgewood Elks.

His UDT training began with "Hell Week" - miles of running, obstacle course and explosions with primary emphasis on endurance swimming. Students went on to advanced demolition courses consisting of two one-week sessions. The first, known as "Standard Week," covered beach reconnaissance techniques and how to quickly and effectively destroy enemy-placed obstacles. The second, the "Pay-Off" course, was the frogman's final exam. Swimmers were assigned their own areas of coastline to survey and had to blow up landing obstacles constructed by Seabees. Many were booby trapped with plastic explosives to simulate real combat conditions. Those successfully completing the sessions were given more advanced instruction before being assigned to an operational UDT. Some went to England to prepare for the invasion of Europe and on June 6, 1944 these demolition units and their Army comrades led the way ashore attempting to clear paths for troops. Over half their number was lost on Omaha Beach alone.

As Pacific operations began to heat up, Bob went overseas with a special reconnaissance detachment aboard the USS *Burrfish*, a Balao Class Submarine. They arrived at Maui in June for advanced training. His UDT Team 10 was reinforced by an Office of Strategic Services (OSS) maritime unit who introduced the swim fin to UDT, leading to universal use of "flippers" by UDT units and, later, by recreational swimmers.

The *Burrfish* hosted the only submarine-launched reconnaissance operation conducted by an Underwater Demolition Team during WWII. The *Burrfish* was outfitted with free flooding, eight-foot long cylindrical tanks, bolted to the deck aft of the conning tower to house deflated rubber boats. The boats were inflated and deflated by a special device originally designated for Army rubber pontoons.

On July 10, 1944, the *Burrfish* slipped out of Pearl Harbor. En route, the *Burrfish* received word that carrier air strikes and bombing raids had been planned for the Palaus, that she was to collect data on ocean currents around Peleliu as well as on reefs, water depths, and underwater obstacles which US reconnaissance had detected. Japanese radar spotted the *Burrfish* which came under air and depth charge attack for two weeks.

On August 11 they were southeast of Pelelieu Island. As amphibious landings in the Pacific were especially hazardous due to the unknown nature of the islands and surrounding waters, five men from UDT-10 were specially selected because of advanced swimming, diving, rubber boat and reconnaissance training they had had as members of the classified OSS Maritime Unit. Black was one of five from the UDT-10 team who, smeared with camouflage grease and equipped with fins, face masks and knives, paddled ashore in rubber rafts. Approximately 1,000 yards from shore four swimmers began to gather hydrographic information for a proposed invasion. On a pre-arranged signal all hands returned to the safety of the submarine.

Five days later the *Burrfish* made a second mission into the southern Yap Islands, the Japanese central command headquarters. All hands again returned safely.

On August 18 they were off Gagil Tomil Island's northeast coast. Enemy radio and radar stations operating from this island were pinpointing Allied shipping in the area. Seven men, five from UDT-10 and two from the UDT training staff in Maui, set out to locate the radio towers and destroy them in anticipation of an invasion of the islands. At 20:00, the *Burrfish* dropped them off and they paddled within a quarter mile of the island for their first reef reconnaissance. Under the noses of enemy beach patrols, they discovered a barrier reef just below the surface where they anchored the raft and swam ashore. Fifteen minutes later, Black returned to the anchored boat with one man who couldn't handle the strong currents. Black then swam back to rejoin the other men.

Several hours after their rendezvous time, five members of the team had failed to return. At midnight, the *Burrfish* surfaced at the pre-arranged rendezvous point and waited to pick up the UDT team. Only at 3:00 did they detect a light from the raft and at 3:50 two more men were pulled aboard. The *Burrfish's* commanding officer gave orders to dive to avoid incoming radar-equipped Japanese aircraft. The *Burrfish* patrolled the area for over two days but strong seas and currents made additional rescue attempts impossible and the *Burrfish* Captain decided that it was better to lose three men than to lose six so he set sail for their next mission. Black was reported missing in action August 19. The three men had indeed tried to rejoin their mates but could not find the rubber boat and had swum back to shore, armed only with sheath knives. They hid all day and then tried again to find their mates at sea but there was no boat to pick them up.

The *Burrfish* subsequently intercepted a radio message confirming their worst fears. Black and two others had been captured by the Japanese and under torture they gave false information concerning UDT capabilities. Black was sent to Palau September 2 for transfer to Manila. During a torpedo attack on a Japanese convoy in the late afternoon of September 7 in the vicinity of Sindangan Bay, Mindanao, the Philippines, the American submarine *Paddle* (SS-263) fired torpedoes and hit and sunk the freighter, *Shinyo Maru* which, unbeknown to the *Paddle*, carried 750 American prisoners of war on board. Most likely, one of those lost was Black. Only eighty-two would be rescued by Filipino guerrillas. These three are the only known POWs from UDT teams. After this incident, there were no further sub-launched UDT operations.

Black was posthumously awarded the Silver Star "for conspicuous gallantry and intrepidity as a member of a special reconnaissance detachment operating in the Pacific area from July 11 to August 18, 1944. He voluntarily participated in the vital task of investigating certain enemy-held islands, obtained valuable information concerning beaches and adjacent waters and contributed materially to the success of operations in the area." He is listed on the Tablets of the Missing at Manila American Cemetery in Manila. At death he was 33 years old.

2 Lt. Bruce H. Bode
O-1060014
881ˢᵗ Field Artillery Battalion
14ᵗʰ U.S. Field Hospital
69ᵗʰ Infantry Division
Liaison Pilot

In WWII, enlisted aviation students who had failed USAAF pilot training were given the opportunity to continue to fly as liaison pilots. Many of them had existing flying skills from civilian life and had already soloed. Their wings bore an "L" in the center. They flew critical yet anonymous missions in unarmored and unarmed puddle-jumpers, usually single-engine Piper Cubs with no radios and very little navigation or flight instrumentation. These pilots flew a variety of hazardous missions in and out of small, rough fields and roads for photographic and intelligence missions to observe enemy positions or troop movements, for medical evacuation from forward areas, to deliver munitions, mail and other supplies to the front lines. They ferried personnel, including saboteurs and spies into remote sites and rescued downed pilots. One such Liaison Pilot was Bruce Bode of Radburn, RHS '39.

"Steve" was born March 21, 1922, was an only child and lived with his parents at 7 Burnham Place. His father worked for the Dictaphone Corporation in New York City. While at Ridgewood High School, between study sessions he played intramural basketball, was in the international club, was treasurer of the German Club, sang in the Second Choir and the A Capella Choir, was in the Red Cross play, on the cafeteria committee, the town council and the library staff.

He went to college and was a senior at Columbia Business School when called to the service in December 1942, entering active service September 19, 1943. He trained at Camp Davis, Camp Edwards and Fort Sill before going overseas as a pilot of a "Mosquito" Piper Cub.

Lt. Bode died February 2, 1945 in Forges-les-Eaux near Rouen, France of third degree burns to his face, legs and arms suffered in an accident the previous day. He was awarded the Soldier's Medal, posthumously "for heroism not involving actual conflict with an enemy on 1 February, 1945, in France. In taking off from a temporary airfield the engine of the plane which he was piloting failed from unknown causes. To avoid crashing into an occupied house with children playing in the yard, Lieutenant Bode deliberately changed his course, fully aware such action would lead to a stalling turn at very low altitude and a certain crash at risk of his own life. In the ensuing crash he received injuries which resulted in death. His unusual courage, self sacrifice and strong devotion to duty reflect the highest credit upon Second Lieutenant Bode and the armed forces of the United States." At death Bruce Bode was 21 years old.

Pvt. Joseph Aloysius Bowen
16th Infantry Regiment
1st Infantry Division

In the heat of the fighting in WWII, the turnover in an Army unit was heavy as the number of wounded or killed in action increased. In order to maintain a level of manpower, replacements were always finding their way on to the front line. Often, this would be their first exposure to combat. Sometimes these greenhorns didn't even get to know their buddies, some didn't even have time to get their uniforms dirty before being hit. Joseph Bowen of Ridgewood didn't last a week in combat. Nonetheless, his impact on his buddies before they went into combat was positive to the point that he is remembered in their poetry.

Joe was born January 5, 1912 in Paterson but moved to Wyckoff with his parents, two brothers and three sisters before moving to 5 Maynard Court in Ridgewood. He was a parishioner at Mount Carmel and graduated from Ridgewood High School in 1930 where he played tennis and soccer.

He later lived in Ridgewood with his wife, the former Effie Macksoud (RHS '29), and 4 year old adopted son Michael. From May 1932 until September 1943 he was associated with his father who owned and ran the Paterson Laundry Company in Paterson.

An "older" recruit, Joe entered the service April 1, 1944, training at Camp Dix and Camp Meade before going overseas in September. The 16th Infantry Regiment had landed on Omaha Beach on D-Day but became a reserve division later that summer. After a brief rest, they moved inland 150 miles to Landry, south of Paris, and then turned north. By mid-November they advanced to the Hurtgen Forest near the small town of Hamich. This is when Bowen joined them as a replacement. The cold and rainy weather in one of the worst winters on record created trench foot problems in the 16th.

The attack on Hamich and its neighboring dominant Hill 232 started on November 16 and ended when the 16th took both on November 18 after tough house-to-house fighting. A German counterattack the next day failed. On November 23, 1944 the 16th attacked through the Wilhelmshöhe Wald to capture the Rösslerhof castle. This is the day Bowen was killed in action – less than a week after entering combat. His body was repatriated in November 1947 and is buried in Veterans Circle 13, Grave 1 at Maryrest Cemetery, Darlington. At death, Joseph A. Bowen, whose name is listed as Joseph E. Bowen on Ridgewood's memorial plaques, was 32 years old.

His friend Pfc. Jerome Berkwitz, who was assigned to the Motor Pool at La Louviere, Belgium, wrote:

My Memory of Joe Bowen
Night after night as I lay upon my bed;
Thinking of buddies of mine who are dead –
Gazing out the window, watching the clouds go by;

And seeing the stars so high in the sky
Sends a feeling of loneliness through my head.

Though I am ever amidst men I know;
My thoughts creep back to dear old Joe –
Our moments together were well spent;
So much so, that he's left a dent
In my heart which will grow and grow.

And so I turn to memories of home;
To my loved ones, who are my own –
For they hold the key to my heart;
Which aches and aches for being apart
From the greatest pal I have known.

As each night falls, another day appears;
Bringing me closer to those who are dear –
For I'm sure their love is so great;
As to mend the dent so made by fate
And then, only then will memories disappear.

Throughout my life a memory I'll keep;
Ever to remain in my heart so deep –
For of all the men I have known'
Only one G.I. named Bowen
Has ever been with me in my sleep.

Now I know that no words can explain;
The feeling which exists, and in my heart pains –
But, I wish to pay tribute to a pal named Joe;
Who gave his life against a fanatical foe
And hope future years prove he died not in vain.

Thomas Milton Boyd

    In a few early autumn weeks in 1918 an epidemic of Spanish Influenza ravaged the United States. It was called the Spanish Flu because it was believed to have been carried to the USA on a Coast Guard Cutter from Spain. You would be working with someone one day, they would go home because they didn't feel well and within days they were gone. The death toll around the world was 21 million of which 548,452 were in the USA – ten times more than the 53,513 American lives lost in WWI. Remote Eskimo villages in inaccessible Alaskan regions were completely wiped out. The flu began with a high fever and aching bones. After about four days, many cases developed pneumonia. The lungs of the victims would fill with fluid, causing death. Highly contagious, "open face sneezing" in public was subject to fines and imprisonment. The Spanish Flu killed its millions and then mysteriously disappeared.

It also circulated in the military, striking first at Fort Riley, Kansas in March 1918 but remaining relatively dormant until the fall. Eventually a call-up of 140,000 draftees was canceled because camp hospitals were full. Two of Ridgewood's 112 Honored Dead died within a week or each other, victims of the flu.

One if them was Thomas Milton Boyd who was born May 18, 1894 in Brooklyn and lived at 8 Brookside Ave. with his parents, two sisters and two brothers. He went to Ridgewood Preparatory School before becoming associated with his father in business in Philadelphia. He married Helen Ward on April 27, 1918. He enlisted June 5, 1917 but it was determined that he was unfit for active military service so ironically, he joined a Medical Detachment in the Sanitary Corps. September 3, 1918 and reported to Camp Dix. He died there a month later at 3:00 a.m. on Wednesday, October 2, 1918 of septic pneumonia, developed from Spanish influenza. He is buried in his family's plot Lot 1136, Grave 2 at Valleau Cemetery. At death he was 24 years old.

1 Lt. Edwin S. Brague, Jr.
O5023617
129th Assault Helicopter Co.
2nd Battalion, 327th Infantry
101st Airborne Division

The Vietnam War was the first real helicopter war as the US used choppers in a new concept called "air mobility". Despite their vulnerability to ground fire, the Army moved massive amounts of troops by air with some combat operations involving over 100 helicopters at a time. But air mobility came at a heavy price as the US lost 4,869 helicopters – 53% of these losses were due to enemy fire costing the lives of 3,007 crewmen.

By 1967 the bombing of North Vietnam continued and American troop strength had grown to 525,000. The South Vietnamese government had stabilized and the communists were being pushed out of many of their strong positions. Despite growing opposition to the war in the USA, the military outlook seemed good. Ridgewood's Edwin S. Brague and others in 'Nam at the time were optimistic.

Brague was born in Wilkes Barre, Pa. February 25, 1943 but moved to Ridgewood with his family to live at 623 Delaware Ave. After attending the Maywood Avenue School in Maywood, where his mother was Secretary in the Junior High School, he graduated from Ridgewood High School in 1961 where he was in the band and on the cafeteria patrol. While at Rutgers he was in ROTC, in Alpha Gamma Rho fraternity and was a member of the marching band, graduating with a degree in general agriculture. He enlisted in the service July 14, 1965 and was trained as a helicopter pilot at Fort Wolter, Texas, going to Vietnam September 14, 1966. He was 6' 2" with brown hair. He married and his wife, Barbara Ann, lived with his parents.

He flew almost every day to transport men, supplies and to pick up the wounded as a member of the 129th Assault Helicopter Co. He flew a UH-1D Iroquois helicopter.

UH-1D

UH was short for "Utility Helicopter", nicknamed a "Huey". These helicopters' main duty was for troop transport, command and communication. It had room for seven men or three stretchers in a cargo compartment behind the pilot. Depending on the model, the UH-1 was 53' long, weighed 4,700 lbs, could cruise at up to 127 mph with a range up to 314 miles. It could carry a payload of up to 4,500 lbs.

Lt. Brague suffered a gun shot wound to the head and was killed instantly January 7, 1967 while attempting to land his chopper after having taken ground fire during aerial action near Kontum in Quang Tin Province while flying a command and control operation in support of the infantry.

He was awarded the Distinguished Flying Cross with First Oak Leaf Cluster and the Legion of Merit, posthumously, which said he "distinguished himself by exceptionally meritorious conduct in the performance of outstanding service during the period September 1966 to January 1967 while serving as an aerial command post pilot, 2nd Battalion, 327th Infantry, 101st Airborne Division in the Republic of Vietnam. Flying an average of six hours a day, he often brought order out of chaos by functioning as an aerial relay station. On numerous occasions, Lt. Brague disregarded his safety to rescue casualties and re-supply combat units, despite adverse weather conditions and intense hostile action. When the battalion was subjected to fierce and continuous insurgent probes, he dauntlessly continued to provide critical aerial support, flying emergency re-supply missions and medical evacuations. In addition, Lt. Brague assiduously advised the Battalion Commander on landing zones, load data, airlift capabilities and armed helicopter support."

The former First Congregational Church of Hackensack created a fund in his memory to sponsor an overseas student in Hackensack. His fraternity at Rutgers University set up the E. Stephen Brague Memorial Award to be given annually to the brother most active in house sports. Brothers and alumni also instituted a memorial brotherhood loan fund in his honor. The Maywood Public schools established the Lt. Edwin Stephen Brague Memorial Award which is still awarded to the highest achieving science student in the 8th grade. Lt. Brague is buried in Lot 615, Section A in Fern Knoll Burial Park. Dallas, PA. At death he was 23 years old.

Pfc. John James Brickell
42001589
63rd Armored Infantry Battalion
11th Armored Division

Jack, sometimes known as "Brick", was born April 12, 1925, was an only child and lived with his parents at 360 Carleton Terrace. As a member of Ridgewood High School's class of 1943, he wrote for the *Spectator* and *High Times*. He was active on prom committees, was on the golf team, booster club and was President of the bowling league. He was also on the rifle squad, shot with the American Legion Junior Rifle Squad and won the expert rifleman's award as a member of the State Guard. He joined the State Guard while in high school, training in Paterson, was a Boy Scout and loved hunting, fishing and sailing. The family worshipped at Mount Carmel Church.

He enlisted a month after graduation and reported to Camp Roberts in California where he won the Expert Rifleman Medal. He was in the ASTP at the College of Puget Sound and later was assigned to Camp Cooke. He went overseas to England in September 1944 and shortly became ill and was hospitalized. While convalescing he did volunteer work with wounded men in one of the wards.

Rehabilitated, he went to France with Company C, 63rd Armored Infantry Battalion, 11th Armored Div. On February 18 Company C captured the high ground west of Leidenborn, Germany and the town was taken the following day. On February 20, the 63rd was attacking toward Reiff. The enemy, coming from the woods, launched a 30-man counter-attack toward Leidenborn with small-arms fire but was repulsed. Hostile artillery, mortar, and small-arms fire were sporadic, accurate, and at critical points, heavy. It was in this action that John died of wounds to the chest and right arm.

His body was repatriated and is buried in Section 9, Block B, Grave 2 at Maryrest Cemetery in Darlington. His parents, then living in Wyckoff, and friends created a memorial room for him in the new Valley Hospital in Ridgewood as a memorial to "Jack". At death he was 19 years old.

Pfc. Charles Elmer Brooks
32771888
Company E
143rd Infantry Regiment
36th Infantry Division

Generally, the minimum age limit for military service in WWII was 18 years old, or 17 years old with parental permission. Many young Americans lied about their age in order to serve, the youngest being a 12-year old sailor. Many joined for the adventure or out of revenge after Pearl Harbor. After a decade of depression, some joined up for economic reasons. Students were pulled out of college, put in to the ASTP and then given a gun. Military academies also furnished their young students to the war effort. In most cases, that meant these youngsters were on the bottom of the totem pole. If there could be any doubt about the role of Willie and Joe or Private Ryan, 34 of Ridgewood's 112 Honored Dead had the rank of Pfc. or under. Their average age was 22 years old. It's no surprise that they were called the "infant"ry. Today we worry about what time our teenagers will

105

be home; in 1943 parents worried IF their teenagers would be home. One such very young casualty was Charles Brooks of Ridgewood.

Charles was born in Robbinston, Maine December 19, 1924 where he did his early schooling. Following the death of his father and mother, he moved with his sister, Helen and brother, Edward to live for the next 14 years with his Aunt and Uncle, Mr. and Mrs. Elmer Hopper, at 294 Bellair Road in Ridgewood. He attended Christ Episcopal Church and George Washington Middle School before attending New York Military Academy in Cornwall on Hudson. Before graduating he joined the Army March 15, 1943. After basic training at Camp Croft, South Carolina he went overseas, arriving in Africa in September with the 143rd Infantry Regiment ("Third Texas").

Later that month the 143rd moved to the Italian front, going ashore near Salerno as part of the 36th Inf. Div. and participated in one of the bloodiest battles of the unit's history. In December, while assaulting the "Winter Line" near San Pietro, Brooks suffered a shrapnel hit in the chest and died December 24, 1943. He is buried in Plot C, Row 12, Grave 26 in the Sicily-Rome American Cemetery, Nettuno, Italy. At death he was barely 19 years old.

Pharmacist M/3 William Robert Burnett
800-19-93
USNR
2nd Battalion
10th Marines
2nd Marine Division

The Navy has had hospital corpsmen since its very beginning. In 1814, Navy Regulations tell of a "loblolly boy" who served surgeons and surgeon's mates. The loblolly boy became the "surgeon's steward". Recognizing the need for truly trained help, surgeons chose candidates for training in basic medicine. But it was only in June 1898 that the Navy Hospital Corps was officially created. The Navy's Hospital Corpsmen provide medical services for Navy and Marine Corps units throughout the world. In World War II, Navy Corpsmen earned seven Medals of Honor, 61 Navy Crosses, 465 Silver Stars, and 982 Bronze Stars.

107

One WWII Navy corpsman was Billy Burnett who was born in Jersey City on February 2, 1925 and moved to Ridgewood when he was a year old to live at 233 North Pleasant Ave. with his sister and parents. Billy graduated in Ridgewood High School's class of 1942 where he played tennis and soccer, was on the First Aid committee and was active in Hi-Y. The family attended Christ Episcopal Church. His father was a former Commander of American Legion Post 53 in Ridgewood.

After a year of pre-medical training at Cornell, where he was a member of Theta Xi fraternity, he enlisted in Syracuse on April 8, 1943 and reported to the Naval Training Station at Sampson, NY. He was known as a "Fleet Marine", a Navy man assigned to the Marine Corps. Medical Division. He also trained at Camp Lejeune.

He went into active service in the South Pacific as support for the 2nd Battalion, 10th Marines as they conducted amphibious warfare at Guadalcanal. While there he contracted an infection involving the central nervous system. On March 12 he was returned to the 75th Army Station Hospital, Mt. View in Hilo, Hawaii. Five weeks later he died in the evening of April 3, 1944 of tuberculoses Meningitis. He was initially buried in Honolulu but later became the first war casualty repatriated to Ridgewood, in October 1947. He is buried in Section S, Plot 99B, Grave 3 in George Washington Memorial Park in Paramus. At death he was 19 years old.

Pfc. Eugene John Busteed
12028710
Company F
161st Infantry
25th Division

The 25th Division was the first U.S. Army division to see combat in WWII when they returned the fire of Japanese aircraft strafing Schofield Barracks, Pearl Harbor on December 7, 1941.

Johnny was born December 27, 1923, lived at 59 Goffle Road, Midland Park and attended Midland Park schools through the ninth grade. His mother then moved to 439 Van Dyke Street in Ridgewood. He enlisted at the age of 17 on March 25, 1941 and went overseas in April to be stationed at Pearl Harbor. As a member of the 161st Infantry, 25th Division he fed a machine gun firing at the attacking airplanes.

In November 1942 he underwent intensive jungle and amphibious warfare training and sailed for Guadalcanal in the Solomon Islands to relieve the 1st Marine Division and began offensive operations against the Japanese on January 7, 1943. At that time the youthful but confident combat veteran wrote his mother saying "Do not worry. We have licked the Japs, and I have come through without a scratch".

The 25th then seized the remaining Japanese held islands in the Solomons and was sent to New Zealand for rest and more training, moving to New Caledonia in February 1944 to prepare for the invasion of the Philippines.

On January 11, 1945 they landed on Luzon at San Fabian and meet fierce resistance from Japanese forces. The 25th fought its way through the Japanese defenses as they liberated town after town in some of the fiercest fighting of the Pacific war.

The Division set the endurance record in the Pacific after 165 days of continuous combat but suffered more combat deaths than any other U.S. Division in the Philippines. Johnny Busteed was one of those casualties. He died March 6, 1945 of abdominal wounds suffered during the battle of the town of Putlon on Luzon. He is also listed on the memorial plaques in Midland Park which named a street after him. In addition to the Purple Heart, he was awarded several Bronze Stars. His body was repatriated in June 1948 and buried in Section 6, Block C, Tier D, Grave 20 at Maryrest Cemetery in Darlington. At death he was 21 years old.

Pfc. John Augustus Cadmus
1210785
Company F,
107th Infantry Regiment
54th Infantry Brigade
27th Infantry Division ("New York")

Of all the army regiments in WWI, perhaps the most populated by New Jersey men was the 107th Infantry Regiment, originally known as the Old Seventh of New York, a descendant of the 27th Infantry Division, the New York National Guard. First organized in New York in May 1806, they were re-designated as the 7th Regiment of Infantry *(National Guard)*, New York State Militia in 1847. They fought in the Civil War and were mustered into Federal service in 1916 for Mexican Border patrol, stationed at McAllen, Texas.

Known as "silk stocking soldiers" because many of them came from wealth Manhattan families, the 7th was then merged with infantries from up-state New York, known as "appleknockers", and mobilized for the war effort July 15, 1917. Re-designated as the 107th Infantry and assigned to the 27th Division October 1, 1917, the regiment consisted largely of men from New York and New Jersey. Brothers and neighbors enlisted together.

10 Ridgewood men were among those originally sent to train at Camp Wadsworth in Spartanburg, SC. On April 28, 1918 the Regiment moved to Camp Stuart at Newport News, Virginia in preparation for their overseas assignment. 3,700 men of the 107th arrived on May 24 and 25 at

111

Brest, France and underwent several weeks of training near Noyelles-St. Omer.

They moved to the Ypres Salient and in early September were in position around Dickebusch Lake to take part in attacks on German positions at Mt. Kemmel, forcing the enemy to evacuate. Then, after 6 weeks in the trenches and having lost 29 killed, they were withdrawn and sent south for rest and training. In September 1918, Australian and British forces took up positions for an attack on the Hindenburg Line, the last and strongest German defense, and on September 18 a first attack was launched, supported by artillery barrages. The battle raged for several days and the 107th Infantry joined in on the 25th at the St. Quentin Canal tunnel.

In what has been called the bloodiest day in the history of any regiment in any war, two Ridgewoodites in the 107th were killed on Sunday September 29, 1918, the day the Allies broke through the Hindenberg Line (a third, Jesse Douglass, was wounded on the 27th and died September 30).

At 6 AM on that foggy morning, the 107th attacked, charging 1,200 yards across fields that, unknown to them, had been mined a year earlier by the British. Also, because the fields were strewn with wounded comrades from the previous days' fighting, the use of close artillery support was excluded. That day the 107th lost 22 officers killed or wounded, 324 enlisted men killed and 874 wounded.

One of the casualties was John Cadmus of Ridgewood who was born March 28, 1891 in Arlington, NJ and lived with his father, brother and three sisters at 90 North Maple Ave. His mother died prematurely. Known as Jack, he was a member of the Ridgewood Methodist Church. He enlisted in the service in New York May 22, 1917.

Because they hadn't heard from him in two months, by November 1918 his family suspected the worst. In the meantime, an Australian soldier had picked up two photos and a portrait on the battlefield, showing an American soldier and a young woman. On the back of the portrait was the photographer's name – Sherman of Newark, N.J. The Australian sent the pictures to him asking if he could locate the subjects. The young woman was Private Cadmus' fiancée. When she received the photos she notified the Cadmus family. At first it was hoped that he had been taken prisoner and had dropped the photos to give a hint of his whereabouts. It was not to be and in early November the family received a letter from a friend of Jack's in the 107th telling them of his death. Jack was originally buried in the Guillemont Farm Military Cemetery, Cambray near where he fell. His body was moved and is buried in Plot A, Row 04, Grave 01 at Somme American Cemetery, Bony, France. There is a marker in his name in Lot S1/2 977, grave 3 at Valleau Cemetery. The Ridgewood Veterans of Foreign Wars post was named in his memory. At death he was 27 years old.

Major William Todd Campbell
O-006985
VMF 211

During World War II, 130,201 Americans were taken prisoner of war. 14,072 died while in captivity. In the Pacific, Japanese troops were ordered not to take prisoners because that would slow their advance. They were told to think of themselves as avengers when they met the enemy, coming face to face with their father's murderer, a man whose death would lighten their hearts. Captured wounded Allied soldiers were often killed and those who had surrendered were also often murdered. With the Rape of Nanking and the Bataan Death March as background, it was best not to be taken prisoner by the Japanese. 27% of all prisoners taken by the Japanese died in captivity (vs. 4% of POWs of the Germans).

Although he was born January 8, 1916 in New York City, Bill Campbell spent all his live in Ridgewood and lived at 40 North Van Dien Ave.

114

with his sister, brother and parents. His uncle, Thomas Boyd, is one of Ridgewood's 112 Honored Dead from WWI.

He attended the Hill School in Pottstown, Pa. before coming home to become President of Ridgewood High School's class of 1934. While in high school, he played football, ran track, boxed, played volleyball, sang in the glee club, the A Cappella Choir and the mixed chorus and was Principal for Senior Day. He was very active in drama and Hi-Y. The summer after graduation he studied at the University of Mexico and then went on to Colgate where he was a member of Beta Theta Pi, played football, captained the wrestling team and was a member of the glee club. He was elected to Konosioni, the Senior Honorary Society and graduated in 1938. He also completed one year of law school at Cornell but left to work for an export company in Panama.

On July 15, 1939 he enlisted in the Marines and was commissioned as a Lieutenant but resigned his commission to go to pilot training in 1940 in Corpus Christi, Texas where he got his wings. He later was a flight instructor there in advanced aviation and on Friday January 28, 1943 he married Katherine Prowse of Corpus Christi in the Naval Air Station Chapel. They honeymooned in Mexico. Shortly thereafter he received orders to report for overseas duty and moved with his wife to California.

He became an F-4U Corsair pilot with the U.S. Marine Corps Reserve in VMF 211, assigned to Midway and Espiritu Santos, Russell Islands. The F—4U was powered by a 2,000hp Pratt and Whitney R-2800-8 radial piston engine, it weighed 8,980 lbs empty, 14,000 lbs. fully loaded. It had a wing span of 41ft., was 33ft. 4in. long and 16ft. 1in. high. Its maximum speed at 20,000 feet was 420 mph. with a cruising speed of 185 mph and a ceiling of 37,000 feet. It was armed with six 12.7mm (0.50 in) machine guns, wing-mounted.

F-4U Corsair

His last base was at Torokina Airstrip on Bougainville, British Solomon Islands where he was promoted to Captain in late 1943. In the fall of 1943 he was injured in an accident while returning to his base in a carryall and spent some time in the hospital.

On January 7, 1944 he was promoted to Major. The following day he was lost over Buka Pass in the Solomon Islands on his birthday January 8, 1944 as he flew with his unit to strafe Buka-Bonis Airstrip. He sighted three float planes and two Japanese fuel barges in Buka passage and ordered the group to attack - he and his co-pilot accounting for the barges while the rest of the unit attacked the planes. All were demolished. However, he failed to return to the rendezvous from the attack. Six weeks later two natives reported that an American plane had come down in that area on that approximate date and that the pilot had been turned over to the Japanese. Post-war searches of Japanese records and interviews with released prisoners of war failed to turn up any trace of Major Campbell. He is listed on the Tablets of the Missing at Manila American Cemetery, Manila.

Major Campbell was awarded the Air Medal and the Distinguished Flying Cross "for meritorious achievement while participating in aerial flight on the central and northern Solomons from October 1943 to January 1944. Leading his division on a strafing mission in the Buka Pass on January 8

Major Campbell aggressively attacked the enemy and aided in starting fires and inflicting casualties on two Japanese barges."

There is an impressive stone in his memory in Section 9, Plot 1136 at Valleau Cemetery. In October 1949 the First Presbyterian Church in Ridgewood dedicated a memorial window to him, the "David the Warrior" window. At death "Major Bill" was exactly 28 years old.

A/2c Howard Raymond Carlough
HQ, 10th Air Base Group

Another of Ridgewood's 112 Honored Dead who died in an accident was Howard Carlough. He was born August 30, 1930 and lived at 143 Pershing Ave. with his parents, brother and three sisters. He was a member of Ridgewood High School class of 1947 where he was an excellent baseball player. He did not graduate and later drove a taxi for Plaza Taxi and worked at the Esso-Linwood Station.

Carlough enlisted in the Air Force in January 1951 and received his first training at Lackland Army Air Base in San Antonio. He later trained at Sheppard Air Force Base and overseas at Burtonwood England, where he was a member of the championship service baseball team. He moved on to Fort Rosière in France where he was assigned to HQ, 10th Air Base Group as an aircraft mechanic, studying to be a flight engineer.

While home on 23-day emergency leave to visit his ailing father, and just a month away from receiving his wings, he was killed instantly on Route 17 in an automobile accident at 2:30 in the morning of April 24, 1953 while returning from a visit to his girlfriend. There was no overpass at the intersection of East Ridgewood Avenue and Route 17, often referred to as "Butcher Boulevard". Carlough ran the red light at that intersection and was hit by a tractor tailor, also killing the truck driver. Witnesses said the traffic light was green for the Route 17 traffic.

Carlough is buried in Block N, Lot 167, Section B, Grave 4 at George Washington Memorial Park in Paramus. At death he was 22 years old.

1Lt. Thomas Edward Carnegie
O5427231
Battery B, 2nd Battalion
199th Light Infantry Brigade
40th Artillery

There is a well known expression about "ships passing in the night". There are a few cases of service casualties from our area who lived here long enough to make an impact on people around them but not long enough to be remembered on local memorial plaques. Thomas Carnegie is one such case.

Born September 18, 1945, Tom lived in Ridgefield, Ct. before moving with his parents and three sisters to Wyckoff where he attended Ramapo Regional High School. While there, he was a member of the fencing team and was active in sandlot football. He then spent the school year 1960/61 at the Augusta Military School and the family moved to 10 Riverview Lane in Hohokus. He came home and attended Ridgewood High School from which he graduated in the class of 1963. He then attended Belknap College in New Hampshire until he enlisted in the service in June 1966 and took his first assignment at Fort Dix. His goal was

119

to use his GI benefits to complete his education, hopefully at the Citadel. He had worked at the Grand Union in Ridgewood, Stamford and in Ridgefield.

Carnegie attended Officers Candidate School at Fort Sill and was commissioned in May 1967. He arrived in Vietnam January 6, 1968 and was assigned to the 199th Light Infantry Brigade's 40th Artillery. Carnegie was fatally wounded April 18, 1968 in Bien Hoa Province near the Cambodian border. His company had become engulfed in small arms and automatic weapons fire when he sacrificed his life going to the aid of his unit's radio operator. He had been promoted to 1Lt. shortly before his death.

Although the Hohokus borough flags were at half-mast upon his death, he is not listed on their memorial plaques. He is listed among the Vietnam casualties at the Community Center in Ridgefield. He was their first casualty of the Vietnam War. Carnegie is buried in Section 8 Grave 6073A at Arlington National Cemetery. At death he was 22 years old.

Pfc. Thomas J. Carroll, Jr.
42001580
Company B
2nd Infantry Regiment
5th Infantry Division
3rd Army

Tom Carroll was an only child, born February 10, 1925 in Princeton. Although his parents moved to Ridgewood in 1938 to live at 307 Heights Road, he stayed behind to continue his education, graduating from Pennington Prep School in Pennington, N.J. in 1943 where he was very active in all sports.

Immediately upon graduation he was inducted into the service July 2nd and trained at Fort Knox, Camp Shaffet in Arkansas and Camp Sill in Oklahoma. He went overseas in November 1943 to join Company B, 2nd Infantry Regiment, 5th Infantry Division ("Red Devils") in Northern Ireland to train for the invasion of Europe. The 5th landed on Utah Beach June 9, 1944 and launched its first attack on Vidouville on July 26. The Division was then assigned to General Patton's Third Army.

With the breakthrough at St. Lo, the 5th advanced rapidly through France. In twenty-seven days they covered 700 miles and eventually ran out of supplies. They seized bridges across the Maine and Loire Rivers, captured the city of Angers and took control of Chartres on August 19th. After taking Etamps, the 2nd Regiment crossed the Marne River and captured Reims on August 29th. The Moselle bridgehead was secured on September 1 and re-supply of ammunition and gasoline was received on September 6.

Metz surrendered on November 21 and Fort Driant fell to the 2nd Infantry Regiment on December 8, 1944, ending the Moselle Operation and opening the road to the Saar River, the Siegfried Line and Germany but the Battle of the Bulge altered their plans. On December 16, 1944, the 5th received orders to move to Luxembourg. On January 18 the Division made a surprise crossing of the Sauer River near Diekirch, Luxembourg, breached the Siegfried Line and drove north to Bitburg, Germany. Carroll drowned March 16, 1945 in the fighting for the Mosel Bridge at Treis. His body was repatriated, ironically on the *U.S.A.T. Carroll Victory*, and is buried in Section 5, Block B, Grave 126 at Maryrest Cemetery in Darlington. At death he was 20 years old.

Deck Cadet Alan Robert Clarke
28 523
S.S. *Meriwether Lewis*

During WWII, members of the Merchant Marine were considered to be civilians, not military. Every member of the Merchant Marine was a volunteer and many men who could not pass the Army or Navy physical examination, or were too old for those services, served their country by joining the Merchant Marine. It was certainly not a service for rejects as evidenced by the fact that superstar professional athletes like Sid Luckman, Bobby Layne, Doak Walker, Jim Thorpe and Charlie Keller all served in the Merchant Marine. Some intentionally joined because they worked for private shipping companies and the pay was much better. Their duty was nonetheless just as dangerous. It was only in 1988 that Congress bestowed the same veteran status to the Merchant Marine as is routinely granted to the other services.

The United States Merchant Marine Academy is the only U.S. service academy whose students can receive an integral part of their training in actual combat, in their case, at sea. In WWII, 142 Merchant Marine cadets lost their lives. In their memory, the Merchant Marine Battle Standard now bears the number 142. Ridgewood's Alan Clarke was one of those lost.

Al was born February 8, 1922 in Paterson, attended the Radburn schools but moved with his parents to Ridgewood in 1936 to live at 131 South Irving Street. He was an only child and graduated from Ridgewood High School in 1940. While there he was on the football, track and golf teams. He subsequently attended Washington & Lee University for two years where he joined Delta Upsilon fraternity and was elected to White Friars, an honor society. He then entered the Merchant Marine Academy. After initial training he was sent to sea October 13, 1942 as a Deck Cadet for a 6-month tour which took him to Morocco and back to New York aboard the Liberty Ship S.S. *Meriwether Lewis* with a complement of 44 merchant crew and 28 Naval Armed Guard.

In a rainstorm in the North Atlantic on March 2, 1943, en-route in Convoy HX-227 from New York to the United Kingdom with a cargo of ammunition and tires, the *Meriwether Lewis* straggled from the convoy and proceeded alone attempting to catch up with the other ships.

Without the safety of numbers, she was sighted by *U-759 (Friedrich)* who attacked and missed but led *U-634* (*Dahlhaus*) to the freighter. She made an initial hit from 800 yards and fired the coup de grâce from 1,000 yards. The torpedo struck under the bridge and then quickly spread over the entire ship. After about 6 minutes a mighty explosion occurred in the forward part of the vessel and the *Lewis* sank rapidly by the head. The USCG cutter *Ingham* searched the area for two days and found only a 30-mile line of floating tires. Clarke died along with the entire crew of 72.

Washington & Lee established memorial scholarships in the name of each of its students who died in the war, including Cadet Clarke. He was awarded the Atlantic War Zone Bar, Combat Bar, Mariners Medal, Victory Medal, Service Emblem, Honorable Service Button and a Presidential Testimonial Letter. Alan Clarke's name is inscribed in the Roll of Honor Book on display in the Mariner's Chapel at the U.S. Merchant Marine Academy in Kings Point, NY. At death he was 21 years old.

Pfc. Thomas Anthony Cobb
32605001
Company D
264th Infantry
66th Division
Troop Ship *Leopoldville*

As Christians worldwide gather on Christmas Eve in the warmth and security of their families – as they gather among themselves at midnight religious services, think for a moment of the tragedy that occurred in the cold darkness of Christmas Eve 1944. On that evening, 763 American GIs died when the troopship *Leopoldville* was torpedoed by U-486 in the English Channel. One of the casualties was Thomas Cobb of 137 Ackerman Ave. in Ridgewood. His family only learned of his true fate over 50 years later.

Tom was born in Reading, Pa. November 22, 1922 and lived in Ridgewood with his sister, brother and his widowed mother. He attended Mount Carmel Church and graduated from St.

Luke's school in Hohokus in 1941. While at St. Luke's he was in the Boy's Athletic Association, the Boy's Glee Club and the Safety Patrol. He was also ad manager for the year book the *"Pindarian"*.

Upon graduation, he worked at the Wright Aeronautical Corp. in Paterson before enlisting in January 1943. He did his basic training at Camp Phillips in Kansas and attended the University of Nebraska Engineering School on the Army Special Training Program, finishing in the top 10% of his class. When the ASTP was disbanded, he was assigned to Infantry School at Camp Rucker, Alabama. His letters home from that time clearly indicated that he was extremely unhappy to find himself in the infantry. In one letter he tells his mother "I dream of the time I can sit at home and not worry about what's going to happen next."

He went overseas in November 1944 and died when the troopship *Leopoldville*, a pre-war Belgian ocean liner taken into service by the British Navy at the outbreak of the war, was torpedoed by a German submarine while most of the soldiers slept.

On December 24, 1944, the *Leopoldville* was transporting 2,235 American soldiers across the English Channel as reinforcements for the Battle of the Bulge. The *Leopoldville* was protected by escort ships, including the British Destroyer *Brilliant*, but no air cover was made available even though the threat of attack by German submarines was high. Just five and one half miles from its destination of Cherbourg, France, the vessel was torpedoed in the number 4 hold by U-486 and sank 2 1/2 hours later.

The British Commander in charge of the convoy ordered the *Leopoldville's* anchor dropped to prevent the troopship from drifting into a minefield outside the harbor. When a tug arrived on the scene, it couldn't tow the sinking vessel because of the dropped anchor. According to many survivors, the order to abandon ship was given in Flemish and the Belgian crew abandoned the sinking ship leaving the American soldiers to fend for themselves. No life jackets had been issued. Delayed radio transmissions for help, delayed response of rescue craft, heavy seas and freezing temperatures were just a few of the many things that sealed the soldiers' fates. And it being Christmas Eve, serviceman at an American base in Cherbourg who could have aided the stricken *Leopoldville* were taking a night off from the war, either partying or attending church. No one seemed to be around to help.

Cobb stood by the rail of the sinking *Leopoldville* with a friend who told him to be sure not to hit the side of the ship when their turn came to jump to *Brilliant,* alongside to off-load the soldiers. He told his friend "visit my family for me because I'm not coming back". By the time their turn came to jump, his friend made it successfully to the *Brilliant* but could no longer find Cobb.

By the end the night, 763 American soldiers were dead (the official casualty count is sometimes given as 802), many drowning or freezing to death in the 48-degree waters of the English Channel. 493 of the bodies were never recovered. Three sets of brothers were killed, including two sets of twins. The survivors spent Christmas Day picking bodies out of the water.

Because of wartime censorship, and to cover-up the mistakes made by the various governments and officials involved, the disaster was not reported to the news media. Survivors were told by the British and American governments to keep quiet. Relatives of the victims were told that their loved ones were Missing in Action, even though the U.S. War Department knew them all to have perished. Later, the men were declared Killed in Action, but even then no details of their deaths were divulged to their families. After the war, the tragedy was considered an embarrassment to the Allies and all reports were filed away as secret by the American and British governments while families of victims searched vainly for information about the deaths of their loved ones. Only in 1996 - over 50 years later - did the British declassify documents relating to the sinking of the *Leopoldville*.

Cobb's body was recovered, buried in France and eventually repatriated to the USA and buried in Section CC, Lot 56, Grave 5 in Gethsemane Cemetery near Reading, Pa. At death he was 22 years old.

Troopship *Leopoldville*

Pfc. Richard Hagaman Condo
12206415
Company G, 2ⁿᵈ Battalion
85ᵗʰ Mountain Infantry
10ᵗʰ Mountain Division

The 10th Mountain Division was the only US Army unit ever recruited by a civilian agency. The National Ski Patrol contracted with the War Department to be the recruiter for the mountain troops. Prospective recruits had to apply for admission with a questionnaire and three letters of recommendation that supported their skiing and mountaineering credentials. The result was a unit top-heavy with college graduates and ski experts. In one regiment 64% of the enlisted men were qualified to be officers. Among them was Norwegian Torger Tokle, who set a ski jumping record within a day of arriving in the US in 1939. In the next few years before his enlistment he became a powerhouse in the jumping world. He was killed in combat with the 10ᵗʰ March 3, 1945. Another famous member of the 10ᵗʰ was 1996 Presidential candidate Robert Dole. Fighting with them was Richard Condo of Ridgewood, NJ.

Dick was born in Ridgewood July 6, 1925 and lived with his brother and parents at 216 Doremus Ave. His family traced its ancestry back to the Chief Officer of the Dutch Colony who conducted the transfer of New Amsterdam to the English. He graduated from Ridgewood High School in 1943 where he was an all-round athlete - a running back on the football team and a superior kicker, having once punted a football 70 yards, a star pitcher and infielder on the baseball team and a basketball player in Hi-Y. He also worked on the senior play, was in Boy Scout Troop 4 at West Side Presbyterian Church and an active member of Ridgewood Methodist Church.

After graduation he enlisted in the Army on August 6, 1943, training at Camp Hale, Colorado and Camp Swift, Texas. In January 1945 he was shipped to Naples, Italy aboard the USS West Point with the 10th Mountain Division.

Condo participated in some of the roughest sectors of the front at Monte Spicolino, Belvedere, Georgiolesco, Della Torreccia and Della Spe in February.. He was awarded the Combat Infantryman Badge. He was also awarded the Bronze Star posthumously for achievements on March 9 when he was assigned to investigate enemy mine fields near Ruffeno Musiolo, Italy. He and a comrade probed deep into enemy territory and contacted a civilian who gave them information about mined areas and warned them that they were near strong enemy positions. His comrade was a Jewish trooper named Pfc. Hans Aschaffenberg who spoke fluent German. When the Germans spotted Dick and Hans in American uniforms, Hans told them that they were on a special mission tracking some Americans in the area and for them to shut up and get the hell out of their way or they would be reported. They did and the mission was completed. Disregarding their own safety, Condo and Hans worked forward and discovered and sketched another minefield. Again they advanced and were within 150 yards of the enemy when friendly artillery forced them to withdraw. The information they gathered was of utmost value. When Dick got back to the bivouac area, he told his friends that he had never been so scared in his life despite already having been in several intensive battle engagements.

April 14, 1945 was the day Bob Dole was wounded - the bloodiest day in the history of the 10th. That same morning Dick Condo was mortally wounded in battle on Hill 909 after coming down from Della Spe to cross the line of defense. Protected by the heavy artillery preparation and the resulting dust haze, the 2nd Battalion had moved from the base of Mt. della Spe at 9:45 and Condo's Company G jumped off for Hill 909. They encountered heavy machine gun fire in addition to mortar and artillery fire. Friendly artillery fire was poured onto Hill 909 until it was taken by Company G.

After the war, veterans of the 10th Mountain Division were instrumental in the popularization of recreational skiing by creating and developing ski resorts that bear names such as Sugarbush, Aspen, Vail.

In 1948 Ridgewood High School established the Dick Condo Trophy dedicated to the cause of good sportsmanship to be awarded to whichever team won three consecutive games in the annual Turkey Day football rivalry between Ridgewood and Fair Lawn (Ridgewood finally won the third in a row in 1961 but no mention is made of the trophy). He is buried in A 120A #3 at George Washington Memorial Park in Paramus. At death he was 19 years old.

Sgt. Charles D. Connolly
32 925 694
Company G
517th Parachute Infantry
17th Airborne Division

Two of Ridgewood's 112 Honored Dead died after the fighting had stopped; one was not even in the service when he died.

Charles "Don" Connolly was born August 7, 1924 and lived at 214 Fairfield Ave. with his sister and parents. Nicknamed "corn", he graduated from Ridgewood High School in 1942 where was on the student council, Hi Y, the art committee for the *Arrow,* did stage and ticket committees, decoration and publicity for the Junior and Senior Proms, was in the senior play, bowled and played intramural basketball. He attended the Citadel for a year and entered the service June 22, 1943, volunteering for service in the paratroopers and was assigned to Company G, 517th Parachute Infantry, 17th Airborne Division - "Golden Talon" - one of the U.S.

Army's first elite combat units. Initially formed in March of 1943, they trained in the backwoods of Georgia.

Don went overseas February 11, 1945 as the 517th assembled near Hurtgen and on March 1 they joined the 13th Airborne Division at Joigny, France for the final thrust into Germany after the Battle of the Bulge.

He returned victoriously to the USA with the 517th August 22, 1945, moved to Fort Bragg and was discharged February 5, 1946. He fell ill the following day. He survived some of the fiercest fighting of the final days of the war but died of tuberculoses September 3, 1946 at the Cornell Medical Center in New York City. As such, he is the only name among Ridgewood's 112 Honored Dead who did not die while on active service. He is buried in J 167C #1 at George Washington Memorial Park, Paramus. At death, he was 22 years old.

Pfc. Thomas W. Connor
1210119
Company C
107th Infantry Regiment
27th Infantry Division ("New York")

Of all the army regiments in WWI, perhaps the most populated by New Jersey men was the 107th Infantry Regiment, originally known as the Old Seventh of New York, a descendant of the 27th Infantry Division, the New York National Guard. First organized in New York in May 1806, they were re-designated as the 7th Regiment of Infantry *(National Guard)*, New York State Militia in 1847. They fought in the Civil War and were mustered into Federal service in 1916 for Mexican Border patrol, stationed at McAllen, Texas.

Known as "silk stocking soldiers" because many of them came from wealth Manhattan families, the 7th was then merged with infantries from up-state New York, known as "appleknockers", and mobilized for the war effort July 15, 1917. Re-designated as the 107th Infantry and assigned to the 27th Division October 1, 1917, the regiment consisted largely of men from New York and New Jersey. Brothers and neighbors enlisted together.

10 Ridgewood men were among those originally sent to train at Camp Wadsworth in Spartanburg, SC. On April 28, 1918 the Regiment moved to Camp Stuart at Newport News, Virginia in preparation for their overseas assignment. 3,700 men of the 107th arrived on May 24 and 25 at Brest, France and underwent several weeks of training near Noyelles-St. Omer.

They moved to the Ypres Salient and in early September were in position around Dickebusch Lake to take part in attacks on German positions at Mt. Kemmel, forcing the enemy to evacuate. Then, after 6 weeks in the trenches and having lost 29 killed, they were withdrawn and sent south for rest and training. In September 1918,

Australian and British forces took up positions for an attack on the Hindenburg Line, the last and strongest German defense, and on September 18 a first attack was launched, supported by artillery barrages. The battle raged for several days and the 107th Infantry joined in on the 25th at the St. Quentin Canal tunnel.

In what has been called the bloodiest day in the history of any regiment in any war, two Ridgewoodites in the 107th were killed on Sunday September 29, 1918, the day the Allies broke through the Hindenberg Line (a third, Jesse Douglass, was wounded on the 27th and died September 30).

At 6 AM on that foggy morning, the 107th attacked, charging 1,200 yards across fields that, unknown to them, had been mined a year earlier by the British. Also, because the fields were strewn with wounded comrades from the previous days' fighting, the use of close artillery support was excluded. That day the 107th lost 22 officers killed or wounded, 324 enlisted men killed and 874 wounded.

One of the casualties was Thomas Connor of Ridgewood who lived at 86 North Pleasant with his parents, two sisters and two brothers. Before joining the service, he had worked for the Bergen Aqueduct Company. He was a member of Mount Carmel Church where his father had been Grand Knight of the Ridgewood Council of the Knights of Columbus before becoming supervisor of the Knights' war activities in the eastern and northeastern sections extending from Canada to North Carolina. Tom and his brother James enlisted in New York April 25, 1917. Tom was promoted to Pfc. December 11.

James hurt his foot in training and did not go overseas but another brother, Leo was also in Europe and met up with Tom and reported that Tom was in good health but had been in some of the thickest fighting. Initially listed as missing in action, his family hoped he might have been taken prisoner; however, his name was listed on the Sunday Casualty List in mid-November indicating that he had been killed. He is buried in Plot B, Row 14, Grave 06 at Somme American Cemetery, Bony, France. At death he was 23 years old.

Meteorologist Mate 1c Harry J. Coyne, Jr.

In 1942 the Joint Chiefs of Staff began to coordinate wartime civilian and military weather activities. At the time of the attack on Pearl Harbor there were 600 Aerographer mates. The Navy gave the Weather Bureau 25 surplus aircraft radars to be modified for ground meteorological use, marking the start of a weather radar system in the U.S. Navy. In early 1942, classes at the Naval Training School, Aerography, at Lakehurst, N.J. grew into a 12-week course for 75 sailors and 7 Marines. By late WWII the Naval Aerological Service counted 6,500 officers and men around the world in 1,400 stations or units. Numbers subsided quickly after the war. Harry Coyne of Ridgewood was a Navy Aerographer.

He was born August 21, 1916 in Brooklyn and moved to New Jersey with his parents and four sisters as a child. The family later moved to Ridgewood in the early 1940s to live at 432 Prospect Ave. on the corner of Grove Street (which actually was in Glen Rock). Earlier he lived at 147 Pasadena Place in Hawthorne. He was a member of the Mount Carmel parish in Ridgewood and attended Central High School in Paterson where his hobbies were football, swimming and skiing. He then attended Forestry School at Syracuse University for a year but went to work for two years as a finger print examiner for the FBI.

Coyne joined the service and began a 10-year Navy career, including a stint as an Aerographer/2 meteorologist in Bermuda (AG2 USNR) during WWII. He re-enlisted one month after his discharge at the end of the war.

In 1952, while stationed at Floyd Bennett Field he was on an official visit at Lakewood when he became ill. After a protracted illness that lasted 6 months, he died of lung cancer in Philadelphia Naval Hospital September 12, 1952. He is buried in Section 12, Block A, Grave 127 at Maryrest Cemetery in Darlington. At death he was 35 years old.

Sgt. John Francis Crikelair
139389004
Company F
75th Infantry
25th Infantry Division

In 1969 President Nixon tried to put in place a program of "Vietnamization", reducing US forces to 480,000. In March, the casualty toll had reached 33,641 – more than the Korean War. Protests in the USA continued and Moratorium Day produced the largest turnout of demonstrators ever to protest the war.

John Crikelair's brother Paul said that what happened to John was like a microcosm of the whole Vietnam War - his team was in a place where they knew they shouldn't have been, they wanted to leave but couldn't get out and the people they were supposed to be helping were the ones who turned against them.

John was raised in Glen Rock and graduated from Glen Rock High School in 1963. He moved to Ridgewood in 1965 to live at 210 Heights Road with his parents, three brothers and three sisters. His father, Dr. George Crikelair, a pioneer plastic surgeon at Columbia University and Director of plastic surgery at Columbia Presbyterian Medical Center, was a leading advocate of fire-resistant coatings for children's sleepwear.

He spent a year at Prep school and graduated from Notre Dame in 1968 with a BA in government. He was an Eagle Scout, Chief of the Ridgewood-Glen Rock Order of the Arrow, was captain of the fencing teams at both Glen Rock High School and at Notre Dame and placed in the top 10 in NCAA fencing competition. He also was in the marching band both in high school and at college. He enlisted for a three-year tour in June 1968 and became a Ranger Paratrooper in Company F, 75th Infantry, 25th Infantry Division. Their mission was to go in small teams for two or three days at a time in an area crossed with North Vietnamese supply routes. They would move at night and hide during the daytime.

On August 6, 1969, "Team 21" was left by a Navy river patrol boat on the west bank of the Vam Co Dong River in knee-deep mud. Their position was discovered by a woman and a man in a sampan and the team asked to be withdrawn because their position had been compromised. They were also seen by peasants who they knew would inform the enemy. They could have killed these civilians for their own safety but instead they radioed saying "They know we're here, come get us out." The team stayed there for the entire day. The woman in the sampan returned, accompanied by a boy and set up a fishing net with bamboo poles in the river near their location. Shortly before dark, the Navy boat returned but instead of taking out the team they removed the bamboo poles and fishing net. Then Team 21 became involved in a fight with the enemy killing three North Vietnamese.

The Navy boats returned and the fight was going well when the team was hit by two rocket propelled anti-tank grenades. Six men were wounded and had to be evacuated. Two died, including John Criklair. He had been in Vietnam 10 months. During his service, he was cited for bravery 11 times, was awarded the Silver Star, Bronze Star and the Cross of Gallantry, South Vietnam's highest award.

He is buried in Section 8, Block A, Grave 35 at Maryrest Cemetery in Darlington. The Ridgewood-Glen Rock Boy Scout Council established a Memorial Fund in his name and dedicated the all-faith chapel in his memory at Camp Yawpaw in Mahwah. At death he was 24 years old.

Pfc. Leonard De Brown
1280035
Co. C, 114th Infantry Regiment
57th Infantry Brigade, 29th Infantry Division

De Brown was born in Passaic but moved to Ridgewood with his sister and a step-brother to live at 39 Union Street and later at 94 Prospect St. He worked at the A&P store after graduating from St. Nicholas School in Passaic. As part of the New Jersey National Guard, on August 31, 1917 he was selected for the 29th Infantry Division, known as the "Blue and Gray" because it was formed from militia companies that had fought in previous wars, in particular the Civil War. The unit trained at Camp McClellan, Alabama where he was promoted to Pfc. November 1.

He arrived overseas June 15, 1918 and assembled in St. Nazaire on the Bay of Biscay before moving on to the final training areas near Poitiers and Prauthoy. They moved to a "quiet area" in Alsace near Belfort in late July and were under French supervision until they moved to the Verdun area in late September. The 57th entered the offensive on October 9 as the only American division serving on the east bank of the Meuse River. Its initial objective was to cover the flanks of the main American effort. Using very sophisticated infiltration tactics rather than a full frontal assault, the division engaged in heavy fighting around such key terrain features as Bois d'Ormont, Morieb Farms, Malbrouck Hill, the Molleville Farm, the Grand Montagne and Etrayes Woods. Under the code name "Mocking Bird" the division advanced seven kilometers in three weeks, fighting elements of six enemy divisions. De Brown suffered a concussion and died at Molleville Farm October 25, 1918; the division was relieved 4 days later in the evening of October 29.

Initially buried at Brabant sur Meuse, he is now buried in Plot G, Row 20, Grave 04 at the Meuse-Argonne American Cemetery, Romagne, France. At death he was 22 years old.

Lt. Lindley Haines DeGarmo
18th Wing
26TH Squadron
Royal Flying Corps.

In 1918, Ridgewood was a much smaller village than it is today – a more intimate place where everybody knew everybody else – where people had almost an insular attitude toward the outside world. Suddenly, in February, the village was rocked by the news that one of its favorite sons had died in the service. Reading reports from the time, one gets the impression that Ridgewoodites felt that nothing like this could happen to them. Reality struck home hard.

Born in 1890, Lindley DeGarmo graduated from Ridgewood High School in 1908 where he played basketball and was advertising manager of the first issue ever published of the *Arrow*. Nicknamed Diggie, he was the class Vice President and gave an oration at the class day exercises. He was also active at the YMCA and was a member of the First Church of Christ, Scientists. He went on to graduate from Cornell in 1912.

More mobile than most people of his time, he and his brother moved to California to operate a grapefruit farm before enlisting in the Aviation Section of the Signal Corps. He graduated first in his aviation class which got him an assignment for further instruction at Oxford, England. He had the distinction of being the first American cadet to fly solo in England, staying up about an hour at 4,000 feet until his face nearly froze and he had to come down. He admitted to having a reputation as a "Stunt Merchant". Regardless, he was well enough thought of to have published a pamphlet entitled *Necessary Preparation for Aviators* which was published in English and in French.

The most popular war plane of the day was the Spad. It was a single seat, 20' 6" long, 8' 6" high, weighed 1,888 lbs and had a wing span of 26' 6". It was powered by a 220 hp Hispano-Suiza water-cooled engine, had a maximum speed of 136 mph, had a range of 250 miles and could reach an altitude of 20,000 feet. It was equipped with two .30 caliber Vickers machine guns and could carry four 25 lb. bombs.

Spad

Communications then were not what they are now. The headline of the *Ridgewood Herald* of Thursday February 21, 1918 read "Lindley

DeGarmo killed somewhere over there". At the time, it was not even known where he died, much less how. We now know he fractured his skull and was killed Saturday February 16, 1918 when his Spad crashed near Ratlett on the outskirts of London while attempting a forced landing on account of his engine missing. While doing a right-hand turn to avoid some trees, his engine stalled at 100 feet. He was the first entry on Ridgewood's Roll of Honored Dead.

A month later, Ridgewood followed a new trend by placing a Gold Star on the Village Service Flag at a well-attended ceremony for Lt. DeGarmo. Subsequently, 13 more gold stars were added to Ridgewood's Service Flag in WWI. Gold Star Banners replaced Blue Star Banners.

The tradition of displaying a Blue Star Banner during times of war dates to 1917 when Army Capt. Robert L. Queissner of the 5th Ohio Infantry, who had two sons serving on the front lines, designed the first such banner. It quickly became the unofficial symbol of a relative in the service with each blue star on the banner representing a service member on active duty. Often the banners were made by hand by the families themselves.

The Blue Star Banner symbolizes pride in the commitment of our youth on the one hand and concern for the seriousness of the war effort on the other hand. By displaying the Blue Star Banner in the window, American families demonstrate their support and pride in the men and women who are serving in the United States Military. A gold star was displayed if a service member was killed in action or died in service and families who lost a loved one in the service became known as gold star families, more specifically gold star mothers. The tradition lasted into subsequent wars.

His cousin Charles DeGarmo wrote the following poem in his memory:

TO THE AIRMEN

Dedicated to Lindley DeGarmo

Thy country lives in thee when borne on wings,
Thou cleav'st the very heavens, for fears forgot,
Thou hast on patriot altars flowing hot
Made sacrifice of all that fair peace brings.
And now thy heart, like hers, exultant sings
Of Liberty through victory; 'tis not
An age for tyranny – thy plunging shot
Shall help her blast the might of ruthless kings
And should'st thou hapless fall, why even then
Life of her life, thou'll live in her, and she
Shall be thy bride, her children thine and when
She calls her roll of fame thy name shall be
Acclaimed among the names of Christ-like men
Who lived and died to keep their country free.

At death Lindley DeGarmo was 28 years old.

1Lt. Michael André Roger de Magnin
133344401
Advisory Team 90
Military Assistance Command, Vietnam, (MACV)

The U.S. Military Assistance and Advisory Group, Indochina (MAAG-Indochina) was created in September 1950 and acted as advisors to the French until their defeat at Dien Bien Phu. In 1962, the command's name was changed to the Military Assistance Command, Vietnam (MACV) and moved the U.S. from advisory roles to combat roles. MACV existed for the remainder of the war in Vietnam, with headquarters in Saigon. Its mission was to assist the Vietnamese Armed Forces to maintain internal security and to resist external aggression. One such advisor was Michael de Magnin.

De Magnin was born April 8, 1945 in Rio de Janeiro, Brazil but moved with his parents and sister to Larchmont, NY when he was three years old. He attended Bucknell University where he was a member of Sigma Chi fraternity and graduated with a degree in business administration. While at Bucknell, he met his wife, the former Peggy Kamuf of Ridgewood. They later lived with her parents at 440 Knollwood Road in Ridgewood. He was 6'1" tall and weighed 165 lbs. and had brown hair and brown eyes.

He first worked at the Continental Insurance Company and then for Columbus Mutual Insurance of Ohio but left to join the service September 6, 1967. He did his officers training at Fort Benning, becoming an advisor in Vietnam April 9, 1969, working directly with the Vietnamese people. This allowed him to participated in the Committee of Responsibility, a committee formed in 1966 in reply to the horrors the war was inflicting on the Vietnamese citizens. Up to 60% of the war's victims were children under the age of 16. The Committee's goal was to bring these children back to the USA for medical attention.

In the late afternoon of November 1, 1969, an Army command and control helicopter (UH1H) in which he was a passenger took ground fire, crashed and burned north of Mo Cong, Tay Ninh Province on the Cambodian border of Vietnam, 65 miles northwest of Saigon. Everybody aboard perished. Lt. de Magnin's body was brought home and buried in the Sycamore Section, Row 8, Grave 49 in Valleau Cemetery. He is also listed on the memorial plaques in Larchmont. At death he was 24 years old.

Radioman 3rd Class John Raymond de Richemond, Jr.
07096159
USS Frederick C. Davis DE 136

Jack or Zeke was born March 25, 1924 in Paterson but moved with his parents and sister to Ridgewood to live at 137 Ackerman. As a member of Ridgewood High School's class of 1942, he was in the A Cappella choir, Glee Club, Dramatic Club, Boosters, was on the bowling team and the property committee for the senior play. He was a Boy Scout, a philatelist, was active in the Junior Cottage Club of Christ Church, sang in their choir and was an acolyte at Christ Church which later dedicated its St. John window to him. After high school he worked for Raffetto's ice cream in Ridgewood. He was also a paperboy for our predecessor, the *Ridgewood Herald.*

Jack joined the service in November 1942. After training at Bainbridge, Md. he studied radio at Auburn Polytechnical Institute in Alabama before being piped aboard the *USS Frederick C. Davis.*

The *Davis* was assigned to escort duty in the Mediterranean between North African ports and

Naples. On January 21, 1944, she sailed from Naples for the Anzio landings and won a Navy Unit Commendation. She patrolled the beachhead for the next 6 months, fighting off many enemy air attacks and coming under shellfire from shore batteries while protecting allied shipping and the Allies fighting ashore.

The *Davis* left Naples August 9 for Corsica in preparation for the invasion on southern France where she patrolled until September 19. She then returned to New York Navy Yard for overhaul.

In April 1945 the *Davis* joined a surface task force to hunt down German submarines in the North Atlantic. On April 24, 1945 the *Davis* made a contact off Nova Scotia and as it prepared to attack, the German submarine *U-546* torpedoed her for its only kill, hitting the *Davis* port side, forward. Five minutes later the *Davis* broke in two and sank within 15 minutes, suffering 115 dead with only 33 survivors recovered. The survivors had abandoned the ship but were pulled from the water within 3 hours. Other navy escort ships sank *U-546* the same day. The *Davis* was the last U.S. warship sunk in the North Atlantic during WWII.

Jack's body was recovered, buried at sea and is listed on the Tablets of the Missing at East Coast Memorial, New York City. At death he was 21 years of age.

USS Frederick C. Davis DE 136

Major Theodore Allison Deakyne, Jr.
AO-2056227
2nd Fighter Interceptor Squadron
52nd Fighter Interceptor Group

Several of Ridgewood's 112 Honored Dead endured the dangers of combat in one war only to die in an accident while still in the service long after the guns had gone silent. Ted Deakyne survived lots of fighting in the Mediterranean area only to die in a training accident several years later in the U.S. He is also one of our several casualties from the Korean Conflict who never set foot in Korea.

He was born in Jersey City March 9, 1921 and moved to 45 Pomander Walk in Ridgewood with his parents and sister in 1927. He was associated with the Emmanuel Baptist Church and graduated from Ridgewood High School in 1939 where he was in the Student Council, wrote for "*High Times*" and the "*Spectator*", bowled, played table tennis, was in the International Club, was football scrub manager and was on the cafeteria committee.

He attended the University of Wisconsin for two years but, anxious to participate in the war in Europe, he left college and enlisted in the Royal Canadian Air Force in February 1941, months before the USA became a combatant. He went overseas in November and spent over 3 ½ years as part of the Mediterranean Allied Coastal Air Force. While based in England he suffered severe head injuries and a broken back when his Beaufighter crashed at Honiley September 23, 1942. He recovered to get his wings on May 1, 1943 in the USAAF and rose to Captain in the 12th AF night fighter squadron, charged with protecting Allied shipping and coastal installations from enemy air attack. He had one kill and was awarded the Distinguished Flying Cross "... for outstanding achievement in action against the enemy" and the Air Medal with one cluster. The French government awarded him their Croix de Guerre with gold star. After the war he was stationed in Germany with the army of occupation.

Several years later he was recalled to active duty while working as a flight engineer with United Airlines. He married Jocelyn Munn of Akron July 19, 1950, a Stewardess with United Airlines. At that time he was also Commander of the 336th Troop Carrier Squadron at Mitchell Field as a Major in the active reserves.

He trained on the T-33, the "T-Bird", which featured a pressurized cabin, dual controls and ejection seats and was capable of speeds up to 580 mph. It was a two-seater manufactured by Lockheed and was used by the Air Force for pilot training. It had a wing span of 38' 10.5", was 37' 8" long and 11" 8" high and weighed 8,100 lbs empty. It could reach a ceiling of 45,000 and had a range of 1,345 miles.

It was when he was with the 52nd Fighter Interceptor Group that he died in an air crash at Ft. Dix (now McGuire Air Force Base). He was a student pilot with an instructor pilot on a local transition mission and crashed August 20, 1951. The fuselage fuel access door had not been secured, causing an explosion in the plenum chamber at 150 feet altitude which made the airplane catch fire immediately upon take off and lose power. In an attempt to land, the T-33 crashed, killing the instructor and student as well as 11 military personnel on ground maneuvers. Another 19 were injured, all within a 30-second time span. Ted Deakyne was awarded the National Defense Service Medal and is buried in Block L, Lot 113, Section C, Grave 1 at George Washington Memorial Park, Paramus. At death he was 30 years old.

T-33

Sgt. Gordon Arthur Dempsey
12136682
754th Bomb Squadron
458th Bomb Group
8th Air Force

The B-24 was a four-engine long range heavy bomber first built by the Consolidated Vultee Aircraft Corporation (Convair) and later by Douglas, Ford and North American Aviation. It was called the "Liberator" because it had a longer range than the B-17. It had a wing span of 110', was 67' 2" long and 18 feet high, and weighed 37,000 lbs empty (65,000 lbs operational). Armed with six 50-calibre guns, two each in the nose and dorsal turrets and in the waist position and four 303mm guns in the tail turret, it could carry an 8,000 lb bomb load and had optional external bomb racks. As such, its crew of 10-12 flew at 290 mph at a ceiling of 28,000' and with a range of 2,200 miles. It was powered by four 1,200 hp, 14 cylinder Pratt & Whitney radial engines. Built at a cost of $366,000, it first flew in late December 1939 and was deployed in 1943.

B-17

Gordon Dempsey of Ridgewood knew the Liberator well. Born July 7, 1921, "Buddy" lived in Paterson with his parents, sister and brother. His father was the founder of the Paterson Steel and Iron Works. The family worshiped at the Presbyterian Church of the Messiah in Paterson and he attended Eastside High School from which he graduated in 1940. While there he was in the Nature Club and served in the Junior Police.

In 1940 the family moved to Ridgewood to live at 333 Meadowbrook Ave. He continued his studies and worked for two years at the Wright Aeronautical Corp. in Paterson. Gordon remained an active member of the Church of the Messiah and became President of the Thursday Night Young People's Club.

He joined the service in March 1943, did his initial training in Tennessee, attended 5 months of Aircraft Engineering School at Keesler Field in Biloxi, Miss. where he received his Aircraft Mechanic's Medal. At 5'8", 163 lbs., he was the right size for a bomber crew. He then spent 9 weeks in gunnery school in Laredo, Texas. It was at the

Army Air Force base in Pueblo, Co. that he received his Good Conduct Medal. It was also in Pueblo that he became engaged to Vauncille Braddy, a student at Boulder College. He finished his training in Topeka.

Dempsey went overseas June 22, 1944 as a B-24 Engineer and top turret gunner in the 754th Bomb Squadron, 458th Bomb Group, 8th Air Force, flying out of Horsham St. Faiths, England. He wrote a letter home every day he was in the service. On his fourth mission, he was in the waist position when his B-24 sustained a direct flak burst and was shot down over Ludwigshafen, Germany on the night of July 31, 1944. The radioman and co-pilot were captured by the Germans and for awhile it was hoped that he and the rest of the crew were prisoners of war. On October 23 it was announced that he had been killed, apparently trapped in the tail of the plane.

His unidentified body was initially buried in a private cemetery in Mannheim but upon identification using dental charts, was moved to the U.S. military cemetery in St. Avold, France and later repatriated in 1951. He is buried in Section 10, Lot 388/389, Grave 4 in Cedar Lawn Cemetery, Paterson. The Church of the Messiah, now the United Presbyterian Church of Paterson, lists him among the WWII casualties from their congregation. At death he was 23 years old.

2 Lt. George Russell Denie
1089515
638ᵗʰ Aero Squadron (Pursuit)
5ᵗʰ Pursuit Group
Air Service, 2ⁿᵈ Army
American Expeditionary Forces

The US Air Force traces its roots to the activities of a group of adventuresome young Americans who volunteered to fight for the French as early as 1914. World War I was the laboratory for military use of aircraft, starting with reconnaissance flights and finishing with dog fights. Early pioneers had familiar names like antagonists Roland Garros of France and the "Red Baron" Manfred von Richthofen of Germany and the Dutchman Anthony Fokker. Then there were the Americans, including Jimmy Doolittle, Eddie Rickenbacker and Jimmy Mitchell who were members of what became the infamous *Escadrille Lafayette* – the Lafayette Squadron.

In April 1916 the *Escadrille Américaine* (N 124) was spun off from the French *Service Aéronautique* to become the first all-American squadron. After the Germans complained, because the USA was officially neutral at the time, it was renamed the Lafayette Squadron. By the end of the war, over 250 American pilots had served, 225 received their wings and 180 flew combat missions. The American flyers were credited with one hundred and ninety nine victories. Fifty one pilots were killed in action, six died in training accidents and six more from illness. As they did not die in the service of the USA, none of these men is recognized by the US government as casualty of WWI.

When the United States entered WWI in 1917 the Army Signal Corps Aviation Section counted 65 officers, 56 pilots and 1,100 enlisted men but had only 250 aircraft – none of which was combat ready. We were not prepared to fight a war. The American aviation industry was virtually

159

nonexistent and, with the exception of the Curtiss Aeroplane and Motor Co., there was neither an industrial base nor a corps of aircraft manufacturers. American industrial ingenuity and the curiosity of young men for the thrill of aviation turned that situation around virtually overnight.

When the men and equipment of the Lafayette Squadron were taken over by the US in February 1918 to become the 103rd Aero Squadron, Air Service, American Expeditionary Force, the United States suddenly had a turn-key air corps of experienced combat pilots. By the summer of 1918 a new and growing industry had been established with several plants mass-producing aircraft and engines. Training facilities were thriving and the industrial infrastructure was in place. By the end of the war, the Air Service had 200,000 personnel and 185 squadrons.

One heir to this legacy was Lt. George Denie whose link to Ridgewood is through his sister, Ida Willcox who lived at 43 North Maple Ave. His mother, Mrs. Frances Denie, lived in Bedminster, NJ.

Denie died after the armistice of multiple compound fractures while piloting a 20' long French built Spad, a single-seat biplane powered by a 180hp Hispano Suiza engine with a maximum speed of 193 kph. It was armed with one Vickers machine gun and would take 6.6 minutes to climb to 2,000m.

Denie was born in Newark and enlisted September 22, 1917 at Essington, Pa. in the U.S.A. Aviation Section, Signal Corps. He went to the School of Military Aeronautics at Princeton until November 19, 1917, trained at Garden City LI until December 22, 1917 and was commissioned April 23, 1918. He was in Texas until going overseas where he passed through Colembey le Belle. Denie was assigned to the 1st Air Corps at Toule before his last assignment, with the 638th Aero Squadron at

Lay St. Rémy, France as pilot of a Spad "Type 7" airplane.

His particular Spad was assigned to the 638th from the 1st Air Depot on January 10, 1919. It had last been flown on November 11, 1918, barely a month after coming out of production. After inspection and repairs, Lt. Denie took her up for a test flight in the afternoon of February 1, 1919. While putting the plane into a barrel roll at 1,000 feet, the right upper and lower wings collapsed, separated from the fuselage and the plane plummeted to the ground, killing Lt. Denie. It was determined that the factory splices on the flying cables had been poorly made and that the spars were very brittle.

Lt. Denie is buried in Plot B, Row 22, Grave 07 in the St. Mihiel American Cemetery, Thiaucourt, France. At death he was 27 years old.

Pfc. Jesse Eddy Douglass
1211680
Co. K
107th Infantry
27th ("New York") Division

Jesse was born March 11, 1890 in Minnesota and moved to Ridgewood when he was very young and lived with his mother, sister and two brothers at 46 South Irving. He attended Ridgewood High School, was active in the YMCA and at Emmanuel Baptist Church where he was Assistant Superintendent of the Bible school and a member of the Christian Endeavor Society.

He was considered a man of exceptionally mild and lovable temperament yet always firm to his purpose in life. He went to work for Hills Brothers in New York and on June 10, 1916 married Elsie Terwilliger, but she died of typhoid fever a year later. Distressed by her death he quit his job and briefly worked on a farm before enlisting in the infantry on September 3, 1917.

After basic training in Spartanburg, SC he sailed for France in May 1918 with Co. K, 107th Infantry, 27th ("New York") Division. His brother Joseph was in the same unit. Fighting with the British in Flanders Fields, their mission was to eliminate the German Salient at Lys during the Somme Offensive in the summer of 1918.

Despite a desperate German defense, the lines were breached and the enemy was driven back 20 miles. Then on Friday September 27th Company K began attacking the Hindenburg Line at Vendhuille in the vicinity of Bony, north of St. Quentin. Jesse was leading his squad when he was wounded. He immediately took refuge in a trench where he lay in the cold and rain spending his time looking at photos in his wallet and reading letters until he was picked up by the Red Cross men.

It was not until he reached the casualty clearing station that he died of his wounds September 30, 1918. His brother Joe was wounded in the same offensive and on October 11th wrote home from the hospital in England that "I don't know where Jesse is; the last time I saw him he was leading his squad across no-mans land just to my right".

Not a natural fighter, Jesse had written home from France "I think I ought to do this thing. If I come back I'll come home to my family and if I'm killed I'll go across to my beloved home in either case".

His body was repatriated in 1921 and buried along side his wife in Plot 1169 at Valleau Cemetery. Emmanuel Baptist Church unveiled a memorial plaque in his honor in October 1921 and his mother unveiled the war memorial shaft in Van Neste Square in 1924. At death he was 27 years old.

"If ye break faith with us who die
we shall not sleep, though poppies grow
in Flanders fields"
John McCrae

Staff Sergeant Richard D. Drager
12038098
419th Bomber Squadron
301st Bomber Group, Heavy

Perhaps there is some closure in finding the final resting place of a long lost friend or relative in the form of a burial plot. However, there must be a very empty feeling in looking for the grave of a friend only to find his name listed on a wall with hundreds of others on the "Tablets of the Missing". Richard Drager had friends close enough to travel 3,000 miles to make such a discovery, albeit anticipated.

Dick was born May 5, 1923 and lived with his brother and parents at 16 Reading Terrace in Radburn and graduated from Ridgewood High School in the class of 1941.

Tall and thin at 5'10½", 145 lbs with brown hair and brown eyes, he entered active service on December 13, 1941. Based in Oudna, Tunisia as of August 6, 1943 as a waist gunner in a B-17, he died November 16, 1943. On that day, the group bombed an airfield at Istres-le-Tube near Marseilles, France.

Returning from the bombing mission, they got in to a running air battle with enemy fighters and his plane was hit over the south coast of France 40 miles south of Marseilles, knocking away a large piece of the vertical stabilizer and the pilot's window. The plane crashed into the Mediterranean Sea. The pilot seemed to have partial control for about five to ten minutes before the fighters put them away and the plane went into a spin and crashed burning in the water. Witnesses said they saw no parachutes.

Drager is listed on the tablets of the missing at Rhone American Cemetery in Draguignan, France. At death Richard Drager was 20 years old.

In 1958, a friend, John Ackerson, visited Draguignan and wrote a poem entitled:

"The Unmarked Grave of Staff Sergent
Richard Drager"

"I'll find him by the sudden, sweeter air,
By roses that he loved, more richly red;
And through the greener turf his yellow hair,
His smiling eyes, his finely modeled head,
The shy, fond look, will stay the maudlin tears,
And silently I shall commune with him,
Defy the dark remembering old years
Till warned by streaks upon the eastern rim;
In casual tones he'll tell me how his plane,
Shot down, delivered him to tender earth;
I'll say how long I sought for him in vain,
And now my heart knows fullness after dearth;
As pale light of farewell breaks on the land,
I'll take in vise-like grip his eager hand."

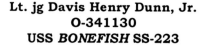

Lt. jg Davis Henry Dunn, Jr.
O-341130
USS *BONEFISH* SS-223

The United States Naval Submarine Force was founded in April 1900 and saw action in every 20th century conflict. In WWII over 50% of Japan's tonnage was sunk by U.S. Navy Submarines including merchant shipping and 214 warships. The human cost was 69,600 Japanese sailors. That success was also very costly to the U.S. submarine service which suffered the highest percentage loss of any U.S. service. Of the 319 boats that saw service, 52 of them never came back. Out of a force of 14,750 officers and men, over 3,500 are on eternal patrol. One of them was Davis Dunn of Ridgewood.

"Bud" lived at 244 Walthery Ave., attended Ridgewood Methodist Church and was in Ridgewood High School's class of 1940 where he played soccer, intramural basketball and bowling. He was in the high school league while also being the *Arrow* representative his senior year and on the ticket committee for the senior play. He was commissioned while a student at Duke University where he was a member of Phi Delta Theta, but left after three years to join the service. He graduated from submarine school in New London, Ct. June 28, 1944 and was assigned to Australia on the USS *BONEFISH*, a Gato Class submarine, eventually patrolling the South China Sea, Celebes Sea and the Sulu Sea.

On May 28, 1945 the *BONEFISH* departed Guam with two other submarines, the *USS Tunny* and the *USS Skate* to conduct their 8th war patrol in the Sea of Japan. It was meant to be their last mission before coming home and they sank one large transport and one medium freighter. For proficiency as a torpedo data computer operator, Lt. Dunn was awarded the Silver Star for service during this patrol "for conspicuous gallantry and intrepidity as Torpedo Data Computer Operator. Lt. Dunn rendered invaluable assistance to his commanding officer in launching a series of devastating attacks which contributed materially to the success of his submarine in sinking and damaging an important amount of Japanese shipping. His heroic conduct under the strain of prolonged war patrol was a major factor in the combat record achieved by the *Bonefish*". It was about this time that Bud was promoted from Ensign to Lt. j.g.

The *Bonefish* and the *Tunny* rendezvoused on June 18. When last seen by the crew of the *Tunny*, the *Bonefjsh* was heading toward Suzu Misaki to conduct submerged day patrol in Toyamo Wan. The *BONEFISH* disappeared that day on its last war patrol before returning home. After other vessels had unsuccessfully tried to contact her, and after she failed to rendezvous on June 23 and failed to return to base on or about July 14 in accordance with her schedule, the *BONEFISH* was reported as presumed lost on June 18, 1945. Japanese records of antisubmarine attacks mention an attack made on June 18, 1945 in Toyama Wan. A great many depth charges were dropped, and wood chips and oil were observed. This undoubtedly was the attack that sank the *BONEFISH*. In total, *BONEFISH* sank 31 enemy vessels and was awarded the Navy Unit Commendation.

Davis Dunn is listed on the Tablets of the Missing at Honolulu Memorial, Honolulu, Hawaii. His name is misspelled on the memorial plaques at Van Neste Square in Ridgewood as Dunne. At death he was 23 years old.

USS Bonefish SS 223

**Yeoman/1 Richard Avery Dwenger
06461848
USS Buck (DD-420)**

Dick lived with his sister and parents at 438 Colonial Road and later moved to 307 Graydon Terrace. He was in the class of 1931 at Ridgewood High School where he had the reputation of being a great bluffer. He was a very active young man: he played interclass basketball, varsity tennis, track and soccer, wrote for the *Arrow*, and participated in various stage presentations and event committees. After graduation he was a playwright and actor by profession and was married at home to Flower Hujer Wilkinson, officiated by the pastor of Emmanuel Baptist Church. She was a solo dancer in the cast of "By Jupiter" on Broadway.

He enlisted in the service a month after Pearl Harbor and was assigned to duty in April 1942 aboard the *USS Buck* which served as a convoy escort between the eastern United States and Newfoundland, Iceland, Northern Ireland, North Africa, and the Caribbean. During his brief tour of duty, the *Buck* was hit by the *SS Atwatea* on

August 22 in a dense fog while trying to escort another ship back to the convoy, severing the fantail and breaking her keel with the loss if seven men. Both propellers were knocked out and the port propeller eventually dropped. The fantail was allowed to sink to avoid having it bang and chafe the hull. The *Buck* was towed to Boston for repairs.

Once again seaworthy, the *Buck* sailed from Boston in November and returned to convoy escort duty in the Atlantic until June at which time they were assigned to patrol duty off North Africa. From July 10th until August 2nd, 1943 the *Buck* participated in the invasion of Sicily and on August 3, while escorting a convoy of six liberty ships from Sicily to Algeria, the *Buck* attacked and sank the Italian submarine *Argento* and took 45 of her crew as prisoners.

After a brief return to the USA, the *Buck* participated in the invasion and occupation of Italy in September. Dick was aboard the *Buck* on anti-submarine patrol when it was torpedoed by German submarine *U-616* in the Gulf of Salerno at 12:45 in the morning of October 9, 1943. The ship sank in four minutes, aided by the explosion of its own depth charges, with the loss of 166 lives. Only 97 of her personnel survived to be rescued by the *Gleaves* (DD-423) and the British *LCT-170*. The *Buck* received three battle stars for her World War II service. Dick is listed on the Tablets of the Missing at Sicily-Rome American Cemetery, Nettuno, Italy and there is a marker in his memory in Section 10, Plot 1158 at Valleau Cemetery. At death he was 30 years old.

USS Buck DD 420

Capt. William Stratton Easterly
O-795921
8th Army Air Force
576th Bomber Squadron &
357th Fighter Squadron
355th Fighter Group

The Distinguished Flying Cross (DFC) was created by an Act of Congress in July 1926 and is awarded to any member of the Armed Forces of the United States who distinguishes himself by heroism or extraordinary achievement while participating in aerial flight. The act of heroism must be above and beyond the call of duty and must have a result so exceptional that the pilot stands out from others in similar circumstances.

President Coolidge presented the first DFC to Charles A. Lindbergh for his solo flight across the Atlantic in 1927. The first DFC awarded to a Navy man was to Commander Richard E. Byrd for his flight to and from the North Pole. The DFC was retroactively awarded to the Wright Brothers; Amelia Earhart was the first civilian awarded the Distinguished Flying Cross but an executive order in March 1927 ruled that the DFC should no longer be conferred on civilians. The medal is identical for all branches of the service and subsequent awards are indicated by an oak leaf cluster for the Army and Air Force. To win one is exceptional; to win two is extraordinary. William Easterly was extraordinary.

Born in Oradell July 5, 1921, he moved to Ridgewood with his family to live at 36 Fairmount Rd. He went to Ridgewood High School but graduated from the Peddie School in 1940, after which he went on to Union College for two years, where he played on the lacrosse team.

He entered the service in January 1942, receiving his commission at Marianna, Fla. 51 weeks later. He went overseas in July 1942 as a P-47D Thunderbolt pilot to complete 50 missions and amass two kills while with the 357th Fighter Squadron, based at Steeple Morden, north-west of Royston, England. He initially named his plane *Sheaf* and it was while piloting this aircraft that he won his first Distinguished Flying Cross, in February 1944. He had already been awarded the Air Medal with 3 Oak Leaf Clusters in 1943.

He moved on to the P-51B Mustang, perhaps the most famous US fighter in WWII. The P-51 was a single-seat fighter/fighter bomber manufactured by North American, 32' 3¼" long, 13' 8" high with a wingspan of 37' 5/16". It had three 50 cal. machine-guns in each wing. Its maximum speed was 445 mph at 24000' over a range of 950 miles with a maximum ceiling of 40000'.

P-51B

Powered by a 1,520 hp Packard V-1650-3 engine, the P-51B was delivered to the 8th Air Force in Great Britain December 1, 1943 and first saw action on December 17th as a fighter. On January 15, 1944, P-51B's were fitted with drop tanks and made their first long-range fighter escort mission as a ramrod for heavy bombers of the 8th AF hitting Germany.

Easterly was lost April 11, 1944 - the Tuesday after Easter, the day the Germans call the "Third Easter Holiday". Leading a formation and piloting a P-51B Mustang *Brenda II*, he dropped down to 200 feet to strafe an airdrome. On his second pass, he was hit by ground fire, suddenly slowed up and his left wing went into some trees. His plane started burning, blew up and crashed one-half mile south of Wilkendorf and one-half mile west of Gartenstadt, a small community a few miles east of Berlin. It was just prior to his death that he was promoted to Captain, although it is doubtful that he had received the news.

173

One day earlier he had written a letter to his parents saying "If you are thinking of my coming home after I complete my time, you might just as well forget about that because I have already put in for another tour of operational missions... There is still a lot of dirt to sweep out and a lot of rats to exterminate, although a lot of them will probably be pretty mouselike before we're through."

He was awarded his second DFC posthumously. Initially buried by civilians in Wilkendorf, his remains were identified and re-interred in Plot A Row 34 Grave 37 in the Ardennes American Cemetery, Neupre, Belgium in 1947. At death he was 22 years old.

Capt. Peter William Ebbert
Headquarter Company
2nd Battalion
58th Infantry Regiment
4th Infantry Division

Pete was born in 1895 in New York City and grew up at 470 Doremus Ave. Glen Rock with his sister and parents. His father was closely associated with Thomas Edison because of his knowledge of electricity. Pete started Ridgewood High School in April 1912 and graduated in the class of 1913 during which he was a reserve guard on the basketball team, in the debating club, participated in school dramatics, playing the role of Baptiste in "A Scrap of Paper" in December 1912 and Luccentio in "The Taming of the Shrew" in

175

March 1913. He also played in alumni football games. He went on to spend three years at Stevens Institute of Engineering but left in his third year when his regiment entered the service in 1917. He was in Company L of the 5th Regiment and had already served nearly half a year on the Mexican border in 1916.

He married in November 1917 and his wife Marion was expecting a child when his unit was mobilized. He would never see his daughter Catherine who was born in October 1918. He did officer training at Fort Leavenworth, Kansas and then served at Camp Greene, NC before going overseas in April 1918 with the 58th Infantry as a Lieutenant transport officer. While at sea, his transport ship was hit by a German torpedo, killing 56 men. After a brief layover in England, the 58th moved on to France and by mid-July was engaged in the Aisne-Marne campaign. He won a Silver Star for gallantry in action on the Vesle River July 28 by personally conducting food details through artillery barrages. He was promoted to Captain.

Peter was awarded the Distinguished Service Cross for his actions on the day he was killed "For extraordinary heroism in action at Ville Savoye, France August 7, 1918. Capt. Ebbert, acting as battalion supply officer, conducted numerous details of food and ammunition through the heavy enemy artillery barrage. Later in the day he volunteered for observation duty and was posted in a prominent tower, where he was killed by a direct artillery hit." That morning he had brought forward an ammunition and ration detail from the vicinity of Les Pres Ferme to Ville Savoye. To do this he had to pass through hostile artillery fire. Shortly after his arrival he and another man visited an observation post in a church tower. These observers had been so accurately pinpointing German positions for U.S. artillery, which was decimating them, that at about 1:15 p.m., enemy artillery retaliated with a direct hit on the tower killing both of them.

Peter Ebbert was Glen Rock's first WWI casualty and his was the first Gold Star affixed to the sanctuary flag at Mount Carmel Church. His daughter Catherine unveiled Glen Rock's memorial to their WWI soldiers and casualties. He is buried in Plot C, Row 5, Grave 9 in the Oise-Aisne American Cemetery in Fere-en-Tardenois, France. At death he was 24 years old.

In his memory, a "friend" wrote:

Gone West

Gone West! In the bright dawning of his manhood,
his life soon ended ere it scarce began
in far-off France our first dear soldier laddie,
has proved himself God's measure of a man.
Gone West, far West into God's radiant presence,
there he shall pass the soldier's last review
there God's reward, eternal decoration,
awaits, crusading knight, for such as you,
who have gone West amidst the din of battle,
and offered up the sacrifice supreme,
to make this earth a safer habitation,
to keep the flag he fought and died for clean.
Immortal fame shall crown him with her laurels,
the High of Heart shall bear his company.
His requiem celestial, angel chanted,
his countersign, his Master's Calvary.

In the summer of 1932 the U.S. government organized a pilgrimage of gold star mothers to visit burial sites in Europe. His mother and daughter went. His wife had remarried by then.

Lt. (jg) William Richard Estell
725th Naval Reserve Fighter Squadron

There are seven casualties from the Korean War listed on the plaques at Van Neste Square. None of them died in Korea; all of them died in the United States. Five of them died in air accidents, one of whom was William Estell. He also is one of several WWII veterans to die in later military service.

Bill was born in Illinois July 10, 1923, moved with his parents, brother and sister to Ridgewood in 1930 and graduated from Ridgewood High School. A popular and active member of the class of 1942, he played basketball and baseball, captained the hockey team his senior year, was on the student council, was home room president, was a salesman for the *Arrow* and a member of the boosters club.

In 1943 he briefly attended Rockford College where he was president of the engineers' group and continued his studies at the Illinois Institute of

Technology while serving as an apprentice seaman at Great Lakes Naval Reserve Station before being getting his commission at Corpus Christi in June 1945. He was released from service later that year. He then went to Purdue University, where he was captain of the soccer team, and received a degree in engineering in 1950. He married Shirley Hopkins of Kirkland, Ill. the same year.

His family lived in Ridgewood for 21 years but moved to Rockford, Ill. in 1951 where he went to work as a buyer for the Sunstrand Machine Tool Corp. Never one to sit still, he was active in the Junior Association of Commerce, was a member of the Second Congregational Church and the American Legion.

While developing his career, he was a "weekend pilot" in the Navy reserve, taking special reserve flight training every three weeks at the Glenview Naval Air Station near Chicago, piloting a McDonnell F2H-3 Banshee.

The Banshee was a single seat, 48'long carrier jet fighter.

F2H-3 Banshee

It was 14' 6" high, had a wing span of 41' 9" and weighed 13,183 lbs empty. Its two Westinghouse axial flow engines gave it a cruising speed of 461 mph, a maximum speed of 580 mph, a ceiling of 46,600 feet and a range of 1,170 miles.

Estell died late in the morning of May 17, 1953 when his Banshee jet fighter dropped out of formation while returning to the naval base and plunged to the ground as the three-plane formation approached the runway during an air show at the Glenview Naval Air Station during an Armed Forces Day celebration. The formation had made two passes over the field and was making a third when his twin-engine fighter faltered, nosed over and burst into flames. It then crashed and exploded. His widow was expecting their first child in June. He is buried in Section 57, Lot 16 at Greenwood Cemetery in Rockford, Ill. At death he was 29 years old.

2 Lt. John E. Faas
O-693655
576ᵗʰ Bomber Squadron
392ⁿᵈ Bomber Group

Paratroopers and skydivers like to say that if you are not scared every time you jump, you are dangerous. So what must it be like to someone who is not a trained jumper? John Faas found out.

"Johnny" was born September 28, 1917 in Passaic, moved to Ridgewood and lived with his mother at 267 Prospect St. for 20 years. His father died when he was just over a year old. He went through the entire local school system and graduated from Ridgewood High School in 1937. A serious vocalist, he participated in the Sophomore Chorus, Junior Choir, Boy's Glee Club, Mixed Chorus, the Amateur Chapel Program and played intramural soccer. He was known as one of the most energetic *Ridgewood Herald & News* paperboys, worked at the Warner Theater, played the guitar and was in one of the local orchestras. He then worked for awhile for the Krug's Bakery and later for the National Cash Register Company in Paterson.

He entered the service in December 1942 and received his commission and wings at Ellington Field, Houston, Texas on October 1, 1943. He went overseas in January 1944 as a B-24 bomber pilot with the 576th Bomber Squadron, 392nd Bomber Group based in Wendling, England. Once, when his plane was in lead position in the squadron, he was forced to turn back and the ship which took his place was shot down. This made him feel that fate was with him.

On July 7, 1944 at 1:30 a.m. and again at 3:00 a.m., 43 aircrews were given a general briefing. A total of 42 planes took off beginning at 4:46 a.m. It was his crew's 30th mission, their first mission to Bernburg. That day the 392nd suffered heavy losses. Fighter opposition and flak was vicious. 38 planes ultimately reached the target, with fair results. But savage attacks from about 140 enemy fighter aircraft as well as heavy and accurate anti-aircraft fire over the target took their toll on the Group. Before this day was over, the Group lost 6 aircraft and 5 aircrews were MIA but their gunners claimed 14 enemy aircraft kills.

The last crew to be MIA on the raid was that of Lt G. E. Jones in aircraft #772. His co-pilot was Lt. John Faas. Their aircraft was shot down by fighter aircraft 400 meters north of Wagenfeld at 10:45 in the morning.

Lt. Jones gave a bail out order and the Engineer went to the waist section to see that all members left by the aft hatch. The Navigator and Bombardier jumped through the nose wheel door opening. 7 of the 8-man crew survived and were captured at Barver-Diephels. Lt. Faas was last seen standing on the catwalk with the bomb bay doors open.

Apparently he was either caught on something in the bomb bay and couldn't jump or he was afraid to jump. His body was found lying in a potato field about 200 yards from the wreckage of the plane which had burned. His chute was unopened and the ripcord had not been pulled, although it was operative. Much later, one of the survivors reported that everybody bailed out except Lt. Faas. The Pilot tried to persuade Faas to jump but he was frozen by fear and wouldn't move in spite of the fire all around him. He went down with the plane.

Initially buried July 7th in the Russian Cemetery at Hannover-Strochlen, Lt. Faas was re-buried in Plot B-Row 10, Grave 3 at the Margraten Netherlands American Cemetery, Margraten, Holland. He was awarded the Air Medal with Oak Leaf Cluster. At death he was 23 years old.

Lt. Commander LeWayne Newcomb Felts
3313
U.S. Coast Guard

Four of Ridgewood's 112 Honored Dead were not from Ridgewood but are listed on our memorial plaques at Van Neste Square because they married women from Ridgewood. One of them was LeWayne Felts, the only Coast Guardsman among our casualties.

He was born February 27, 1921 in Waterloo, Iowa and later moved with his family to Dayton, Ohio. He had one sister but neither ever lived in Ridgewood. He attended the University of Cincinnati and graduated from the U.S. Coast Guard Academy. He was an Ensign when married Ethel Sproul, Ridgewood High School class of 1940 at Emmanuel Baptist Church in November 1943. They had three children. He stayed in the service after WWII and got his wings in April 1947.

On July 5, 1953 he was on a training flight piloting a twin engine Beechcraft C-45B from Sioux City, Iowa to his home station at Wright-Patterson Field in Ohio.

The C-45B was 34'. 3" long, 9' 2" high, weighed 8,725 lbs loaded and had a wing span of 47' 8".

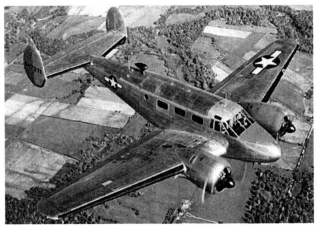

C-45B

The crew of 2 could carry up to 7 passengers. The plane was powered by two Pratt & Whitney 450 hp engines which took the plane to a maximum speed of 218 mph. It had a range of 1,200 miles and a ceiling of 18,500'.

A planned refueling stop in Madison, Wis. was canceled due to bad weather and he was forced to land early and spend the night in LaCrosse, Wisc. The next day he refueled and took off for Wright-Patterson. Shortly after take-off the left engine went out and Felts started a steep turn back to the field in an attempt to land but the plane crashed one mile short of the runway near Sparta, Wisconsin. He was thrown out of the cockpit and died of a skull fracture and burns. Two other officer-students and a passenger also died. Felts had over 1,500 hours as a pilot the day he took off on his last flight, as did his co-pilot.

Felts is buried in Section 7, Grave 10173-A at Arlington National Cemetery. At death he was 33 years old.

2 Lt. Howard Holmes Ford, Jr.
O-321103
Company E, 60th Infantry Regiment
9th Infantry

Born February 15, 1912, Howy lived with his parents and brother at 300 McKinley Place and was in Ridgewood High School's class of 1930. While in high school he participated in tennis, interclass track, the Triangle Club, Hi-Y and had a role in the "Pirates of Hoppergrass" his senior year. He went on to Lehigh and graduated in 1934 where he was a member of Pi Kappa Alpha. Having become a reserve officer before the war, he was called to active duty in February 1942.

He married Marion Heckel of Castanea, Pa. in October 1943 and made his home in Lockhaven, Pa. After serving at several posts in this country, he was sent overseas in March 1944 as a platoon leader of veterans of North Africa and Sicily in

Company E of the 60th Infantry Regiment, 9th Infantry Division "Old Reliable".

The division trained in England for the invasion of Europe and landed on the Normandy beaches on D-Day plus four - June 10, 1944. The 9th then drove across the Douve river and reached the coast of France near St. Lod'ourville and Barneville on June 17, 1944. Through the 9th's efforts, the Cotentin peninsula was successfully cut off. Next, the division turned north toward Cherbourg, seizing Octsville and capturing the senior army and navy commanders of the Cherbourg area. By July 1 the division had cleaned up the Cap de la Hague area and later that month spearheaded the St. Lo break through. Lt. Ford was killed in Ste. Mère Eglise, France July 10, 1944.

He is buried in Plot E, Row 3, Grave 37 at the Normandy American Cemetery, St. Laurent-sur-Mer, France. At death he was 32 years of age.

Pfc. William R. Francis
USAAF

Many of us remember the miracle of the polio vaccine when it was introduced in the mid-1950s/early 1960s. The incidence of polio in the Americas, Europe and Australasia ever since is negligible. Generally thought to be a crippling disease, there are strains of it which are fatal. Polio is usually fatal if the nerve cells in the brain are attacked, known as bulbar poliomyelitis, causing paralysis of essential muscles such as those controlling swallowing, heartbeat, and respiration. One local man who never lived to see the Salk or Sabin vaccines was Bill Francis.

Born in Paterson December 31, 1923 and known to some as "hot dog", he was the only child of Mr. & Mrs. William S. Francis of 206 Hamilton Ave. in Glen Rock. He did his elementary schooling in Glen Rock and graduated from Ridgewood High School in the class of 1942 where he played football his junior year. He was a member of the Community Church of Glen Rock.

Interested in aviation, he enlisted in the Army Air Corps in February 1944 and shortly thereafter took a course in master mechanics at the Roosevelt Aviation School at Mineola, Long Island. He further trained in Florida and Sheppard Field, Wichita Falls, Texas. At the Boeing Aviation School in Seattle in February 1944 he qualified to receive his technical aircraft training certificate on the B 17.

He was transferred to Avon Park, Fla. where he was stricken with bulbar poliomyelitis. He died September 27, 1944 after a short illness. His parents had been alerted to his illness and were at his bedside when he died. He is buried in George Washington Memorial Park in Paramus. At death he was 21 years old.

Sgt. Walter Joseph Freund, Jr.
11082414
Company I
335ᵗʰ Infantry Regiment
84ᵗʰ Infantry Division

In anticipation of lowering the draft age from twenty to eighteen, the Army Specialized Training Program (ASTP) was created in December 1942 by the War department in collaboration with civilian educators. Launched early in 1943, its purpose was "to provide the continuous and accelerated flow of high grade technicians and specialists needed by the Army." Qualified enlisted men (generally meaning college students) were sent to major colleges and universities to study in fields where the Army's own training facilities were insufficient. Two main disciplines were medicine and engineering. While in ASTP the soldiers were on active duty, in uniform, under military discipline, and received regular army pay. But due to the substantial manpower needs for the invasion of Europe, the program was disbanded in early 1944. Most of these "soldier students" were then assigned to the infantry. Several of Ridgewood's 112 Honored Dead went through the ASTP. One of them was Walter Freund.

He was born in Jersey City March 19, 1924 and moved with his parents and two brothers to Ridgewood in 1929. The family lived at 364 Hillcrest Road. He attended the Willard School, George Washington Elementary School and Ridgewood High School before graduating from Mercersburg Academy in 1941. He was active in the Boy Scouts, was an avid reader and would read a book a night. His father served several terms as an Assemblyman, was on the Board of Chosen Freeholders and was Bergen County Counsel and State Superior Court Judge.

Walt was in his junior year at M.I.T., studying aeronautical engineering when he went into the service in February 1943. After training at Camp Hood he was assigned to Lehigh University in the ASTP. When that program was eliminated, he was assigned to Company I of the 335th Infantry Regiment, 84th Infantry Division ("Railsplitters").

He went overseas in September 1944 and the division landed on Omaha Beach from November 1-4, 1944. The 335th Infantry was detached and fought in Wuerselen, the Geilenkirchen salient north of Aachen, Prummern and won the Battle of Mahogany Hill November 19-22. On November 29, the 335th Infantry reached Lindern in the push to the Roer River and took Beeck the following day. Freund, whose name in German means friend, was promoted to Sergeant and awarded a Purple Heart for wounds suffered in this action.

The division started its offensive to help reduce the German Ardennes salient on January 3, 1945 as it followed the 2nd Armored Division toward Houffalize. Freund was a sniper and died of a head wound received near Beffe, Belgium January 7, 1945. He was initially buried by Belgian civilians and thus was listed as missing in action. Evidence sufficient to establish the fact of death was received on August 11, 1945. His body was repatriated in 1949 and buried in Section 34, Grave 1873 in Arlington National Cemetery. At death he was 20 years old.

Lt. Bruce Carlton Fryar
328386720
Attack Squadron 196
USS *Ranger* CVA 61

The final disposition of 23 of Ridgewood's 112 Honored Dead remains a mystery. They are missing in action. Of the hundreds of thousands of U.S. servicemen who went to Southeast Asia in the 1960s and 1970s, over 1,900 are still unaccounted for. Unlike veterans from previous wars, Vietnam veterans have made a concerted and very visible effort to locate their buddies who are POW/MIA. We see the black flag everywhere. On the other hand, the American Battle Monuments Commission, which is responsible for operating and maintaining permanent American military burial grounds in foreign countries for other 20th century conflicts, talks of MIAs as well as "Americans who gave their lives in the service of their country but whose remains were never recovered or identified" and comingles them on their "Tablets of the Missing". The result is that if you do a web search on "Missing in Action" you will find little relating to Korea, WWII or WWI but you will find hundreds of sites dedicated to MIAs from the Vietnam War. There are even "adopt-an-MIA" sites. One name frequently mentioned is Bruce Fryar of Ridgewood.

Although more than 700 MIAs have been identified since the shooting stopped in 1973, hundreds of families still have not received final news of their loved ones, including Carroll Fryar and his wife Belle who lived at 35 East Glen Ave. in Ridgewood from the late 1960s to the early 1970s while he was on assignment here as Manager for Continental Can Co. and their son Bruce was flying for Uncle Sam over Southeast Asia.

Bruce Fryar was born March 28, 1944 in Seattle, WA and grew up in Chicago. After graduation in 1962 from Proviso East High School in Maywood, Ill he attended the U.S. Naval Academy where his fine tenor voice gave him an important role in the Glee Club, which toured the country and appeared on the nationally televised Bell Telephone Hour, and the Chapel Choir. He also participated in intramural handball and lightweight football. An outstanding student and a Superintendent's List regular with a cumulative 3.2 GPA, he graduated in 1966 with a B.S. in Aeronautical Engineering.

After a month of primary flight training with Training Squadron 1 at Saufley Field Naval Auxiliary Air Station in Pensacola, he flew his first solo flight in a T34 "Mentor" trainer aircraft in early 1967. Then followed 13 months of advanced flight training before he received his "Wings of Gold". He reported to the Naval Air Station Whidbey Island, Oak Harbor, WA in early 1968 for training accompanied by his wife Diane and their infant daughter. Whidbey was the West Coast training and operations center for medium-attack bomber squadrons. He was granted "Top Secret" clearance and selected for the postgraduate education program, to be undertaken after his first sea tour. He missed the opportunity. Attack Squadron 196 (VA-196) became Whidbey's first squadron to receive the Grumman A-6A Intruder on Nov. 15, 1966. The A6 Intruder was considered to be the best ship-based attack aircraft.

He moved to Vietnam with VA-196 in late 1969 as part of Air Wing TWO on the USS *Ranger*, arriving at Yankee Station in November where they settled down to the daily routine of flights over the Ho Chi Minh Trail as the enemy moved anti-aircraft artillery into southern Laos. Bruce confided in a friend that he did not expect to survive the cruise; he nonetheless had the courage to pilot his A-6A every day in combat. VA-196 flew more A6 sorties and suffered greater losses than any other carrier-based squadron.

A-6A Intruder

Powered by two Pratt & Whitney J52-P8B engines with 9,300 lbs. of thrust each, it was 54 feet, 8 inches long, had a wing span of 53 feet, was 15 feet, 6 inches high and weighed 28,000 lbs. empty, with the capability of a maximum weight of 60,400 lbs. Its top speed was 563 knots with a ceiling of 40,600 feet.

In 1969, as had become the custom, a 24-hour cease-fire was announced for the New Year's holiday. As had also become the custom, there were 111 enemy violations. On January 1, 1970 full-scale offensive operations resumed as 30 B52 bombers undertook raids in South Vietnam, near the Cambodian border. The next day, warplanes from the carrier USS *Ranger* again tried to close the Ho Chi Minh Trail.

That day, January 2, Lt. Fryar and his Bombardier/Navigator Lt. Nicholas G. Brooks, with a load of six MK82 bombs, were on a raid on a storage dump along the Ho Chi Minh Trail in the Mu Gia Pass area. At approximately 5,400 feet, on his second 40° dive during a visual dive-bombing attack, the plane exploded and the starboard wing separated from the fuselage, perhaps after being hit by 23mm flak. It is also possible that the bombs exploded prematurely. The plane crashed, exploded and burned. Other planes in the flight saw two parachutes and heard beeper signals from two survival radios, indicating that both crewmen had safely ejected.

Search and Rescue efforts began immediately. One man was sighted lying on the ground still wearing his parachute. A SAR helicopter crewman was lowered to attach a hoist to the man but heavy enemy ground fire forced the helicopter to take off before getting hold of the man. The SAR crewman was able to identify the flier as Lt. Fryar and indicated that he was dead.

The next day the SAR helicopter returned to find that the flier and the parachute were gone. An emergency beeper was heard but attempts to identify a pattern of transmission or voice contact were unsuccessful. After five days, SAR efforts were called off. Both crewmen were initially declared missing in action and eventually both were declared killed in action.

Captain Brooks' remains were identified and repatriated in April 1982. In February 1986 the Joint Casualty Resolution Center received information that remains had been recovered from this crash site but could not be identified as those of Lt. Fryar. In May 1991, a joint U.S./Lao investigation of a crash site believed to be Lt. Fryar's included an interview with witnesses who said the bodies of two crewmen were recovered after the incident and were buried in an adjacent bomb crater. The joint team recovered remnants of two survival tests, one flight suit and other artifacts but no remains. As no firm determination of his death has yet been made, he is listed as presumed dead, body not recovered – the official handle for MIA.

Bruce Fryar was awarded the Air Medal with Numeral "2" for "meritorious achievement in aerial flight... Lt. Fryar contributed materially to the success of the United States efforts in Southeast Asia. His skill, courage and devotion to duty in the face of enemy fire, under hazardous flying conditions, were in keeping with the highest traditions of the United States Naval Service". He was also awarded the Navy Commendation Medal with Combat "V", "for heroic achievement as a pilot of jet aircraft ... during combat operations in Southeast Asia. On 22 December, 1969 Lt. Fryar was assigned the mission of destroying active enemy gun positions. He courageously piloted his aircraft within the lethal envelope of the antiaircraft artillery, purposely drawing fire to himself in order to pinpoint the weapons and execute the attack. A dive-bombing attack was made through an intense barrage of enemy fire, and his weapons were observed to detonate precisely on target. Lt. Fryar's actions significantly decreased the enemy threat to the other strike aircraft in the target area and allowed the primary target, enemy supplies, to be destroyed."

He also was awarded the Purple Heart, Combat Action Ribbon, Meritorious Unit

Commendation, National Defense Service Medal, Vietnam Service Medal with one bronze star, Republic of Vietnam Meritorious Unit Citation (Gallantry Cross Medal Color with Palm) and the Republic of Vietnam Campaign Medal, all posthumously. When lost, Bruce Fryar was 26 years old.

Cadet Herman Giraud Garritsen
27 964
SS *William Clark*

The first Liberty ship built was the *SS Patrick Henry*, launched in 1941. President Roosevelt delivered a speech using 'Liberty' as the theme. He referred to Patrick Henry's quote "*Give me liberty...or give me death*", stating that these ships would bring liberty to Europe.

Liberty Ship

199

The name stuck and the ships were forever thereafter referred to as 'Liberty Ships'.

Designed for rapid construction at minimum cost (utilizing welded hulls which were faster to produce than riveted hulls), 2,770 Liberty Ships were built during WWII specifically as cargo ships. All had a life expectancy of 5 years, were 441' long, 57' wide, displaced 14,100 tons and could carry 10,000 tons of cargo. They were powered by reciprocating engines because turbine engines were reserved for the Navy. The Captain was supported by a crew of 39 sailors and a Naval armed guard ranging from 15 to 30 men.

Professional sailors of the Merchant Marine manned them and cadets trained on them. The United States Merchant Marine Academy is the only U.S. service academy whose students can receive an integral part of their training in actual combat, in their case, at sea. In WWII, 142 Merchant Marine cadets lost their lives. In their memory, the Merchant Marine Battle Standard now bears the number 142. One of these cadets was Herman Garritsen of Ridgewood.

Herman, the only boy and youngest of 5 children, was born in Paterson February 23, 1922 and moved with his family to live at 67 Godwin Ave. and later 131 South Irving Street. He graduated from Mount Carmel Parochial School and Ridgewood High School in the class of 1940. While there he wrote for the *Spectator, High Times* and the *Arrow*. He played intramural and Hi-Y basketball and was in the photography club. He went on to Columbia University.

Upon the outset of WWII, he initially wanted to enlist in the Army Medical Corps but joined the Merchant Marine, doing his training at the Great Neck Training School on Long Island. On his first trip as a Midshipman in the engine room, he sailed from New York August 24, 1942 on the Liberty Ship

SS *William Clark*, stopped at Boston where they joined Convoy BX-35 for Halifax. The ship left Halifax in Convoy SC-99 arriving Iceland September 19, 1942 to await orders. She carried a merchant crew of 41 and a Naval Armed Guard of 30.

More Liberty ships were lost in 1942 than any other year of the war. The War Shipping Administration indicates the Merchant Marine lost 1,554 ships due to war conditions. 562 ships were lost in 1942. Cadet Garritsen was lost November 4, 1942 when the *Clark,* en route from Hualifiordur, Iceland to Murmansk, Russia, was torpedoed by the German submarine *U-354* off Iceland. This ship was one of ten ships selected to sail to Murmansk without a convoy because the previous convoys had suffered terrible losses. None of the ten ever reached their destination. The Master of this ship was advised he would be contacted by an escort vessel 5 hours after leaving Iceland but the only thing sighted were two fishing boats.

The *Clark* was transporting a cargo of airplanes, tanks, tires and ammunition. At 12:35, a torpedo struck amidships on the port side in the engine room. The explosion killed five men in the engine room, disabled the engine and flooded the engine room spaces. After the ship was abandoned, two more torpedoes hit the starboard side amidships, breaking the ship in two, forward of the midship house. A distress call was sent but not acknowledged. The ship was abandoned in three lifeboats, the fourth having been destroyed in the explosion of the first torpedo. The *Clark* sank around 1:00 in the afternoon.

The three life boats got together and the motor lifeboat attempted to tow the other two. Because of the danger of swamping, the master ordered the lines cast off and told the other two boats he was going to try to sail to Iceland so he could send them help. His boat was never seen again. It was presumed to have swamped with all hands lost. 25 survivors in #2 lifeboat were picked up on November 7 about 20 miles from where the ship went down. Lifeboat #3 containing 15 survivors and two dead crew members was picked up on November 12.

Garritsen, whose name is misspelled on the memorial plaques at Van Neste Square, was awarded the Atlantic War Zone Bar, Combat Bar, Mariners Medal, Victory Medal, Merchant Marine Service Emblem, Honorable Service Button and a Presidential Testimonial Letter. At death he was 20 years old.

Lt. Col. James Hamilton Gilson
O-6461848
779th Bomber Squadron
464th Bomber Group, 15th AAF

James Gilson was born January 21, 1917 in Chicago and graduated from Evanston Township High School in Illinois. He won the Northern California Junior A.A.U. swimming championship at 11 years of age and was the undefeated Illinois State high school diving champion.

His parents, brother and sister moved to Ridgewood in 1939, his senior year at Colgate, to live at 659 Wall St. In college he was a six-letter man in baseball and basketball and was manager of the Colgate *Maroon*. He was a member of the Junior Honorary Society, the Maroon Key and the Senior Honorary Society "Konesioni "– elected to these honorary societies because of his scholarship and prominence in all phases of campus life. He was also a member of Delta Upsilon before graduating in 1939. With his degree in business administration, he went to work for Lamson Corp. in Syracuse as assistant advertising manager.

He joined the service in September 1940 as an air cadet and received his wings at Barksdale

Field in Shreveport in April 1941. He was an instructor at Turner Field in Albany, Ga. after which he made Captain. He was then assigned to the staff of the Commander of the 559th Squadron at navigation school at Selma Field in Monroe, La. where he was promoted to Major August 18, 1943. He married Jean Tait April 26, 1941, they had a son and moved to Wyoming, Ohio. Her sister married Col. Gilson's brother.

After three years in the states, his wish came true in July 1944 and he became a B-24 pilot and Squadron Commander of the 779th Sq., 464th Group, 15th AAF in Italy. Piloting his Liberator "Stevanovitch", he was awarded the Air Medal in 1944 for having knocked three enemy planes out of the sky over Blechhammer, Germany. "It was one of the roughest missions our group has ever flown. Enemy fighters? There were 40ME 109s after our box alone. I saw three of our bombers go down, but the boys on my ship got three of the enemy. Our group knocked down 28 enemy planes that day". He was then promoted to Lt. Colonel, based at Pantanella Air Base in Italy.

After leading formations in missions over Vienna, Belgrade and Budapest, he was killed April 10, 1945 piloting "Black Nan" on his 34th mission, one short of the required 35 missions. On that raid, 648 B-24s and B-17s, in support of British Eighth Army forces, hit artillery positions, machine gun nests and infantry defenses along the Santerno River in Italy. This effort represented the largest number of Fifteenth AF heavy bombers attacking targets in a single day. Gilson was shot down over Bologna, near Lego when his plane lost its right wing to flak. Only one member of his crew survived.

Lt. Col. Gilson was awarded the Distinguished Flying Cross, the Presidential Unit Citation, the Air Medal with Oak Leaf Cluster and two campaign stars. He is buried at plot A row 3, grave 13 in the Florence American Cemetery, Florence, Italy. At death he was 28 years of age.

Pfc. Donald Jacob Goris
Quartermaster Corps

Donald lived at 102 Stanley Place with his brother and parents and graduated from Ridgewood High School in 1938. He was an artist and his work on play scenery, prom decorations and chapel programs made him an invaluable member of his class. He was an avid hunter and fisherman and was associated with the First Reformed Church. He took up electrical work and was employed by Burnett & Hillman.

He was inducted into the service in June 1941 and went to Fort Dix and Camp Lee where he received his basic training in the Quartermaster's Corps. He was later transferred to Fort Slocum New York where, in March 1942, he was injured in a fall while training to climb telephone poles. His spurs slipped and, despite his safety belt, he bounced down the pole to the ground and was hospitalized. He developed intestinal cancer (Lymphosarcoma) and six weeks later was transferred to the hospital at Fort Dix where an operation proved unsuccessful. He was then transferred to Walter Reed Hospital in Washington. In November 1942 he was given an honorable discharge and sent home where he died February 13, 1943. He is buried in Section 3, Lot 263, Grave 4 in Fair Lawn Cemetery. At death he was 23 years old.

Capt. Lindol French Graham
O-791302
79th Fighter Squadron
20th Fighter Group
8th Air Force

To become an "Ace" in WWII a pilot needed to have at least 5 kills. Less than 1% of all pilots ever became an Ace yet Aces accounted for over 40% of aircraft destroyed in WWII. Ridgewood claims two aces among its WWII casualties: Thomas McGuire and, with 5½ confirmed kills and two damaged, Lindol Graham. Both are featured among the Flying Aces in the Aviation Hall of Fame and Museum of New Jersey in Teterboro.

Lindy was born November 15, 1918 and lived at 76 Crest Road with his parents, two brothers and one sister. He went to high school in Watertown, Mass. where he was in the band and orchestra, played tennis and basketball, was Treasurer of the class of '36, was on the class day committee and in the class play. He then went to Dartmouth where he got a degree in economics in 1941 and was a member of Phi Delta Theta. 11 days after Pearl Harbor he was called to service and reported to Maxwell Field in Alabama. After basic training in Greenville, Miss. he received advanced flight training at Selma, Ala. where he received his commission. At this time, he was engaged to Marjorie Smith, the sister of a Dartmouth classmate.

He arrived overseas August 31, 1943 as part of the 79th Fighter Squadron, 20th Fighter Group 8th Air Force based in Kings Cliffe, Northamptonshire, England where he was given a bicycle so he could tour the English countryside while waiting for war planes to arrive. "Lucky Lindy", 5' 8" and 147 lbs., was initially the Operations Officer but became a P-38J "Lightning" pilot Ace.

The P-38 was a twin-engine high-altitude

P-38

interceptor, built by Lockheed. A long-range escort fighter, it was also used for dive bombing, level bombing, ground strafing and photo reconnaissance missions. It could out climb and out dive nearly every enemy fighter. The first fighter with two engines, the first fighter with tricycle landing gear and the first American fighter to shoot down a German aircraft after the US entered the war, its maximum speed was 414 mph with a range of 2,260 miles. It was powered by two 1,425 hp Allison V1710 engines and weighed 21,600 lbs. It was armed with a 20mm cannon and four machine guns.

His first three kills occurred on January 29, 1944 on an escort mission to Frankfurt for which he was awarded the Distinguished Flying Cross. The citation reads "The courage, aggressiveness and superior flying skill displayed by Captain Graham in destroying three enemy aircraft during one mission reflect highest credit upon himself and the armed forces of the United States".

Three weeks later on February 20 he knocked down two Me-110s in the Koblenz area to become the 79th Fighter Squadron's first ace. He had named his plane "Susie" for his fiancée. "Take today for instance. Susie got plenty worked up when two Messerschmitt 110s started acting crazy up there and thumbing their noses at us. Lt. Marion Bench and I were helping to protect some heavy bombers and those two Jerries circled up to within 300 yards of us before taking any sort of evasive action. They were really asking for it. Bench and I started blasting away and knocked out both engines of one of the Nazi ships in short order. But the prettiest sight was when the ship broke in two. It went down in flames, with its whole tail assembly shot off. Then we skidded over and gave the other guy the works. We kept shooting until we saw him go down in smoke".

In March 1944, as part of a new Allied tactic, 79th pilots swept target areas after the bombers had departed, earning the squadron its nickname "Loco Squadron". Lindy's last victory occurred on the day he was killed during just such a strafing mission near Ulm, Germany. At about 2:00 in the afternoon of March 18, he had descended from 20,000 feet to attack two M110s that had just taken off. He went after one plane and made repeated attacks until the enemy plane crashed. Flying low, he returned to strafe the plane when his propellers hit the ground. The plane pulled up and then crashed on its back and burned.

Lindy was also awarded the Air Medal with three Oak Leaf Clusters. He is buried at Plot F Row 7, Grave 28 in the Lorraine American Cemetery, St. Avold, France. At death he was 25 years old.

Lindol Graham and crew

Major David James Gunster
44644
56th Combat Support Group

Ridgewood High School class of 1944 lost 3 of its classmates in combat. Two died in World War II. David Gunster died almost 24 years to the day after graduation. David Gunster died in Vietnam.

David was born August 5, 1926 and lived at 405 East Ridgewood Ave. with his brother, two sisters and his parents. He was active in his church, went to Ben Franklin Junior High School, played football at RHS and basketball at the Y, was in the high school band and was very active in lighting and decorations for school plays, Christmas programs, variety shows and the prom. He graduated from RHS in the class of 1944 with the intention to go into the U.S. Army Air Corps. He joined the Army reserve in 1943, was activated into the Air Corp. in January 1945, and was honorably discharged as a Corporal in August 1946.

After his WWII service he went to Fairleigh Dickinson for an AA degree and then to Michigan State where he graduated with a BS in 1951. He was recalled to active duty in February 1952 and commissioned upon completion of Air Force ROTC. He got his wings in June 1952. Later in his career he got a masters degree from George Washington University and also graduated from the U.S. Air Force Command and Staff College at Maxwell Air Force Base in Alabama.

During his 18-year military career he was a B-52 commander as well as personal pilot for many high-ranking military and civilian personnel attached to military operations. He was aide and executive officer to Lt. General Richard Montgomery and personal aide to Generals Preston, Reynolds and Agan. Then he volunteered for a combat tour in Vietnam. While there he was awarded numerous decorations for gallantry and unselfish devotion to his country far and above the call of duty. In December 1967 he received the Silver Star while with the 1st Air Commando Squadron at Pleiku Air Base and was cited for gallantry while helping save an entire Army special-forces team during a battle with North Vietnamese army regulars.

On June 6, 1968 he was piloting an A-1E Skyraider fighter-bomber on his 318th mission, this one over Khe Sanh, accompanied by one other Skyraider. It was a bombing and strafing mission again in support of Marine ground forces which were surrounded by hundreds of enemy troops. Over the next two hours he bombed and strafed against intense ground fire, killing or wounding between 300 and 500 enemy soldiers and destroying four gun positions.

As a result, the entire special-forces team being protected by Major Gunster got out alive. However, he was killed when his plane collided at 4,500 feet with the other Skyraider and pancaked into a mountain ridge. His flight companion ejected and survived. Major Gunster had completed 317 combat missions and was scheduled to take a new assignment as Plan Directorate at the Pentagon just four days later.

Among his awards are the WWII American Campaign Medal, Army of Occupation Medal, WWII Victory Medal, the Distinguished Flying Cross with Oak Leaf Cluster stating that he "...penetrated through mountainous terrain to deliver ordnance on hostile forces who were attacking friendly ground troops occupying a forward fortification. With complete disregard for his own safety, Major Gunster pressed his attack through heavy hostile antiaircraft fire to lay down his ordnance accurately. This courageous attack, blunted the attack by opposing forces and prevented subsequent hostile movements.". He was also awarded the Bronze Star, Silver Star, Air Medal with 15 Oak Leaf Clusters, the Air Force Commendation Medal with Oak Leaf Cluster, citing "...outstanding initiative and professional competence in the planning and execution of policies in conjunction with the official visits of many high ranking foreign and United States civilian and military dignitaries throughout this command.". His Purple Heart was posthumous.

He was buried with full military honors in Block D, Lot 332, Section A, Grave 2 at George Washington Memorial Park in Paramus. At death he was 41 years old.

A1-E

Cpl. Charles Joseph Haeberle
32146168
Battery B
633rd Field Artillery Battalion
5th Army

"Habe" was born March 9, 1919 in Paterson and lived for awhile in Allendale. His parents divorced when he was one year old so he moved to Glen Rock to live at 140 Harding Road with his mother and stepfather, Mr. & Mrs. Joseph Dockray. They attended All Saints Episcopal Church. After elementary schooling in Glen Rock, he graduated from Ridgewood High School in the class of 1938 where he was the alternate pitcher his senior year. He also participated in intramural basketball, football and bowling. After high school he pitched for the Glen Rock Athletic Club and worked for Mathieson Chemical Company of New York and

214

later with the Wright Aeronautical Corp in Paterson.

He was among the first boys from Glen Rock to enter the Army, on April 28, 1941. He trained at Fort Dix and Fort Bragg. While there he was voted most popular soldier and therefore was asked to act as escort for visiting movie celebrities who toured the camps. He was offered the chance to go to Officer Candidate School but turned it down so he could stay with his friends among the enlisted men. He continued his baseball career as a pitcher for the regimental team, touring many bases. His second season was cut short when his unit was sent overseas August 6, 1942 arriving in Scotland with the 2nd Battalion, 36th Field Artillery Regiment, later redesignated the 633rd Field Artillery Battalion They moved to England in October where he pitched well but only briefly as he was shipped out and arrived in Africa on Christmas. The unit fought in Oran and later in Fondouk Pass, Kairouan, Beja and Mateur. He suffered a leg wound in Africa, was put back together and then participated in the invasions of Sicily and Italy. The 633rd is credited with having fired the first shell on the mainland of Europe, on August 16, 1943 – across the Straits of Messina, the day before American troops took Messina.

The 633rd went on to participate in the battle of Monte Casino which was actually four different battles, starting in early 1944. These battles allowed allied forces in Northern Italy to join with allied forces in Southern Italy resulting in the capture of Rome June 4, 1944. Haeberle was killed March 18, 1944 in the third battle for Casino.

All Saints Episcopal Church in Glen Rock engraved his name on an oak communion rail and dedicated it in his memory. He is buried in S 7C 3&4 at George Washington Memorial Park in Paramus. At death he had just passed his 25th birthday.

Ensign Donald Cameron Haldane
326421
VF 81

Of all of Ridgewood's 113 Honored Dead, Donald Haldane was arguably the best athlete and certainly warrants a spot in Ridgewood High School's Sports Hall of Fame.

Don was born in Allendale September 22, 1923 but moved to Ridgewood in 1925 and lived at 181 N. Pleasant Ave. as an only child. He was a Boy Scout and while at Ridgewood High School he wrote for *"High Times"* and the *"High School Spectator"*. A gifted athlete, he captained the basketball and baseball teams and also played football and soccer. His level of play was high enough for him to be recruited by colleges for football and by the New York Giants baseball team. He should have graduated with the class of 1941 but complications from a broken leg suffered playing football his sophomore year held him back and he graduated in the class of 1942, receiving the School Athletic Award.

Two months later he entered the service, took his pre-flight training at Chapel Hill, where he again played football. His primary training was at Squantum, Mass. followed by training in Pensacola where he was commissioned in December 1943. After a brief assignment to Daytona Beach, he arrived at Otis Field, Cape Cod, Mass., which gave him frequent opportunities to hop home on 24-hour passes.

He piloted a single seat Grumman F6F Hellcat which had a maximum speed of 380 mph and a range of 945 miles. It was 33 feet long, had a wingspan of 42 feet was armed with six .50-caliber machine guns and could carry 3,000 pounds of bombs or rockets. It was the Navy's most successful fighter in WWII, accounting for over 6,000 air-to-air kills.

F6F

Piloting a F6F Hellcat in a flight of 12, he died July 3, 1944 when the aircraft he was ferrying went down in a storm near Callahan, Georgia, 35 miles west of Jacksonville, Fla. Although neither of the flight leaders was qualified to proceed on instruments, nor were most of the other members of the flight, they were flying on instrument clearance with the understanding that they would only need to be on instruments about 5 minutes. They flew into thunderheads, showers and reduced visibility and several of the flight became disoriented, only to regain control after losing considerable altitude. Ensign Haldane lost control and crashed.

Donald Haldane was elected to the Ridgewood High School Sports Hall of Fame in 2006. He is buried in 12 Park, Plot E1/2 1475, Grave 1 at Valleau Cemetery. At death he was 20 years old.

SP/4 Charles Randolph Hall, Jr.
U.S. Army Ordinance Depot
Fontenet, France

Here is another Ridgewood man who gave his life in the service of his country, but whose name is not listed on our memorial plaques because he died outside and official period of combat. As with the other Ridgewood service casualties whose names cannot be included on a war memorial because their deaths occurred during peacetime, we honor and remember him because of his willingness to dedicate a part of his life in the service of his country. His premature death was no less painful for his friends and families and his full potential will never be known.

Known as Chucky, Charles Hall was born July 30, 1935 in Ridgewood. He lived at 440 Hawthorne Place with his sister Suzanne and their parents. He went through the entire Ridgewood school system and graduated from Ridgewood High School in 1953 where he was active in basketball and football. Upon graduation, he attended and graduated from Lafayette College in 1957 with a Bachelor of Sciences degree in Business Administration. He was a member of Delta Upsilon and in the ROTC. In September he enlisted in the army, doing his initial training at Fort Dix.

He had been in France about a year at the time of his death. He had gone to Paris to buy a Triumph TR 3 and was killed February 27, 1959 when he hit a tree while driving it back to his duty station. In the pre-seat belt and air bag days, the steering post pierced his chest. He was picked up by some French civilians who took him to a local hospital where he was pronounced dead.

Chucky is buried in Section 6, Block B, Grave # 95 1B in Maryrest Cemetery, Darlington. At death, he was 23 years old.

Pfc. Mandeville E. Hall
32461729
Battery B
445th Anti-Aircraft Artillery
Auto Weapons Battalion (Mobile)
Coast Artillery Corps
8th Infantry Division

Although the concept of big fixed artillery guns for seacoast defense exists since the War of 1812, the Artillery Corps was only divided into two branches in 1901 with the creation of the Field Artillery and the Coast Artillery. Because older, larger guns at seacoast installations were practically useless against long-range bombers or carrier-based aircraft, by World War II the Coast Artillery Corps had shifted its emphasis to antiaircraft artillery. Fort Monroe, VA was the principal training center for the Coast Artillery branch of the Army. Mandeville Hall of Ridgewood was in the Coast Artillery Corps. in WWII.

Hall was born in New York City November 21, 1920, grew up in Westfield with his sister and parents, graduating from Westfield H.S. He eventually moved to Ridgewood with his wife, the former Catherine Carter and lived at 234 West End Ave. After being employed by Western Electric in Kearney he joined the service in September 1942 and went overseas in February 1944 with the 445th Anti-Aircraft Artillery Battalion (Mayfair 445), 8th Infantry Division.

The 8th Infantry Division landed on the beaches of Normandy on D-Day plus 28, July 4, 1944 and entered combat on July 8. The 445th protected advancing columns from air attack through Normandy and Brittany until late September. In early October 1944 they were hastily moved to the Our River, the border between Luxembourg and Germany, in relief of 5th Army forces which had met with considerable enemy resistance. They established a number of observation and listening posts on the high ground of the "Hoesdorf Plateau" facing the well-camouflaged German "Westwall" (Siegfried line) fortifications across the Our river.

It was there that Hall was killed by shrapnel Saturday October 7, 1944. He is buried in Plot D, Row 2, Grave 48 in the Henri-Chapelle American Cemetery, Henri-Chapelle, Belgium. At death he was 23 years of age.

Pfc. Frank Luther Hamilton
32305418
47th Armored Infantry Battalion
46th Infantry Regiment
5th Armored Division

The Purple Heart was established by General George Washington August 7, 1782.

It is authorized for the first wound suffered in an armed conflict by any member of the U.S. Armed Forces or any civilian national of the United States who, while serving with one of the U.S. Armed Services, has been wounded or killed or who dies after being wounded. For each subsequent award, an Oak Leaf Cluster is given and worn on the medal or ribbon. One of the unlucky servicemen to be awarded the Oak Leaf Cluster was Frank Hamilton of Ridgewood but he never saw it.

Frank was born in Ridgewood January 26, 1921. His father was killed in an automobile accident on Maple Avenue when Frank was young. His mother remarried and raised Frank and his four sisters at 58 John Street. A member of First Presbyterian Church, he graduated from Ridgewood High School in the class of 1938. Although he played intramural basketball and various other home room games, he was noted mainly for his ability to kick a soccer ball.

After graduation he worked at Wright Aeronautical Corp. before entering the service June 1, 1942. He did his basic training at Fort Knox and Camp Cooke in California and sailed for England on February 10, 1944. Hamilton participated in the liberation of France, was wounded in Luxembourg September 21st and hospitalized for several weeks with an injury to his back for which he was awarded the Purple Heart. He was deemed fit to return to active service and joined Company C, Combat Command R of the 47th Armored Infantry Battalion, 46th Infantry Regiment, 5th Armored Division ("Victory Division") which had quickly moved through France, Belgium and Luxembourg after landing on the beaches of Normandy July 26.

They ran into heavy resistance in the Hurtgen Forest as the 5th faced its most difficult fighting. Enemy snipers, intense enemy mortar and artillery fire and anti-personnel mines made movement of tanks almost impossible and dismounted advances very difficult, causing heavy casualties in the 47th Armored Infantry Battalion, including several Tank Commanders.

Hamilton earned his Oak Leaf Cluster when he was again hit in the back. This time it was fatal. He died November 30, 1944 near Kleinhau in Germany. His body was repatriated in December 1947 and buried Section 13, Lot 833, Grave 2 at Laurel Grove Cemetery in Totowa. At death he was 23 years old.

Flight Officer Philip Westenfelder Harris
T-123913
492nd Bomb Squad
7th Bomb Group

     Harris was born in Westfield November 13, 1915, moved to Ridgewood in 1926 and lived with his sister and parents at 419 Upper Boulevard. After attending Ridgewood secondary schools, he became a student at Franklin & Marshall Academy in Lancaster, Pa. He was 5' 10", 162 lbs. and an avid bowler.

     He was employed in the bond department of the Central Hanover Bank in New York City when he enlisted in December 1943. He qualified as an expert aerial triggerman during training in aerial gunnery warfare at Harlington Army Air Field in Texas. He then went to Big Spring Bombardier School in Texas and eventually became a B-24 Flight Officer and Bombardier in the 492nd Bomb Squad, 7th Bomb Group (H).

     Initially their mission was to destroy enemy communications in Burma by bombing anything in sight - bridges, docks, warehouses, locomotives and rolling stock, railway marshalling yards, cargo vessels and naval craft, airdromes, barracks areas, depots, gasoline plants, landing strips, supply dumps and troop concentrations.

For awhile in the summer of 1944 they ceased combat operations and began transporting thousands of tons of fuel and supplies over the "Hump" to the Fourteenth Air Force in China.

After just three months in combat Harris drowned in an air accident near Kurmitola, India on August 18, 1944 while returning from ferrying gasoline to Kunming, China. On approaching the airdrome, the pilot called the tower for landing instructions, giving no indication of possible trouble. While circling the field preparing to enter the traffic pattern, all four engines quit. Unable to reach the runway, the pilot attempted a forced landing in a water-filled rice paddy and crashed. Only one member of the 8-man crew survived.

Harris was awarded the Purple Heart posthumously with a citation, signed by General H. H. Arnold, Commanding General Army Air Forces, which read "Citation of Honor – United States Army Air Forces – Flight Officer Philip W. Harris: who gave his life in the performance of his duty, August 18, 1944. He lived to bear his country's arms. He died to save its honor. He was a soldier ... and he knew a soldier's duty. His sacrifice will help to keep aglow the flaming torch that lights our lives ... that millions yet unborn may know the priceless job of liberty. And we who pay him homage, and revere his memory, in solemn pride rededicate ourselves to a complete fulfillment of the task for which he so gallantly has placed his life upon this altar of man's Freedom." He also received a memorial citation signed by President Roosevelt.

His body was repatriated in June 1948 and buried in the family plot in the Hillcrest Section, Lot 1220 in Fairview Cemetery, Westfield, NJ. At death he was 29 years of age.

Lt. Charles Kenney Harvey
Attack Squadron 72 (VA 72)
USS Shangri-La

The name Shangri-la has a deep history in the air service. It was the name of USAAF ace Don Gentile's P-51 Mustang. It was also the mythical point of departure for the bombers of Doolittle's Raid on Tokyo in April 1942 - a name chosen by President Roosevelt whose retreat, now known as Camp David, was then called Shangri-la. Shangri-La is defined as Utopia, a remote, beautiful, imaginary place where life approaches perfection. Ridgewood High School graduate Kenney Harvey of Hohokus learned otherwise.

He was born January 13, 1944 in Pittsburgh, moved to Glen Rock at age 2, where he began his elementary education, before settling in Hohokus in 1952 with his brother, sister and parents to live at 241 Blauvelt Ave. He finished elementary school there and graduated from Ridgewood High School in the class of 1962 where he was very active. He was on the student council for three years, American Field Service committee two years, served as co-chairman on the social committee his senior year, played soccer three years and tried JV baseball, JV basketball and baseball one year each. He forewent a full soccer scholarship at Denison to attend the University of Virginia where he received a N.R.O.T.C. scholarship. He still managed to play lacrosse and soccer for U. Va. and was first Treasurer and then President of his fraternity, *Chi Psi*.

Upon graduation in June 1966 he was commissioned in the Navy, did initial training at Pensacola and completed engineering and navigation training and night instrument flying, cross-country flights and aircraft carrier landing training as well as air-to-air gunnery tactics in Beeville, Texas. He was awarded his "Wings of Gold" receiving an "E" for excellence in Air-to-Ground weaponry. He was subsequently stationed at Cecil Field Naval Air Station in Jacksonville, Fla., joining VA 72, the renowned "Blue Hawks" flying off the *U.S.S. Shangri-La*. At that time, the *Shangri-La* was assigned to the 2nd and 6th fleets, alternating deployments to the Mediterranean and operations in the western Atlantic.

Just prior to holiday leave at his sister's home in Rochester, which would have coincided with his father's and sister's birthdays, he was lost in the early evening of December 18, 1968 30 miles south of San Juan, Puerto Rico during a night training session while piloting a Douglas A-4B

A-4B

Skyhawk as he missed on a carrier landing, catching the undercarriage on the tail-end of the *Shangri-La* and skidding off the port side of the flight deck into 6' waves. Despite an extensive search and rescue operation, his body was not recovered. He had been promoted to Lieutenant 6 days earlier but had not yet received the news.

The following October the Commander of the *Shangri-La* created the Ken Harvey Memorial Award to be presented to the Lieutenant or man of lesser rank selected by each out-going Commander for junior leadership and contribution to the welfare of the squadron. 18 men received the award before VA-72 was disestablished on June 30, 1991. The last recipient was James Wetherbee who became a NASA astronaut who logged over 1,592 hours in space in six space flights and was the first American to command five space missions. At death Ken Harvey was 24 years old.

Flight Officer Thomas Lawson Hawkins
T-63113
100th Fighter Squadron
332nd Fighter Group
15th AAF

Fighter Group 332, known as the Tuskegee Airmen, was composed entirely of African-American pilots. Between May 1943 and June 1945, the Tuskegee Airmen flew bomber escort and ground assault missions. Their skills and tenacity laid the groundwork for the integration of the United States military. Tuskegee-escorted aircraft downed 251 enemy aircraft without losing a single allied bomber. Tuskegee pilots fought with such fervor that many American bomber squadrons requested them over other escorts.

Because 332nd pilots wanted to be certain that Allied bomber crews and enemy pilots could quickly identify them, they painted the tails of their P-51 Mustangs with the reddest of red paint available. Bomber crews started referring to them as the "Red Tail Angels." The 332nd flew 15,553 sorties completing 1,578 missions with the 12th Tactical, and the 15th Army Air Force, was awarded over 850 military medals - 150 Distinguished Flying Crosses, 744 Air Medals and 14 Bronze Stars. A total of 926 pilots earned their wings of whom 450 pilots went overseas to fly P-39, P-40, P-47 and P-51 fighter aircraft in combat. 66 pilots were killed in action. One of those killed was Thomas Hawkins of Glen Rock.

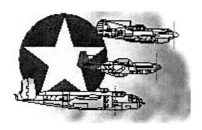

    He was born November 19, 1923 in Springfield, Mass. and moved with his parents to Glen Rock to live at 35 Dean Street. He was an only child after a brother died in infancy. The family attended Mount Bethel Baptist Church where he was responsible for creating the Junior Choir. He attended Glen Rock elementary schools and graduated from Ridgewood High School in the class of 1942. While in high school he was known as Hawk, was homeroom Vice President his sophomore year, played football, ran track, was in the boosters Club and the Willow Club and sang in the A Cappella choir, the combined choir and the Glee Club. Despite his love of singing, his high school quotation was "men of few words are the best men".
    He then attended Temple University where he studied dentistry for two years before enlisting in the Army Air Corps in March 17, 1943 as an aviation cadet. At induction, he was 5' 7" tall and weighed 170 lbs. He did his basic training at Kessler Field, Biloxi, Miss., graduated from the

Army Primary Flying School at Moton Field, Alabama and then completed Advanced Flight Training School at Tuskegee Air Field and received his wings in Class SE-44-E May 23, 1944. He then moved on for training at Eglin Field in Florida and finally took P-47 training at Waterboro, S.C. He came home briefly in October before going oversees. He married Gloria Brown of Bayonne on Christmas Day in the Tuskegee Air Base Chapel.

Upon arriving overseas, his initial training was in Africa. He was then assigned to the 100th Fighter Squadron, 332nd Fighter Group – the celebrated Tuskegee Airmen – in Cattolica, Italy. As of January 1, 1945 he had 28 missions and 3 kills to his credit. Hawkins received the Air Medal and Oak Leaf Cluster for meritorious achievement in bombing installations and trains carrying German supplies to the Russian front from December 20, 1944 to January 8, 1945 and from January 15 to February 15, 1945. He was then named Flight Leader of his group with nine officers under him. Two weeks later on March 7, 1945 he was killed near San Severo when his plane crashed on the runway while taking off on a mission.

There is a monument to the Tuskegee Airmen in the Memorial Park at the Air Force Museum at Wright-Patterson AFB, Ohio and a Tuskegee Airman statue in the Honor Park of the U.S. Air Force Academy in Colorado Springs, Colorado.

His body was repatriated and buried in Plot 792 in Valleau Cemetery. At death Thomas Hawkins was 22 years old.

**Pfc. Elwood H. Hearne
32762155
Company D
503rd Parachute Infantry**

The Browning Automatic Rifle (BAR) was considered by many to be one of the best weapons ever used by the US Army in WWII.

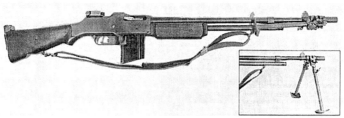

BAR

A .30 caliber, gas operated and air-cooled rifle that required special training, it was 47 inches long, weighed 15½ pounds and could fire 450 shots per minute. The BAR could be adjusted to fire semi-automatically, which was more accurate but much slower than automatic firing, and did not heat the weapon as automatic firing would. As the ammunition was heavy, a second man acted as ammunition carrier and fed the ammo to the BAR man. Normally, there was one BAR man per squad. One such sharpshooter was Elwood Hearne of Ridgewood.

Woody was an only child, born November 28, 1922 and lived with his widowed mother at 131 Ackerman. He went through the entire Ridgewood public school system and in high school was known as El. He was a member of the student council and was active in track, soccer, bowling and basketball before graduating in 1940. He attended West Side Presbyterian Church and was active in the YMCA and Boy Scouts. He then spent three years at Rutgers University where he was an oarsman on the crew and joined Delta Kappa Epsilon until he left for the Army on February 3, 1943.

After basic training, he was assigned to anti-aircraft artillery training at Camp Stewart in August 1943. Then he went to The Citadel in Charleston, S.C. in September 1943 for the Army's Special Training Program (ASTP). Later he was assigned to the 100th Division, 397th Infantry, an anti-tank company at Fort Bragg where he was awarded a medal for good conduct and made Sergeant but gave up a stripe when he decided to become a paratrooper. He went to Fort Benning in September 1944 as a member of Co. B, 541st Parachute Infantry and got his paratrooper's wings on October 7. Christmas 1944 found him doing his final training at Fort Ord, then at Camp Stoneman. He was awarded the Combat Infantryman Badge.

He went overseas in the middle of March 1945 to New Guinea and then on to Leyte in the

Philippines as one of 27 replacements that arrived on March 24, 1945 at San José Mindoro, Philippines to replace losses suffered during the February 16th parachute assault on Corregidor Island. He ended up on the island of Negros with Company D of the 503rd Parachute Infantry. He was a Browning Automatic Rifle Man (BAR) sharpshooter. The BAR was the US Army's principal light automatic weapon in WWII. It fired a .30 caliber bullet (meaning the bullet measured 30/100 of an inch in diameter), was fed from a 20-round magazine, had an effective range of over 600 yards and weighed 10 lbs.

Despite many months of paratrooper training, his jump on to Negros was canceled and he arrived by landing craft at the provincial port of Pulupandan on April 8. Three days later, the 2nd Battalion was ordered to attack a heavily fortified defensive position in the rolling open plain leading to the mountains that ran down the center of the island at the base of massive mountain peaks at the end of Tokaido Road. The prolonged, bloody attack lasted for two and a half rainy weeks.

On April 28th he advanced to the front, firing his BAR down the road to support the 2nd platoon and was crouched on the edge of the road while his assistant lay at his feet, passing ammunition up to him. He would empty one clip after another at enemy positions. His weapon was hot from continual rapid firing and, as often happened with BARs, it jammed. As he crouched to clear the weapon, he was hit and killed instantly.

Elwood Hearne was awarded the Bronze Star and the Purple Heart. His body was repatriated and is buried in Plot 1276 at Valleau Cemetery. His mother agreed to unveil the memorial when the Phi Chi chapter of Delta Kappa Epsilon at Rutgers dedicated a plaque to her son - and 13 other fraternity brothers - who died in WWII. At death Woody was 23 years old.

Pfc. Ronald William Helps
12102675
Co. K, 406 Infantry
102ⁿᵈ Division
"Ozark Division".

In WWII the Army's maximum permissible height for induction was six feet six inches tall. Ronnie Helps slipped under the bar at 6'4".

Ronald William Helps was born April 22, 1924, moved to Ridgewood when he was in the fourth grade and lived at 315 North Murray Ave. with his parents and brother, an accomplished pianist. He attended West Side Presbyterian Church, was active at the YMCA, went to Ben Franklin and George Washington Junior High Schools and then Ridgewood High School for his freshman and sophomore years. He went away for the last two years and graduated from the Peddie School in 1942.

He played on the tennis teams in high school and college, won the American Legion Tennis Championship as well as the Ridgewood Country Club Senior Tennis Championship in September 1941. During the summers he worked on a farm in Pennsylvania, became a Western music fan and learned to square dance.

Then he went to Cornell, was a Chi Phi and played basketball. Before finishing his freshman year, he left school and joined the Army on April 8, 1943. After basic training at Camp Croft he went to Georgetown University in the Army Special Training Program.

On June 25, 1944 he shipped out to Fort Dix, N.J., got a pass and married Joan Shaw on the 4th of July. At the bus stop in Ridgewood, on his way back to Fort Dix, he boarded, walked back about three-quarters of the length of the bus and leaned out of the window to kiss Joan goodbye. She was a short person so someone had to hold her up to reach him, but they managed a long final kiss, much to the delight of the local assemblage, until the bus driver released the brake and drove away.

After helping with a police action to calm transportation strikers in Philadelphia, he shipped out and was one of about 140 men who arrived in Weymouth, England on September 22, 1944. The next day, September 23, 1944, he arrived at Cherbourg and staged in Valognes, Normandy. He was in Co. K, Second Platoon of the 3rd Battalion, 406 Inf., 102 Div. "Ozark Division". They moved to the old Roman city of Tongeren, then got back into trucks for a quick and bumpy ride through Holland until he saw signs for Aachen, just 12 km away.

Immendorf had just fallen easily but the defense at Apweiler was stiff. His unit got orders for his first attack assignment, on Apweiler for

November 17 but overnight the Germans had reinforced their position.

On November 18, he was ordered to attack Apweiler at 11:00 but got delayed and moved in from Immendorf just before noon. On November 20 they followed the 1st Battalion in reserve to join the attack on Gereonsweiler. He was delayed in Apweiler an hour and a half by heavy enemy artillery fire. Two sergeants and he took shelter in German trenches but the trench took a direct hit. It took three weeks to identify him. Ronnie Helps is buried in Plot F, Row 11, Grave 20 in the Netherlands American Cemetery, Margraten. At death he was 20 years old.

Lt. Betty Jo Hicks
Army Nurse Corps

In WWII, more than 265,000 women served in the U.S. Army, Navy, Coast Guard, and Marines, mainly during the period of fighting. Betty Jo Hicks of Glen Rock nonetheless saw a side of WWII that few others did – the humanitarian aftermath. She is the only woman on Glen Rock's memorial plaques and died of an illness a year after the war was over.

"B.J." was born in Chicago November 11, 1923 and moved to Glen Rock with her brother and parents in 1934 to live at 52 Emerson Place. She attended Glen Rock schools before going to Ridgewood High School from which she graduated in the class of 1941. A very active high schooler, she was in the Girl's Club, Girl's Mariners, did folk dancing, swimming, basketball, baseball, was on the decoration committee for the junior prom, the publicity committee for the junior play, the chapel program committee, the clean-up for the publicity committee and the senior prom, the cafeteria committee, wrote for the *Arrow*, performed in Cabaret and was in the Spanish Club. In 1940 and 1941 she had been named "official hostess" for

Glen Rock with the task of welcoming newcomers to town. She also taught Sunday school at the Community Church of Glen Rock.

She entered the School of Nursing of Paterson General Hospital and received her diploma to become a registered nurse and entered the Army Nurse Corps in May 1944, serving first at Fort Dix and in the England General Hospital in Atlantic City.

In January 1946 she was assigned to the USS *Goethals* and made several trips back and forth across the Atlantic, assisting with returning wounded GIs and war brides and their children coming to the USA. She came home in August and immediately fell ill. She died August 25, 1946 in Paterson General Hospital of uremic poisoning as a result of advanced kidney failure. She is buried in Plot Aster, Section 206, South 14424 in Woodlawn Cemetery, New York. At death she was 22 years old.

2 Lt. David Ellsworth Himadi
O 859844
15th Bomb Maintenance Squadron
468th Bomb Group
20th Bomber Command
20th AAF

David was born in Hackensack November 15, 1918 and lived at 666 East Ridgewood Ave. with his brother and his mother. His father lived in Los Angeles. He graduated from Ridgewood High School with the class of 1936 where he ran track and played intramural football. He was a slight 5' 5" and 150 pounds with brown hair and brown eyes. He then went to Duke University, was a Kappa Sigma and graduated in 1940.

After working for awhile at Wright Aeronautical Corp. in Patterson, he enlisted and was sent to communications school at Yale where he was commissioned in 1942. He entered active service on March 4, 1943, received his wings that same month in Boca Raton, Florida, trained on the

B-29 in Salina, Kansas and was assigned overseas in spring 1944.

The B-29 "Superfortress" had an 11-man crew, was 99' long, 29½' tall, had a wingspan of 141.2', and a maximum take off weight of 124,031 lbs. It cruised at 290 mph at a maximum ceiling of 31,857'. Powered by four 2,170 hp Wright engines, it had a range of 2,824 nautical miles. With a bomb load of up to 20,000 lbs, it was armed with 10 machine guns and a rapid-firing 20 mm cannon although many B-29s had their machine gun turrets removed in 1945 to increase speed and bomb load.

B-29

As a communications Officer in a B-29 crew with the 20th Bomber Command Himadi flew the "Hump" in the China-Burma-India command. On June 15, 1944 he was in the first plane of the first super fortress squadron of 60 China-based planes to bomb Japan after Jimmy Doolittle's famous raid in early 1942. Hurried into combat from airfields at Chengtu, Western China USAAF B-29s bombed the Yawata Steel Mills, northern Kyushu, Japan, marking the first time that B-29s were used in distant support of an ongoing amphibious operation. Modeled on the American air campaign in Europe, these daylight raids were high altitude precision bombing missions. But they involved many fewer bombers - less than 100 - and also suffered from the treacherous wind currents above 30,000 feet over Japan.

The Bomber Command in China had other special problems. It was totally dependent on supplies flown in over the Hump from India. And it had no defense against the offensive launched in April 1944 by the Japanese in Southern China that eventually overran its bases. Sometime later Himadi's B-29, the "Gertrude C" was damaged so they were grounded for repairs. One subsequent mission had to be aborted.

On his second bombing mission, he was killed during a raid over the Imperial Iron and Steel Works, again at Yawata, Japan August 20, 1944 when his plane was rammed and destroyed by a small enemy pursuit plane. He was initially buried in a mass grave with the rest of his crew in Japan. Because they could not be identified individually, they were repatriated in 1951 and buried as a group in Section 79, Grave Row O, Grave Site 508 in Jefferson Barracks National Cemetery, St. Louis, Mo. At death he was 25 years old.

S/Sgt. Robert Ainsworth Hird
42012613
467 Bomb Group
788 Bomb Squadron
8th Air Force

Bomber crews flying out of England in WWII wee given a certain number of missions they had to fly before being reassigned to less dangerous duty. Often that number was raised as the need for crews grew. Crew members would mark on their planes and on their jackets the number of missions already flown. Bob Hird's quota was 25.

Bob was born in Ridgewood April 16, 1924 and was confirmed at West Side Presbyterian Church in 1939. He lived at 401 Mountain Ave. with his two brothers, his sister and his parents. He was also a Boy Scout. At Ridgewood High School he was president of the camera club. After graduation in 1942, he briefly attended Lehigh University with the hope of studying aviation engineering. Although drafted in February 1943, he didn't enter the service until September.

After basic training, he took a course at the Roosevelt Aviation School and in January 1944 he was in Laredo, Texas with the 8th G.S.S. L.A.A.F. In March he was promoted to Pfc. and the crew that he would fly with over Europe started to take form at Hammer Field near Fresno, Cal. In a letter he wrote at that time he said: "The training I am getting here is the last before combat overseas. I was assigned to a crew when I arrived here and will remain with them for the duration. There are nine or 10 men in the crew of a B-24. My position is 2nd gunner assistant engineer in charge of the Sperry Ball turret. I have plenty to do with the plane as assistant so that what knowledge I had of airplanes and mechanics will come in handy. We fly about 6 hours a day. Our missions consist of cross-country air to air firing, air to ground firing, high and low altitude bombing and night bombing. I often think of the good times we had in New York and sure wish I could get home again."

A month later they were known as Squadron T of the 422nd A.A.F. and he was in gunnery school at Tonopah, Nev. After D-Day they were off to England, via Camp Miles Standish in Boston. In July they sailed in a convoy to Liverpool, England. He was now a Corporal. His Crew # 6 was assigned a B-24 heavy bomber unofficially known as "Vibratin' Cremator" based in Rackheath, Station 145 near Norwich, England. His first mission was on August 25 to Lubeck. 36 aircraft took off at 7:30 in the morning and they all got back, despite a dogfight. They proceeded to fly 23 missions, always with the same 9-man crew at 18,000 to 28,000 feet altitude against heavily defended targets, although many missions were flown at much lower altitudes. He was awarded the Air Medal & Oak Leaf Cluster for "meritorious achievement in accomplishing with distinction several operational missions over enemy occupied continental Europe, displaying courage, coolness and skill". He was promoted to Staff Sergeant.

When the "Vibratin' Cremator" was being repaired they used other planes. On his 18th mission they were named deputy lead plane in "MASSACHUSETTS GAL", leading more than 60 other bombers. As deputy lead this time they had a crew of 10. He was the right waist gunner, just behind the bomb bay.

They set out early in the morning, expecting an easy mission because they only had to penetrate Germany by about 60 miles. They were headed for a railroad bridge at Güls in Koblenz on January 1, 1945 at 25,000 feet. But they were uneasy because they had been there before and had been severely battered by flak. They arrived about an hour late due to heavy head winds.

When they got over the target they turned right directly into more severe head winds which slowed their ground speed to 100 knots. Normally they crossed targets at over 200 knots. That meant they would be in range of the very accurate flak for a long time. At 13:20, just 30 seconds before they got there the pilot said "boys, they're tracking us. Flack at two o'clock. Hell, they have us zeroed".

They got peppered for about five or six minutes by the most accurate 88mm flak they had ever seen. They were knocked full of holes and tossed about in the air, but nobody was hurt and it began to look like they were going to make it all right. German artillery missed with the first shot but they had the altitude right. The second shot missed too but the third one didn't.

Over the next half-minute, they took several hits: first the front end got blown off, killing three. All the controls were knocked out, forcing them to keel away from the formation in only semi-control. They put the plane on autopilot but it too had been partially damaged. The bombardier managed to get rid of all of the bombs before they got hit in the number four engine and then in the bomb bay. The fourth shot was in the right waist window where Hird was and he was hit with shrapnel. Two buddies stripped off his flack jacket, helping him with his parachute before they jumped. The last thing he said to them was "save yourself". He refused to jump. The plane exploded at about 7,000 feet and was scattered over one kilometer between Missenheim and Saffig near Andernach.

First he was reported missing in action. Two months later the German Government, via the Red Cross, advised his family that he had been killed in action. Two days later he was buried in the community cemetery of Ochtendung, Germany. His body was moved to Margraten, Holland in April 1946 and repatriated to the family plot in Section 10, Lot 164/165, Grave 8 at Cedar Lawn Cemetery in Paterson, New Jersey in June 1949. At death, He was 20 years old.

Hine, Hogarth, Hurst,
Benner, Hird

Cpl. Jon Hampton Holley
81st Maintenance Battalion

When one accepts the obligation to serve in the military, one accepts the risk of death. Death usually comes from hostile action confronting the enemy but can also come from accidents or illness. But nobody goes into the military service with the thought that they will die at the hands of a fellow American. Such was the fate of one of Ridgewood's Honored 112.

Jon Holley was born April 15, 1945 in North Haledon and moved with his parents and sister to live at 120 Walton Street in Ridgewood. He was a scout, attended the Union Street School and George Washington Junior High School before graduating from Ridgewood High School in 1963 where he ran track and cross-country and participated in the Far East Seminar. He was a member of the West Side Presbyterian Church and also belonged to the local

250

Junior Masons, the Order of DeMolay. His high school quote describes this intelligent, imaginative, quiet and self-controlled gentle person well: "Fools make noise, the wise remain quiet".

Immediately after receiving a B.A. in Geology from Lafayette College in 1967, he was drafted in to the Army. After training at Fort Dix, he felt fortunate to be sent to Germany just as the conflict in Vietnam was escalating. He went overseas in November 1967 with the 81st Maintenance Battalion.

Jonny was killed in Mannheim, Germany August 4, 1968. Originally reported as an accident, he died of injuries sustained when assaulted in his barracks by a drunken soldier. He did not fight back. His assailant was convicted of involuntary manslaughter. In his memory, his family established the Jon H. Holley Memorial Scholarship Fund of Lafayette College. He is buried in Block J, Lot 184, Section C, Grave 1 at George Washington Memorial Park. At death he was 23 years old.

Seaman James Robert Hubbard
1718638
U.S.S. Arizona

Every fall we are warned to get our flu shots to counter the danger of the impending flu *du jour*. We have learned that all flues are not created equal. In a few weeks in autumn 1918 an epidemic of Spanish Influenza ravaged the United States. It was called the Spanish Flu because it was believed to have been carried to the USA on a Coast Guard Cutter from Spain. You would be working with someone one day, they would go home because they didn't feel well and within days they were gone. The death toll around the world was 21 million of which 548,452 were in the USA – ten times more than the 53,513 American lives lost in WWI. Remote Eskimo villages in inaccessible Alaskan regions were completely wiped out. The flu first appeared in March 1918, began with a high fever and aching bones. After about four days, many cases developed pneumonia. The lungs of the victims would fill with fluid, causing death. Highly contagious, "open face sneezing" in public was subject to fines and imprisonment. By May it had consumed two continents as US troop ships, unaware that they carried with them the virus, transported it to Europe and by July was officially pandemic. The Spanish Flu killed its millions and then mysteriously disappeared. It also circulated in the military, striking first at Fort Riley, Kansas in March 1918 but remaining relatively dormant until the fall. Eventually a call-up of 140,000 draftees was canceled because camp hospitals were full. Two of Ridgewood's 113 Honored Dead fell victim to this flu. A stellar Ridgewood High School graduate from Allendale also died of this epidemic.

Born in 1896, James Hubbard lived on West Crescent Avenue in Allendale where his father was President of the Board of Education for many years. He finished the Allendale School in 1910 and graduated from Ridgewood High School in the class of 1914 where he won the prestigious Frank A. Thayer Prize for good citizenship. His classmates named him Best Student, he played football, was on the *Arrow* staff for two years and was class treasurer his Junior and Senior years. The Mary A. Hubbard School in Ramsey was eventually named for his sister.

He went on to graduate from Rutgers, enlisted in the Navy in Philadelphia October 22, 1917, trained at Norfolk and then was piped aboard the USS *Arizona* January 25, 1918. The *Arizona* was commissioned October 17, 1916 and her fate was written in infamy December 7, 1941 at Pearl Harbor.

Operating out of Norfolk throughout the war, the *Arizona* served with the Atlantic fleet starting in March 1917, initially as a gunnery training ship, and patrolling the eastern seaboard from the Virginia to New York. She proudly sailed

253

out of Hampton Roads for Portland, England in November 1918 – one week after the armistice – to rendezvous December 12 with the *George Washington* which was transporting President Wilson to the Paris Peace Conference. She thus became part of the honor escort that arrived in Brest, France on December 13.

On that same December 13th day, as the *Arizona* sailed from Brest for home with 238 WWI veterans, Hubbard became ill. He died December 23, 1918 of Spanish Meningitis aboard the *Arizona*. The official report states "illness commenced December 13, 1918 with mental symptoms, followed later by partial hemiplegia. On December 19, 1918 meningitis set in. A gram-negative diplococcus was found in the spinal fluid, not intracellular. Fluid clear and under pressure. Serum treatment instituted." Because of the number of deaths, the US Navy issued a directive that men who died at sea be shrouded in the US flag and released overboard. Seaman Hubbard is listed on the memorial plaques in Allendale. At death he was 22 years old.

Lt. Arthur Morris Hughes, Jr.
O 432962
22nd Bombardment Group
408th Squadron

The loss of America's youth in the brutality of war is perhaps a necessary evil but is always difficult to accept, regardless of the reason or the cause. But sometimes the irony of a serviceman's death exceeds comprehension. What logic is there to the death of a highly experienced, respected and decorated combat pilot in an accident? Particularly if his death is a result of "an act of God" and the serviceman is a minister's kid. It is a test of our faith.

Dr. Arthur M. Hughes was the head pastor at West Side Presbyterian Church from 1933 to 1957. In November 1942, the "Service Supplement" to West Side's newsletter was begun and was circulated through Christmas, 1945 communicating letters, photos and address changes of local service personnel. Throughout the war, Dr. Hughes faithfully sent it to as many people as he could, peaking at 287 men and women in the service plus 250 families in January, 1945, all the while bearing the substantial burden of his own personal loss. The Service Supplement was begun the month after it was reported that his eldest son, Lt. Arthur M. Hughes, Jr. was killed in the South Pacific.

"Juni" was born March 15, 1918 in Mansfield, Ohio. In 1933 his family moved to Ridgewood where his father served as minister of West Side Presbyterian Church for the next 24 years. He lived in the Manse at 119 Sheridan Terrace with his wife, two daughters and two sons. Juni graduated from Ridgewood High School in 1936 and, after two years at Lehigh University, transferred to the University of Alabama where the Civil Aeronautics Authority had a program he wanted to take. He graduated in June 1940 and immediately went into the Army Air Corps as a cadet at Randolph Field, moving to Mitchel Field, New York in February 1940. He got his wings in class 41-B in March 1941 at the Gulf Coast Air Corps Training Center at Kelly Field in Texas and joined the 408th Bomb Squadron, assigned to the 22nd Bombardment Group at Langley Air Base, Virginia in the summer of 1941.

The day after Pearl Harbor the group flew to Muroc Dry Lake in the Mojave Desert where they were permanently equipped with 44 B-26 Marauders. They moved to the Southwest Pacific early in 1942 as part of the Fifth Air Force and finally arrived at a Royal Australian Air Force base in Brisbane, Queensland, Australia. They then headed for Reid River, about 25 miles from Townsville in the Australian bush. He was given B-26 # 40-1481 and named it "Dumbo" after the

Disney character, partly because Walt Disney was his mother's cousin.

Now known as Art, he earned the Distinguished Flying Cross on the fourth of July 1942. Six Marauders were preparing to head out to bomb grounded Japanese aircraft at Lae Airdrome. He was cited for "extraordinary achievement while participating in an aerial flight over Lae Airdrome, New Guinea, on July 4, 1942. This B-26 type aircraft of which this officer was the pilot, was one of a three-plane formation engaged in a bombing attack on the enemy airdrome at Lae. This crew took off from its base during an enemy air raid, eluded the hostile aircraft and proceeded to the target area. After the runway and installations had been heavily bombed, this aircraft was intercepted by twelve to fifteen Zero fighters which made frontal attacks. In the ensuing engagement during which this aircraft protected another B-26, which had become vulnerable, the gunners of this crew shot down two enemy fighters, which crashed into the sea. Though this plane was damaged by enemy cannon and machine gun fire, it was safely returned to the home base. The courage, ability and devotion to duty displayed by First Lieutenant Hughes are in keeping with the high standards of the service."

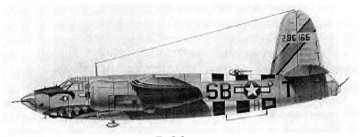

B-26

The B-26 was a twin-engine bomber built by Martin. Officially called the Marauder, it was unofficially called the incredible prostitute because the wings on early models were so short it was said the plane had no visible means of support.

The B-26, which first flew in early July 1942, had a wingspan of 70', was 50' long, 18'6" high and weighed 35,000 lbs. Its two 2,000 hp Pratt & Whitney engines gave its crew of six a range of 1,400 miles, a top speed of 355 mph. It was armed with eight 50 inch machine guns, fourteen 5" rockets and had a 5,000 lb. bomb load.

Their base of operations was moved to Iron Range in late September 1942. On Wednesday, October 14, 1942 Lt. Hughes was flying some men out on furlough. They had striped one of the older planes to silver and would fly it to Sydney for R and R. Two other planes accompanied him. Despite the fact that he was a decorated combat pilot and a veteran of 31 combat missions, his plane went down in a bad storm. The place was Williamtown NSW, an RAAF Air Base adjoining Newcastle municipal airport south of Brisbane and about half way to Sydney. He ran into extremely bad weather. The pilot of the lead plane spotted an airport and buzzed the runway. Hughes thought that was a signal to land and, without taking a chance of losing sight of the runway, brought the plane down in the direction the lead pilot had indicated. There was no radio communication with the tower. It turned out he came in downwind with a 50 mile per hour tailwind. The normal landing speed for a B-26 is 140 mph so his wheels did not touch down until well over half way down the runway. He hit the brakes hard but couldn't stop, hit a tree stump at the end of the runway with the nose gear and flipped the plane upside down. Everybody except Hughes got out of the plane through the bottom hatch at the waist gun position that was now facing up. Another plane from the flight landed very much as he did and was headed straight for him. At the last second, the plane skidded to the right and missed them but was also a complete loss. The lead plane circled and landed normally in the right direction. Everybody on both planes escaped with minor injuries, except Hughes. He suffered severe lacerations and died later that day in Newcastle Hospital.

Lt. Hughes is buried in Section A, Grave 23 in the Beverly National Cemetery in Beverly, NJ. West Side Presbyterian Church created the Arthur M. Hughes, Jr. Memorial Fund a month after his death to provide scholarships for young men and women to study for the ministry. At death he was 24 years old.

Paratrooper Walter William Jackson

A few Ridgewood's 112 Honored Dead survived combat only to die later of an illness. Others, although trained and ready to fight for their country, did not get that chance because they died as a result of an illness before heading for battle. Walter Jackson never met the enemy.

Walt was born October 22, 1911. Originally from Ashtabula, Ohio, where his late father was a railroad official, he move to Ridgewood with his brother, sister and mother and lived at 33 Sherwood Road. He was in the graduating class of 1929 at Ridgewood High School where he was active in various interclass sports, played varsity basketball, helped with many school events, performed in plays, was in the public speaking club and ushered at class day and the commencement.

With a clever wit and a nonchalant manner, and known affectionately as "cueball" or "baldy", he went on to Lehigh University where he was a member of Lambda Chi Alpha, played football and swam for three years, captaining the swim team as a senior. He graduated in 1934 with a degree in business.

In May 1942 he enlisted in the Navy, doing his initial training at Newport, R.I., eventually graduating to the Navy Air Force as a paratrooper. It was at San Diego Naval Station that he died July 8, 1943 after several months of illness from chronic nephritis, a persistent destructive inflammation affecting both kidneys simultaneously, accounting for over 60% of the deaths from terminal kidney failure. He is buried in the family plot in Section 6, Lot 1029, Grave 4 in Chestnut Grove Cemetery, Ashtabula, Ohio. At death he was 32 years old.

Lt. Harold Parkinson Johnston
0791699
449ᵗʰ Bomb Squadron
322ⁿᵈ Bomb Group

Known as Hal or Johnny, Lt. Johnston was born March 21, 1920 in Jersey City but lived most of his life at 521 South Maple Avenue in Glen Rock with his sister and parents. He attended secondary schools in Glen Rock, was in Boy Scout Troop 17 and graduated from Ridgewood High School in 1937. He was an active member of All Saints' Episcopal Church where he sang in the choir and had served as an acolyte. Always a serious artist and musician, he was a violinist in the high school orchestra and sang in the choir three years, won the Orpheus Award his sophomore and junior years, was in the rifle club, on the junior prom committee and, as president of the student council his senior year, was on the senior executive committee. His high school quote of "While melting music steals upon the sky" seems like an eerie premonition.

Hal then went on to Rutgers where he was a member of Zeta Psi, the Scarlet Key and the orchestra and choir. He was a member of the Scarlet Rifles and joined ROTC, officially entering the service the day after the attack on Pearl Harbor in December 1941. He also took flying lessons through the Civil Aeronautics Authority and graduated with a degree in ceramics in 1942.

He trained at Maxwell Field, Alabama, Sahaw Field, SC and Lakeland, Fla. He was commissioned at Moody Field, Georgia August 5, 1942, qualified as a B 26 pilot, married Janet Smith in September 1942 and was promoted to 1Lt. February 1, 1943. He and his wife moved to Tampa to be near his new base at MacDill Field.

Shortly after a visit from his parents to Tampa, and despite good weather and a normal takeoff, he and five others were killed February 28, 1943 when the B-26B he was piloting crashed approximately one minute after takeoff from Hunter Field in Savannah while on a cross country navigation flight. The cause of the accident was never determined although pilot error was ruled out. Hal is buried in plot 946 at Valleau Cemetery. At death he was 22 years old.

Lt. Paul Joseph Jordan
O 443770
Company G
317ᵗʰ Infantry Regiment
80ᵗʰ Infantry Division

Transfusing blood remains an inexact science today, despite substantial progress in the past century. As early as the year Columbus discovered America doctors were administering blood transfusions to the ill and injured but only in 1818 was the first successful transfusion of human blood to a patient performed. Nearly a century later, in 1907 it was determined that the safety of a transfusion could be improved by matching blood types between donors and recipients to exclude incompatible mixtures. In 1916, because of the exceptional needs arising out of World War I, the British established the first blood "depot" and in 1937 the first hospital blood bank in the United States was established. Three years later the Rh Blood group system was discovered and determined to be the cause of the majority of adverse reactions to blood transfusions and the dangers of blood transfusions quickly subsided.

Have we progressed over the past 60 years? It is an understatement to say that World War II saw an increase in the demand for blood. The public constantly saw posters with slogans like "Give Blood Now," "Your Blood Can Save Him," and "He Gave His Blood. Will You Give Yours?" The response was massive. During World War II, some 13,000,000 units were donated in the United States in addition to 68,500 gallons in London. Then, as now, blood transfusions carried a number of health risks. One unfortunate witness to this problem was Paul Jordan, one of Ridgewood's 112 Honored Dead.

Paul was born November 16, 1920 and grew up in Lyons Falls with his parents and brother. He did his early schooling there. Upon graduation, he was in the insurance business before entering the service.

He attended Plattsburg Civilian Training Camp which enabled him to get his commission and he joined the Army April 12, 1942. In August of that year he married Angela Cavagnaro, a Ridgewood High School graduate in the class of 1936, at Mount Carmel Church in Ridgewood. They met when she was teaching at Lyons Falls High School. Before he went overseas they lived off-base at Camp Croft, SC and later had a daughter. Their Ridgewood address was at her parent's home at 68 Wildwood Road. Paul was an expert pistol marksman and could have represented the USA in that venue at the 1944 Olympic Games, had circumstances been different.

Paul went overseas in July 1944 with Company G, 317th Infantry Regiment, 80th Infantry Division (the "Blue Ridge Division"). They landed in Greenock, Firth of Clyde, Scotland, trained in Northwich, England and crossed the Channel to land on Utah Beach August 2. The 80th went into combat August 8 at Le Mans and during the next nine months served in General Patton's 3rd Army fighting its way across Northern France, Belgium and into Germany. Lt. Jordan suffered a leg injury in action on September 20 near Dieulouard, Meurth-et-Moselle, France.

What should have been his ticket home turned into a tragedy. He was transferred to the 67th General Hospital in England where his brother-in-law was stationed. Despite optimistic letters home from both of them, Paul died December 4, 1944 of blood poisoning after surgery performed December 3. He is buried in Plot B, Row 4, Grave 21 in the Cambridge American Cemetery, Cambridge, England. At death he was 24 years old.

2 Lt. Charles John Kartz
O-831952
16th Bombardment Operational Training Wing
235th AAF Base Unit, Section II

Although there are some celebrated stories of aerial combat from WWI, it was only in WWII that the potential of air power was fully understood and used. Unfortunately, after a decade of nation rebuilding during the depression, in 1941 the Air Corps was ill prepared; further, there was resistance from traditional militarists who felt a war should be fought on the sea and on the ground. Fortunately, the flyboys won out and in a reversal of the traditional "hurry up and wait" philosophy, development of an American Air Force became hurry up and hurry up. An unfortunate consequence is that many young lives were lost simply testing the new equipment. In WWII, more American pilots were lost in training accidents than in combat. Out of a total of 120,000 USAAF casualties, only 40,000 died in combat; 15,000 airmen died in accidents in the USA. Unquantified

267

is how many lives were saved by gallant pilots who sacrificed themselves to give their crew mates the chance to escape. One such hero was Charles Kartz of Rutherford and Ridgewood.

Kartz was born October 31, 1922 and lived with his parents and brother at 20 Courrier Place in Rutherford, N.J. "Kartzie" graduated from Rutherford High School in 1941 where he played football and was in the Latin Club. His ambition was to be an art director and he attended Pace Institute while also taking evening courses at Fairleigh Dickinson. His family later moved to Ridgewood and lived at 227 Kemah Road. He worked for the Eclipse Pioneering Division of Bendix Aviation Corp. in Teterboro before entering the service in October 1942. He trained at Amherst College, Maxwell Field, Alabama and was an instructor at Biggs Field near El Paso for three month before he got his wings at Blytheville, Arkansas May 23, 1944 as a B-17 pilot.

While with the 16th BOTW Wing, he was killed in a crash 4 miles east of Biggs Field on December 13, 1944 a during routine transition training flight that entailed formation flying and camera gunnery. At 10,000 feet a fire broke out in the top turret and the plane was thrown into a steep dive. Realizing the crew could not escape while the plane was diving, Lt. Kartz leveled off the plane at approximately 2,000 feet allowing the crew, including the instructor pilot, to escape. All members of his crew were saved but there was not time for him to escape. He bailed out at an altitude insufficient to assure a successful parachute jump. For his he was awarded the Distinguished Flying Cross, posthumously for "courage and heroic devotion to duty". The Kartz family was told that Lt. Kartz "... was first a pilot. All of the members of his crew were out of the plane and were saved and in doing so it seems it was too late for him to save himself. This action is according to the highest traditions of the Commanding Officer of all nations.

That is, his own safety must come last and that of his crew and passengers must come first."

Lt. Kartz, who is also listed on the memorial plaques in Rutherford, was initially buried in Flower Hill Cemetery, North Bergen, but was moved in March 1945 to Section F, Lot 67A, Grave 4 at Hillside Cemetery, Lynhurst, N.J. At death he was 22 years old.

Pfc. Donald B. Koukol
42106065
Battery B
604th Field Artillery Battalion
10th Mountain Division

    In 1943, the Selective Training and Service Act, which governed the draft, lowered the minimum age for conscription from 20 to 18. Anybody enlisting before their 18th birthday needed parental consent. Some forged their parent's signature and enlisted illegally (the nation's youngest military retiree stopped after a 20-year career at age 34). In most cases, Uncle Sam promised not to send these "under-aged" men overseas for a year. It was a promise that was not always kept. Donald Koukol's high school quote "I'd rather be different than right" was an eerie premonition.

    Sometimes known as Koke, he was born in New York City April 13, 1926 and moved to Ridgewood as a small boy to live at 170 Hope St. with his parents and sister. He went through the entire Ridgewood school system and graduated from the High School in the class of 1944. In high school he ran track, was active in most of the drama programs and was also an accomplished magician.

He entered active service July 17, 1944 and went overseas six months later at age 18 to join the 10th Mountain Division as a replacement in a radio unit of the 604th Field Artillery in support of the 85th infantry regiment fighting in Italy in mid-April 1945. On April 19th the 10th captured and occupied positions overlooking the Po Valley. The following day they broke out of the Apennines and continued their rapid dash across the Po Valley.

The 10th was determined to reach the Po by nightfall and seize an area for a crossing on April 22, 1945. That same day, with the Russians 40 miles from Berlin, Hitler admitted that the war was lost and that suicide was his only recourse. With the end of the war in sight, the 10th crossed the Po on the 22nd. In that action Koukol was hit in the head and neck and killed near Ansola.

Private Koukol had been in combat less than a week. He is buried in Section J, Grave 16224 in Long Island National Cemetery, Farmingdale. At death he was barely 19 years old.

Pvt. William Kruskop
1748435
Company A
311th Infantry Regiment
156th Infantry Brigade
78th Infantry Division

One of the most significant battles of WWI was waged at St. Mihiel and was fought from September 12 to September 16, 1918. It was the first battle of the war in which the American Army fought as a separate army, in its own sector and led by its own generals, under the ultimate command of General John J. Pershing. About 500,000 Americans were engaged at St. Mihiel, the largest battle involving Americans since the Civil War. Among his commanders were two men who would lead American forces to victory in WWII. In an ironic look at the future, it was at St. Mihiel that Lt. Colonel George S. Patton Jr. met Brigadier General Douglas MacArthur. Other American participants providing air support at St. Mihiel were Eddie Rickenbacker and Billy Mitchell who gathered the largest air force ever assembled for a single operation - more than 1,400 aircraft for the battle of St. Mihiel.

At 1:00 in the foggy and drizzly morning of September 12, Allied guns began a five-hour artillery barrage supported by Patton's 327th Tank Battalion. It was in this battle that American tanks were first used in combat. By 6:30 MacArthur was 800 yards into enemy territory. Under constant shelling, Patton advanced to the town of Seicheprey, southwest of MacArthur's position. MacArthur made his way through the Sonnard Woods towards Seicheprey. Patton spotted MacArthur on a small hill and went to meet him, just as an artillery barrage began and everyone else ran for cover.

Together, they faced German armies who were defending a network of trenches that started southeast of Verdun, ran south to St. Mihiel and then east to Pont-à-Mousson. American casualties were comparatively light, costing only about 7,000 wounded or killed. One of the latter was William Kruskop of Ridgewood.

He was born July 27, 1888 in New York City. His father died when he was 12 years old and his mother spent 34 years in a sanitarium so he and his sister moved to Ridgewood and lived thereafter with their cousin Mrs. F. W. Milliken at 46 Kenilworth Place. He was in the taxi business in Ridgewood until called into the service April 26, 1918.

After training at Camp Dix he arrived overseas May 19, 1918 and fought in the Argonne and St. Mihiel with the 311th Infantry Regiment, 78th Infantry Division ("Lightning"). During the summer and fall of 1918, the 78th was the "point of the wedge" of the final offensive that defeated Germany.

First reported missing in the action at St. Mihiel, he died on September 24, 1918 and was eventually included on Ridgewood's Sunday Casualty List. Initially buried in Bois de Grande Fontaine – Preny, he is now buried in Plot D, Row 16, Grave 22 in the St. Mihiel American Cemetery, Thiaucourt, France. There is a marker in his memory in Plot 895 at Valleau Cemetery. At death he was 30 years old.

Lt. Thaddeus Chester Kulpinski
AO 1683354
59th Fighter Interceptor Squadron
ADC, EADF
4707th Defense Wing

Lt. Kulpinski was born July 13, 1920 and grew up in Willow Grove, Pennsylvania with his parents, two brothers and two sisters. He attended Ursinus College and married Lois Deakyne, Ridgewood High School class of 1942. She was Theodore Deakyne's sister, another of Ridgewod's 112 Honored Dead. Deakyne and Kulpinski were close friends and had served together in Africa during WWII after Kulpinski had transferred from the Polish Unit of the RAF to the US Army Air Force.

He served in North Africa and Corsica before becoming a radar instructor in Florida and California. After WWII he remained in the Air Force Reserve and attended St. Joseph's College in Philadelphia and Temple Law School. He was recalled to active duty in May 1951. He and his wife then lived in Hempstead, NY.

At the time of his death he was assigned to the 59th Fighter Interceptor Squadron, ADC, EADF, 4707th Defense Wing at Otis AFB. The 59th FIS converted from F-84Cs to the F-86A during Spring of 1950 at Otis AFB, MA. The squadron then received F-94As in late 1950. 59th FIS was assigned to 33rd FIG until 6th February 1952, when it reassigned to 4707th ADW, flying the Lockheed F-94B Starfire.

The F-94B was powered by one Allison turbojet, had a wingspan of 37 feet 6 inches, was 40 feet 1 inches long, 12 feet 8 inches tall and weighed 10,064 pounds empty, or 13,474 pounds loaded. Its maximum speed was 606 mph at sea level with a ceiling of 48,000 feet and a normal range 665 miles (maximum range 905 miles). It was armed with four 0.50-inch M-3 machine guns in the nose.

F-94B

As Radar Observer returning from an air to air gunnery training mission at the Nantucket Range, he died April 9, 1952 as his F-94B dove through a hole in the clouds just as a C-47, based at Stewart Air Force Base in New York but flying out of Otis AFB to Niagara Falls, rose up into the same hole in the clouds. The mid-air collision at 7,000 feet over Edwards AFB on Cape Cod cost 12 lives. Kulpinski is buried in Block L, Lot 113, Section C, Grave 2 at George Washington Memorial Park, Paramus - next to his friend in life and death, Ted Deakyne. At death he was 31 years old.

Lt. Christopher William Lambert
12046696
Aviation Cadet
Cadet Attachment
382nd Sch. Squadron

Another long-time Ridgewood resident who is not one of Ridgewood's 113 Honored Dead is Christopher William Lambert. Because he and his family were living to Trenton when he died, this RHS graduate is not listed on our memorial plaques.

Billy was born December 30, 1919 in Kearny and later moved to Ridgewood with his parents and two brothers to live on North Pleasant. He was in the boy scout troop at Mount Carmel and graduated from Ridgewood High School in the class of 1938. While there he was on the varsity track team for three years, played junior varsity football, was on the bowling team, played intramural basketball as well as church league basketball. He then went on to Wake Forest College. His parents moved to Trenton and he was working as a postal clerk there when he enlisted in the service.

He was accepted as an air cadet in the air corps January 14, 1942 and was scheduled to get his wings at graduation on October 8, 1942. He then volunteered for combat duty with the possibility of first becoming an instructor at Craig Field in Selma, Alabama.

Late in the afternoon of October 7, the day before his graduation, he volunteered to take his P-39D into the air. He pulled the airplane into a planned stall at a safe altitude of 10,000 feet at which time the plane did indeed stall, slid backwards and went into a forward tumble, then into a flat spin and then into a normal spin, losing between 5,000 and 6,000 feet of altitude. At 4,000 feet, with the plane still in a normal spin, Lambert apparently over-controlled, recovered from a left spin and then went into a right spin. Sensing the futility of his situation, he bailed out at about 2,000 feet but his parachute was struck by the plane's tail, slicing it in two. The plane crashed and he plunged to the ground, dying of his injuries. His parents had come to attend his graduation, only to learn that he had been killed the previous day.

Billy was awarded his wings posthumously. He is buried in Holy Sepulcher Cemetery, Paterson. At death he was 22 years old.

1 Lt. Richard Soutter Lane
O-558308
498th Bomber Squadron
345th Bomber Group
5th Air Force

Atrocities are a part of war; some are spontaneous – some are a matter of policy. We shudder when hearing stories of atrocities; we gasp in disbelief when a victim of an atrocity is someone we know.

In August 1942 Japan passed the Enemy Airmen's Act which authorized the execution of captured enemy airmen. Prior to May 1945 it had been the policy at Japanese headquarters to forward captured American flyers to Tokyo after local interrogation. But that month a telegram was sent from the Intelligence Section of the General Staff HQ in Tokyo instructing that American flyers of no further intelligence value be disposed of locally. Therefore, with the end of the war in sight, Japanese commanders received official orders to annihilate all prisoners of war by any means without allowing any to escape and without leaving

278

any trace. Thus, after being condemned for "indiscriminate bombing" 19 flyers were taken from their detention barracks at Fukuoka, first on June 20 and again on August 12, and beheaded. Nine others were turned over to Kyushu Imperial University where they died while undergoing medical experiments, including autopsies while they were still alive. Among the war crimes committed by the Japanese in WWII are many cases of decapitation, butchery and even cannibalism of Allied POWs. The pace of these atrocities accelerated between the cease fire announcement of August 15 and Japan's formal surrender on September 2. These acts were to be judged as war crimes after the war.

Shortly after the second atomic bomb was dropped on Nagasaki on August 9, the Japanese government realized there was no hope for victory and communicated to the allies their acceptance of the terms of surrender. A Japanese news service had made the announcement but the Japanese people wanted to hear it from an authoritative voice – the Emperor himself. When that message came several days later, on August 15, Japanese commanders carried out their bloody orders and butchered an American air crew. A member of that crew was Dick Lane of Ridgewood.

Dick was born December 7, 1922, lived at 232 Claremont Road with his parents. His father was an aeronautical engineer. At 5' 10" tall, 150 lbs. with blue eyes and brown hair, Dick was manager of the football team and graduated from Ridgewood High School in 1940 where he was in Hi-Y and on the decoration committee for the Junior and Senior Proms. He was also a Senior Day teacher. His sadly prophetic high school quote was "tis good to be abroad in the sun". His fate abroad in the land of the rising sun was not good.

Dick attended Boston University but was called to duty in the Army May 15, 1942 during his junior year. He trained at Wolters Field, Texas but transferred to the Air Corps, graduated from the AAF Navigation school at San Marcos, Texas and was commissioned on September 25, 1944. He joined the 498th Bomber Squadron, 345th Bomber Group Medium (Air Apaches), married Priscilla Walker of Marblehead, whom he met at Boston College, on August 26, 1944 and went overseas to be based in Tsu Shima, Okinawa.

The first atomic bomb was dropped on Hiroshima August 6, 1945. The following day, on August 7, four squadrons of the 345th sent a total of 32 aircraft on sweeps against railroad and highway bridges at Matsubase, Kyushu Island. Lt. Lane's B-25 was hit by anti-aircraft fire and disappeared, last seen by other squadron members over the target area. The aircraft failed to respond to radio calls and crash-landed in Kumamoto Prefecture, Kyushu, where the entire crew was captured by the dreaded KempeiTai, the Japanese Army's rogue Secret Police, their equivalent of Germany's SS. Within a few days they were transferred to Japan's Western Army Headquarters at Fukuoka.

After the voice of Emperor Hirohito was August 15th announcing the Japanese acceptance of the terms for an unconditional surrender, 16 American prisoners, including Lt. Lane and his 5-man crew, were taken to a nearby field at Aburayama where, upon orders from Major Kusumoto, they were stripped naked, decapitated and hacked to pieces with samurai swords. Because the country had been alerted nearly a week earlier that Japan would surrender, the KempeiTai knew these remaining prisoners could incriminate them for the earlier atrocities. Their bodies were among the 32 bodies of American flyers cremated in the night of August 15-16 and buried by Minoru Nakamura and Sadayoshi Murata.

From the remains of 13 bodies the Japanese took a piece of a skull, hand, rib, pelvis, spine and leg to represent each of the prisoners executed, placed them in a small box which they kept. Everything else was buried in the box in the military cemetery at Ropponmatsu. Nakamura and Murata subsequently were ordered by Major Kusumoto to give the remains to Kenjo Mizushima, Head Priest of Miyoko Temple, along with a list of the names of the executed flyers. A week later Kusumoto ordered that the remains be removed from the Temple. They were subsequently vandalized and buried in the mountains near Hirao. The list of names destroyed. The U.S. Graves Registration eventually recovered the ashes but individual identification was impossible.

Lane was awarded the Air Medal with Oak Leaf Cluster and is listed on the Tablets of the Missing at Honolulu Memorial. The Boston University chapter of (ironically) the Scabbard and Blade Society, a national honorary society for members of advanced ROTC units, established a memorial trophy known as the Hubbard - Lane Award in memory of Neal Hubbard and Richard Lane, the two Scabbard and Blade Honor Society members of the class of 1944 who died in the war. It is awarded annually to the outstanding senior ROTC Cadet. At death Dick Lane was 23 years old.

Crew of B-25J-32: Lt. Robert G. Neal,
Lt. Louis J. Winiecki, Jr., Lt. Richard S. Lane,
S/Sgt. Robert W. Goulet, S/Sgt. William Cohen

S/1 Arthur Webster Lanigan
02017044
USS *Houston (CA-30)*

After the shock and disaster of Pearl Harbor in December 1941, which destroyed most of the U.S. naval fleet, allied forces in the Pacific had to organize themselves as quickly as possible, certainly not something that could be accomplished overnight. On the home front, we needed reassurance and any good news possible. That is why Lt. Col. Jimmy Doolittle's raid on the Japanese mainland barely four months later on April 18, 1942 was so important. The effect on the American people was an electrifying moral booster. We had hit back and crews had survived to report the results. On the other hand, details of catastrophic news, where we had no survivors to report the results, left the country and concerned families in suspense for years.

The Battle of Sunda Strait in late February 1942 has been called the most serious Naval disaster suffered by the allies in WWII. The entire crews of a dozen allied vessels were reported as missing in action. Families waiting for news of their loved ones were left in the dark for more than three years. In the case of Arthur Lanigan, the suspense effected two families in different towns.

Lanigan was born January 3, 1922 and lived in Waterville, Maine with his mother, Mrs. Christine Roundy. His stepfather was an athletic coach at Colby College and his father Donald Lanigan lived in Ridgewood. Arthur was a marksman and a charter member of the Sons of the (American) Legion. He graduated from Waterville High School and studied at the Coburn Classical Institute before going to work at the Haines Theater. At age 13 he saved the lives of two youths who had fallen through the ice on a frozen pond.

He enlisted in the Navy January 8, 1940, trained at Newport News and was assigned to the Pacific Fleet aboard the carrier *Saratoga*. He then became a submariner aboard the *U.S.S. Henderson* out of Mare Island, Cal. He was transferred to the cruiser *USS Houston* CA-30 in the summer of 1941. The *Houston*, known as the "Galloping Ghost of the Java Coast" because it had twice been reported sunk by the Japanese, had been fitted out as a flagship for President Roosevelt who traveled 24,445 miles on her over a period of 8 years.

USS Houston (CA-30)

Immediately after Pearl Harbor the *Houston,* based in the Philippines, sailed into Australian and Dutch East Indies waters. As the largest Allied vessel in the area, she was actively engaged in fighting the Japanese East Indies' offensive. In early 1942, as the Japanese were landing transport of troops on the northern coast of Java in Banten Bay, an enemy bomb disabled the *Houston's* after gun turret on February 4, 1942 but she remained in the combat zone, fighting off air raids and taking part in the Battle of the Java Sea on February 27.

Lanigan died February 28, 1942 in this fighting, known as the Battle of Sunda Strait. Along with the *Houston,* one U.S. destroyer, 4 Dutch vessels, 5 British ships and 2 Australian vessels were lost. They were passing through an area which hosted a 56-ship Japanese transport convoy at the time. Initially attacked, and hit, on February 27, the *Houston* and the *H.M.S. Perth* tried to escape under cover of darkness the following day. Although they managed to sink four Japanese transports, both allied ships were lost off St. Nicholas Point as Japanese fighting ships converged on the area and mercilessly pummeled them with every sort of artillery imaginable for 90 minutes. The doomed ship, which had become target practice for the Japanese fleet, imploded but remained afloat for 30 minutes while what was left of the crew abandoned ship.

Two weeks later the entire crew of 1,012 was listed as missing and presumed lost. To amplify the suspense, rumors of survivors quickly began to circulate and approximately 300 survivors of the *Houston* were eventually reported to be in Japanese prisoners of war camps in Thailand or Java. The *Houston's* final death toll was 368 survivors taken prisoner and 644 lost. 68 died in captivity in labor camps in Burma and 145 were sent to Japan as "technicians" and were never heard from again. Although it is unknown whether Lanigan's fate was from combat, at the hands of hostile Javanese natives or from the Japanese, no *Houston* survivors ever mentioned having seen him subsequent to the attack.

Arthur Lanigan was the first WWII casualty from Waterville, Maine where American Legion Post No. 5 is now named in his honor. In September 1945 his mother was chosen to christen the *U.S.S. Waterville Victory,* named for the city of Waterville. He is listed on the Tablets of the Missing at Manila American Cemetery. At death he was 20 years old.

Pfc. Roger Colby Lawn
32783623
353rd Bombardment Squadron
301st Bomber Group (H)
15th AAF

The Soldier's Medal is awarded to Army personnel who distinguish themselves by heroism involving personal hazard or danger and the voluntary risk of their life under conditions not involving conflict with an armed enemy. Roger Lawn was awarded the Soldier's Medal, posthumously.

Known as Pinocchio for reasons obvious to anybody looking at him, he was born in Brooklyn December 7, 1922 and later lived on Bancroft Place in Radburn with his mother and brother. His parents divorced and his mother eventually re-married and moved to Asheville, North Carolina. His father moved to New York City and was a member of the news staff of the *New York Times.*

Roger graduated from Ridgewood High School in 1939 where he was on the Town Council, the International Club, Class Gift Committee and participated in the League of Nations Competitive Examination. He attended the University of Michigan for two years but went to work first for the Wright Aeronautical Corporation and later for the Raw Materials Commission of the British Publishing Agency in New York.

He joined the service in North Carolina January 26, 1943 and went overseas in September of the same year, being stationed at various posts in North Africa and Italy. Lawn died May 20, 1944 in Foggia, Italy while trying to rescue the pilot of a plane that had crashed and was burning. At 2:00 in the afternoon, four planes – two P-38s and two P-51s - were in formation over the airfield. Suddenly, the motor of a P-51 conked out and began to smoke. The pilot immediately began circling the field to make an approach. He overshot the landing strip and crashed on a taxi strip as his wing caught the ground, spinning the plane 180°. The pilot was trapped in the burning ship as ground crews tried to put out the fire. But their equipment failed and the fire intensified. Then the plane's guns started going off, wounding several of the ground crew and killing four, including Private Lawn.

The citation on his Soldier's Medal speaks of "heroism at great risk of life at an Allied airfield in Italy on May 20, 1944. Observing a P-51 type aircraft crash and burn, Private First Class Roger Lawn rushed to the scene. Heedless of the burning fuel and the imminent danger of explosion, with complete disregard of his personal safety, he made his way through the wreckage in an effort to extricate the pilot who was trapped in the cockpit. Attempting to cut through the fuselage, he was forced by spreading flames to cease his efforts. Securing fire extinguishers, he attempted to suppress the flames from the front of the burning aircraft when he lost his life as the guns of the fighter began firing wildly. By his outstanding courage and devotion to duty, his heroism in sacrificing his life to save a service comrade, Private Lawn has reflected great credit upon himself and the armed forces of the United States".

Roger Lawn is buried in Plot G, Row 1, Grave 26 in the Sicily-Rome American Cemetery, Nettuno, Italy. At death he was 21 years old.

S/1c Charles Upham Leonard
02255075
USS SHARK II SS-314

In WWII the Japanese were taught that surrender was dishonorable and they would therefore fight to the death. This same thinking was generally also applied to enemy prisoners taken by the Japanese – but not always. Many were killed immediately and some died after being subjected to medical experiments. Many lived to tell of their experiences. Stories from survivors of Japanese prison camps tell of reprehensible conditions beyond imagination. Perhaps worse yet was the ordeal of getting there. Beyond the Batan death march, thousands of Allied prisoners were transported to Japan in "Hell Ships". Prisoners were crammed into the hold of ships with no sanitary facilities and very little to eat. Many did not survive the trip. Worse yet, because the ships flew the Japanese flag, they were targeted by Allied war ships which could not distinguish them from any other Japanese vessel. The result was the death of uncounted thousands of Allied servicemen who went down in a Hell Ship. At least one of Ridgewood's 112 Honored Dead is believed to have died while a prisoner on a Hell Ship, sunk by his countrymen. One such "victory" may have been claimed by Charles Leonard of Ridgewood.

Charles was born October 16, 1925 and lived with his parents, two brothers and three sisters at 549 Wyndemere Avenue. He lettered in soccer in high school and was one of several members of Ridgewood High School class of 1944 to leave school early to join the service. All of them graduated in absentia. He joined the Navy in September 1943, did basic training at Great Lakes, Ill. followed by submarine training at New London, Ct. In September 1944 he went to San Francisco to board the *USS Shark II*, a Balao Class submarine.

Leonard died aboard the submarine *SHARK II* on its 3rd war patrol October 24, 1944 in the channel between Hainan and Bashi Channel. On that day, *SHARK II* reported having made radar contact with a freighter, and that she was going in to attack. This was the last message received from *SHARK II*. On November 13, 1944 the Commander Naval Unit, Fourteenth Air Force stated that a Japanese ship en route from Manila to Japan with 1,800 American prisoners of war had been sunk on October 24 by an American submarine. It is assumed that the *SHARK II* made the attack and perished doing so. Four such "Hell Ships" were sunk by the allies with a total loss in excess of 4,000 allied POWs.

Prisoners on the Hell Ship who survived and subsequently reached China stated that conditions on the prison ship were so bad that they prayed for deliverance from their misery by a torpedo or bomb. Because many prisoners of war had been rescued from the water by submarines after vessels in which they were being transported were sunk, U.S. submarines had been instructed to search for Allied survivors in the vicinity of all sinkings of Empire bound Japanese ships. The *SHARK II* may well have been sunk trying to rescue American prisoners of war. All attempts to contact *SHARK II* by radio failed and on November 27 she was reported as presumed lost.

Leonard is listed on the Tablets of the Missing at Manila American Cemetery, Manila, Philippines. There is a marker in his memory in Section 10, Plot 1184 at Valleau Cemetery. At death he was barely 19 years old.

USS Shark II *SS-314*

T/5 Jeremy Leonard
12162705
Medical Department
644 T.D. Battalion
415th Infantry Regiment
104th Infantry Division

There are several men from Ridgewood who moved away before going away to war. As a result, they are not listed on our memorial plaques. Fortunately, they have not been forgotten because they are listed among the casualties in their new home. Jeremy Leonard is such a case.

Jerry was born October 10, 1923 and lived on Brookside Ave. with his parents, three sisters and two brothers. He graduated from Ridgewood High School in 1942 where he played football, ran track, was in the camera club, archery club, booster club and was in the Christmas Play. A regular kid just like yours or mine. His family moved to 202 Grove Street in Montclair the summer he graduated from high school and he enlisted in the Air Corps on October 7, 1942.

He changed his mind and transferred to the Medical Corps, taking ASTP at NYU. It is estimated that a wounded soldier in WWII had an 85% chance of surviving if he was treated by a medic within the first hour – a success rate three times higher than in WWI. Unfortunately, the red cross worn by unarmed medics on their helmet and arm bands became visible targets for enemy snipers.

Leonard went overseas in August 1944 with the Canadian Fifth Army but it was as a medic with the 104th Inf. (Timberwolves) that he suffered a gun shot wound to the abdomen and died near Stolberg, Germany November 16, 1944 during "Operation Queen". On that day a massive Allied attack began as 4,500 planes, mainly heavy bombers, of the 8th Air Force and the Royal Air Force flying out of England undertook the biggest air assault of World War II since the St. Lo breakthrough.

Leonard is listed on the WWII Memorial Plaque in the courthouse in Montclair. He was awarded the Bronze Star and is buried Plot A, Row, 18, Grave 36 in Henri-Chapelle American Cemetery, Henri-Chapelle, Belgium. At death he was 21 years old.

Lt. Harley Benton Lewis, Jr.

Harley was born November 12, 1919 at the Naval Air Station at Coco Solo, Panama Canal Zone where his father, a WWI pilot, was base commander. While he was in high school, he moved from Hamden, Ct. with his parents and sister to live on Cottage Street in Ridgewood, eventually settling in Hohokus at 402 Enos Place. In Connecticut he had been active in the student council, was on the class executive board and in the Hi-Y. Harley then attended Ridgewood High School and graduated in the class of 1938, running the sprints for the track team and participating in the German Club.

He went on to Rutgers pre-med with the intent to do cancer research. While there he was a member of Lambda Chi Alpha and again ran track, winning the Middle States track championship in the 100 and 220 yard dashes in 1940. After two years of college he entered the service in June 1940, was commissioned in November and promoted to Lt. jg in June 1942. During this time he married his high school classmate and sweetheart, Betty Thomas. He then attended midshipman's school on the *USS Illinois,* which served as a Naval Reserve Midshipmen Training School at New York, and then served 16 months as a line officer on battleships. Harley then joined the submarine service and graduated from sub school in New London, Ct. He was promoted to Lieutenant.

Sub trainees were required to jump into large water tanks wearing a diving apparatus called a rebreather. At that time these apparatus contained lye and the rebreather Lewis was using broke. He absorbed the lye and developed cancer as a result. He died of cancer October 7, 1943 in the Brooklyn Naval Hospital after undergoing two major operations during the year.

Harley Lewis is buried in Section D, Lot 953 in Pine Lawn Memorial Park and Cemetery, Farmingdale, Long Island. At death he was 24 years old.

2 Lt. Walter Francis Livingston, III
O-024299
3rd Marine Division

War is indiscriminate in its selection of casualties. We can never know how many captains of industry, intellectuals or government leaders were lost prematurely because of the madness of war. Walter Livingston had all the credentials to become a leader in any of his endeavors. He was leading when he died.

Walt was born in Brooklyn January 29, 1921 and lived at 20 South Irving St. with his mother and sister. They attended First Presbyterian Church. He was President of the Student Council in 1939, his senior year at Ridgewood High School. While in high school he was captain of the football team, on the Town Council and was Chairman of the Junior Class play.

He then went on to Franklin and Marshall College and graduated in 1943 with a B.S. in Economic Distribution and was in the Industrial

296

Management Association. In college he was a member of Alpha Delta Sigma and was treasurer of his fraternity, Lambda Chi Alpha. He played intramural sports and was a lineman on one of F&M's best football teams and was President of the Varsity Club.

He was also in the Marine Corps Reserve. He trained at Parris Island and received his commission at Quantico, Va., took combat training in California and was an instructor at Camp Pendleton. He was part of the "Hollywood Commando" who put on exhibitions for university Army and Navy men during bond drives. He went overseas in January 1944 with a replacement unit. As part of the Third Marine Division he was killed on Guam while leading his men in Operation STEVEDORE July 21, 1944. A naval attack force landed Marines and Army forces on Guam in an assault preceded by intensive naval gunfire and carrier-based aircraft attacks. The simultaneous use of naval gunfire and aircraft in the same coastal area marked the first time that the two have been used in this fashion in a Pacific amphibious operation. While enemy opposition was small at the outset, determined resistance developed inland. Lt. Livingston was advancing up a draw in the face of enemy artillery and was hit in the chest by a piece of shrapnel. He died within an hour and was buried in a Marine Cemetery on Guam.

His body was moved and buried in National Memorial Cemetery of the Pacific, Honolulu and there is a marker in his honor in Section 7, Plot 453 at Valleau Cemetery. At death he was 23 years old.

Colonel Douglas C. MacKeachie
O-905098
General Staff, Service of Supply
HQ SOS ETOUSA

On January 17, 1943 a C-87 Liberator Express, the transport version of the B-24D bomber, of the 9th Ferrying Group, Air Transport Command left Accra in what is now Ghana on a flight to Natal, Brazil with 12 U.S. military personnel and 13 RAF personnel on board. It disappeared into the south Atlantic, out of sight and reach of search and rescue teams. Several on board survived to drift in life boats in the Equatorial current, which runs across the Atlantic from Africa to Brazil at approximately 1-2 knots, only to die one by one until the last body was found in a life boat that drifted ashore at Ponte Negra, Brazil – 18 days after the plane was reported missing.

Among them was Colonel Douglass MacKeachie, Ridgewood High School class of 1917. Although born in Brooklyn December 4, 1900, he became a well known son of Ridgewood and lived on Beech Street (now Cottage Place), was on several sports teams in high school and was School Notes Editor for the *Arrow*. He established what high school principal Somerville called "one of the finest scholastic records in school history". He had a gift for Latin and often helped classmates with their difficult passages. He spent the next four years at Colgate, earning a degree in 1921. It was about this time that his family moved to East Orange.

For a number of years he served as Vice President, Director of Purchases, New England Division, Great Atlantic & Pacific Tea Company, living in Medfield, MA. In 1940 he went to Washington D.C. as Deputy Director of Purchases for the Office of Production Management, later serving as Director of Purchases for the Office of Personnel Management (OPM) and the War

Production Board before becoming a civilian employee of the War Department as Deputy Director of Procurement and Distribution for the Services of Supply (SOS).

From the very beginning of the war it was policy in the European Theater of Operations (ETOUSA) that the United States would purchase as many of its supplies as possible in the United Kingdom in order to save shipping space. Local procurement was therefore destined to be an important function, and to handle such matters a General Purchasing Board and a Board of Contracts and Adjustments were created in June 1942, both of them headed by a General Purchasing Agent. Colonel MacKeachie was commissioned in May 1942 and sent to the United Kingdom to fill this position.

The shortest distance over water between the western hemisphere and Europe or Africa is between Brazil and French West Africa. Natal, Brazil was the largest United States air base outside US territory and became known as the "trampoline to victory" as military activities in Europe as well as in the Indian sub continent transited through this base to and from the USA.

MacKeachie was a passenger on a plane which was reported missing on January 20, 1943 - having gone down about 700/800 miles east of the Brazilian coast. Search and rescue was abandoned on January 29. On February 4 a life raft was found adrift at sea by the USS *Kearney* about 60 miles east of Recife. The raft contained the remains of a man later identified as the pilot. An inventory of articles found in the raft included five life jackets, indicating that at least four RAF personnel had made it to the life raft. The next day, a second life raft was found on the beach at Ponte Negra, Brazil. One body was found in the raft and was identified as an American member of the flight crew. Among articles found in the raft was an American Express Travelers Cheque bearing the signature of Colonel

MacKeachie. Also found was one insignia of rank of Colonel, USA. Six life jackets were also found indicating that the raft originally had six occupants. It is clear that, as each survivor died, the remaining survivors buried him at sea until there was nobody to bury the last casualty.

As neither of the two bodies found had evidence of injuries, it is assumed that the plane was forced down but did not explode or crash violently. Hunger and thirst are assumed to be the cause of death as there was no means to collect rain water. Attempts to catch fish were made by using a Colonel's eagle insignia as a hook. The bones and tails of several small fish were found in the raft.

The official date of death for the eleven who are assumed to have survived the crash but perished at sea was established as February 3, 1943. Col. MacKeachie, who left a widow and one daughter, is listed among the Missing in Action or Buried at Sea at Cambridge American Cemetery in Cambridge, England. He is also listed among the service casualties in Medfield, MA. At death he was 42 years old.

Lt. Stephen Sherwood MacVean
155323112
US Naval Advisory Group
Coastal Group-36

No one is born a warrior. Some are raised to be warriors – maybe 2 out of 100. Most service people are civilians in military uniform, trained physically and mentally for combat but looking forward to restarting their civilian life. When push comes to shove, and the recycled civilians are first faced with a life and death combat situation, the odds are probably at best 50/50 that their reactions and instincts will carry them through. Most live to tell of their baptism of fire but many don't. Often, newly arrived replacements in combat never got their uniforms dirty, never had time to unpack or to introduce themselves to their new mates before they died, lonely and anonymously in the chaos of battle. Occasionally, those with more combat experience manage to avoid impending danger by arranging to be replaced by someone newly-arrived, confirming the adage that field experience is something you don't get until just after you need it. Stephen MacVean grew up in the comfortable surroundings of Ridgewood and got an Ivy League education but wasn't a fighter. In his first encounter with the enemy, he gave the unknown the benefit of the doubt and allowed the enemy to shoot first.

MacVean was born January 30, 1944 and grew up in Ridgewood with his brother and parents. His father was Ridgewood Village Commissioner from May 1959 to December 1962 and was also the mortgage banker who closed the first GI loan for World War II veterans, in 1945.

Stephen attended the Willard and George Washington schools and graduated from Ridgewood High School in 1961. While in high school he managed the football and track teams, was in the junior class cabinet, was chairman of the junior prom Queen and Court, senior play-reading chairman, campus patrol chairman and was in the student council cabinet his senior year. Always active, he graduated from Dartmouth in 1965 where he was a member and Vice President of Delta Kappa Epsilon fraternity and was awarded the Reed Descriptive Geography Award. He was active in ROTC and was an Inter-dormitory Council member. Stephan was commissioned in June 1966 and given a leave of absence to continue his studies. He received a B.E. degree from the Thayer School of Engineering at Dartmouth in 1966.

Upon graduation, he trained with the Naval Advisory Group at the Amphibious Warfare Base in Coronado, CA. and was fluent in Vietnamese. He was assigned to the USS Nicholas (DDE 449) out of Pearl Harbor for replenishment activities off the coast of Vietnam. In March 1969 he was the main propulsion assistant on the *Nicholas* when it was one of the Apollo 9 secondary landing zone recovery ships (the primary splash down was in the Atlantic). He was then sent to Vietnam as a replacement and phoned home with the news. It was Sunday. He was immediately given a command and sent into combat and was killed the following Wednesday. Warfare in the waterways of the Mekong Delta was learned, for the most part, by on-the-job-training. Because of this, the first few months of one's tour were probably the most dangerous. Once you'd been there a while, and if you were lucky, your chances of survival began to increase.

The evening before his death, he went in a Kenner small-boat to the Ba Sac River, about a 150 yards out from Long Phu /"Foxtrot-India." Foxtrot-India was situated on the west bank of the Bassac River at the confluence of the Long Phu River and overlooked Dung Island at its mid-point. The people on Dung Island were sympathetic to the Viet Minh. The local Viet Cong were dangerous, but the North Vietnamese Army had thoroughly infiltrated the Mekong Delta.

At dawn on the morning of October 29, 1969 Stephen lead a squad of nine Navy, Coast Guard and Vietnamese sailors from Coastal Division 36 "Foxtrot-India" against elements of the North Vietnamese Army (NVA) and Viet Cong on a board and search operation at the south end of enemy infested Cu Lao Dung Island in the Bassac River. Dung Island lay midway between the west and east banks of the Bassac River, was about 13 miles long by 3 miles wide, had two primary canals that ran its entire length, was heavily jungled, as well as cultivated, and was laced with irrigation canals, creeks and mud flats. Its southern-most end extended almost to the sea and the ocean tide affected the water levels far up river, even beyond Dung Island.

What caught MacVean's attention were two large junks which appeared to be moving east into the river from the mouth of the canal. The junks were spread out quite a bit and, holding his fire, MacVean's boat went after the one to the right and closest to the island, a large junk piloted by a woman. NVA and VC troops had been ferried across the Bassac at the southern tip of Dung Island each morning at dawn, just as all the civilian traffic and fishing boats started moving about the river.

MacVean wasn't going to fire on what could possibly be a civilian vessel, even though it fit the profile of what he was looking for. Mac Vean's crew signaled for the junk to stop, but it did not. As he neared, the junk fired an anti tank rocket at the fiberglass boat killing a Vietnamese Lieutenant and a Navy Gunner's Mate out-right. His boat was then raked with AK47 fire, ruining the boat and mortally wounding him. The junk, most probably transporting NVA troops, then disappeared into the bushes. Despite losing a lot of blood, Stephen nonetheless remained alert and in charge throughout the incident. But as his medevac helicopter gained altitude above the river, his mates wondered why it was not heading for the hospital. The pilot radioed that Stephen had died. Lt. MacVean had only been in country 4 days and hadn't had enough experience to be in a place that evil. Had he been willing to fire on the junk and the woman steering it when she failed to stop, he might have survived. But there were rules of engagement, and the Lieutenant risked his life and his crew rather than take the chance of killing innocent civilians.

Two months later, as part of President Nixon's Vietnamization program, the US transferred inland waterway combat responsibility to the Vietnamese Navy by giving them 125 vessels, marking the end of the US Navy's four-year responsibility for inland waterway combat, and eventually allowing US troops to be withdrawn.

Stephen MacVean was awarded the Bronze Star and the Navy Achievement Medal. Because his family had moved to Hohokus, he is listed on the memorial plaques there as well as in Ridgewood. He is buried in Plot 1693 at Valleau Cemetery. At death he was 25 years old.

1 Lt. Donald W. Maddox
O-1167963
387th Field Artillery Battalion
104th Infantry Division

Another Ridgewood boy who once lived here and died in combat but is not listed on our memorial plaques is Donald Maddox. Like many others, his family had moved away.

"Minsk" was born in New York City January 25, 1921, attended Cherry Valley School in Garden City and moved to Ridgewood with his two brothers and parents and lived for five years on North Maple Ave. He graduated from Ridgewood High School in 1939 where he was on the soccer team.

The family moved to Holmdel in 1940 where he served in the National Guard while working in Newark for the Beneficial Management Corporation. He entered active service August 11, 1942 and went overseas in August 1944 as an aerial observer with the HQ Battery, 387th Field Artillery Battalion, 104th Infantry Division ("Timberwolf Division"). The 104th landed in France on September 7 and had moved into a defensive position near Wuustwezel, Belgium by late October, becoming the first American regiment to fight under the command of an Allied Army on this front. On the 25th they went on the offensive and liberated Zundert, Holland, gaining control of a major road and overrunning the Vaart

Canal defenses. Victory followed victory as they advanced on Aachen. On November 16 they attacked and took Stolberg. Eschwiler fell on the 21st as they pushed on to the Inde River. German radio broadcasts called it the "most terrible and ferocious battle in the history of all wars" and the "*Stars and Stripes*" described the German shelling of the town of Inden as "the heaviest artillery concentration ever experienced by American troops". Time Magazine stated that "the Germans fought like wild men for the Inde". It was in this chaos that Maddox lost his life. After a month of intense combat, he died of multiple wounds and 3rd degree burns received in the Inde River area of Germany November 30, 1944.

Maddox is buried in Plot F, Row 2, Grave 48 in Henri-Chapelle American Cemetery, Henri-Chapelle, Belgium. He left a widow and a young daughter in Eugene, Oregon. He is listed among the WWII casualties in Holmdel and by the Monmouth County (NJ) Historical Association. At death he was 24 years old.

Pvt. Joseph Charles Mallory
32771823
Headquarter Company
1st Battalion
25th Infantry Regiment
93rd Infantry Division

When we look at our neighbors at home and our colleagues at work, it is difficult to imagine the racial dichotomy that existed in the USA 60 years ago. Manpower needs in WWII made it necessary to call on every able-bodied man and woman but the country was not ready to have blacks working or fighting side by side with whites. Military units were segregated, the best-known manifestation of this being the Tuskegee Airmen. In the infantry, African Americans fought together in what were known as Negro Army units, the largest of which were the 92nd and the 93rd Infantry Divisions which fought in both WWI and WWII. Joseph Mallory of Glen Rock has the dubious distinction of being the first WWII casualty of the 93rd.

Mallory was born January 22, 1922 in Glen Rock and lived with his parents and sister at 43 Dean Street. He attended Glen Rock public schools and graduated from Ridgewood High School in 1941. He was active in youth activities at Mount Bethel Baptist church. He married Elsie Linton in 1942 and they had a daughter. The family moved to Paterson and before being called to service in March 1942 he worked at Schweinfurth Florist.

He enlisted March 3, 1943, trained at Camp Croft, South Carolina and later in California and was assigned to the segregated Negro Army Unit, the 25th Infantry Regiment, 93rd Infantry Division in the Pacific. On March 21, 1944 the 93rd Infantry Division was ordered to move its Combat Team to Empress Augusta Bay Perimeter on Bougainville Island. The combat team included the 25th Infantry Regiment. By March 31, the Combat Team was in position and on April 2 the 93rd Infantry Division was in combat. The next day four men were lost from A and P Platoon while returning from a supply mission to the American Division on Hill 500, one of whom was Joseph Mallory.

Initially listed as missing in action, they were the first men of the 93rd to be killed in action in this war. Mallory is buried in Plot H, Row 16, Grave 121 in the fully integrated Manila American Cemetery, Manila. At death he was 22 years old.

Lt. John Mansfield Mason
O-825664
91 AAF, 9th Squadron
3rd Combat Cargo Group

It has been said that if one has a choice between skill and luck, one opts for luck. It has also been said that timing is everything. In the case of John Mason, his death was unlucky and his timing was tragic in every sense.

Born July 5, 1921, he lived at 287 Gardner Road with his brother and parents. John went through the entire Ridgewood school system. In High school he ran track and played football. He also played bass violin in the high school orchestra and was selected for both the county and state orchestras. He was also a member of the senior cabinet, was active in the Ridgewood YMCA and was participated in the youth groups at West Side

Presbyterian where he was confirmed on April 28, 1935. He was also a master scout.

After graduating from the high school in 1939 he went to Cornell to study Chemical Engineering and again was active in track and football. He was 5'9" tall and weighed 160 lbs with brown hair and blue eyes. He was a member of R.O.T.C. and Kappa Sigma Fraternity but didn't graduate because he joined the service Feb. 1, 1942 as an enlisted man.

He did his pre-flight training at Maxwell Field, Ala. in the summer of 1943, at Fletcher Field in Clarksdale, Miss. in the fall and in Greenville, Miss. in the winter. From February to May 1944 he was at George Field in Lawrenceville, Ill., getting his commission on March 12, 1944. For a time thereafter he was a flight leader and lead 65 cadets. He went to Malden Airfield in Malden, Mo. in March 1945 for transition school to learn how to fly the C-47 "Gooney Bird" and gliders. The C-47 Douglas transport was the military version of the DC-3 passenger plane.

Then he went overseas to Karachi, the city in which he was born when his father was working there for the Standard Oil Company. He proceeded to fly the perilous "Hump" in the China-Burma-India route. More than 400 supply planes crashed flying the Hump – either shot down by the enemy or forced down by bad weather.

Mason flew his first combat mission into Imphal, India and then moved on to Myitkyina, Burma June 3, 1945 at the northernmost terminus of the Ledo Road and switched from the C-47 to the C-46 because it had a greater range and could carry a bigger load.

In a letter written in June 1945 he said: "We've gotten to see lots of Burma and one corner of China has been well covered - from the air anyway. We are a combat cargo squadron and up until last month all of our work was concerned with supplying the Chinese, Americans and Indians that

310

were driving the bloody Japs southward. We dropped to them, and landed supplies at small airstrips, and had quite a busy time of it. We have been over Jap lines often but there are so few Japs left in Burma now, and those that are left keep pretty well hidden during the day so the "dramatic adventure" of offering yourself as an easy target never proved any more unusual than a bus ride to Paterson. We missed most of the serious fighting along the Ledo Road so things have been pretty soft for us. We are now primarily concerned with flying stuff into China which is also a lot easier than I had expected after hearing of all the "dangers" of Hump flying. I guess it used to be rough, but now it's pretty much routine."

One month later, August 15, 1945 - the day U.S. forces were ordered to cease-fire to end World War II - after 144 missions, 560 hours and with the Air Medal with one Cluster on his chest and shortly after being promoted to 1st. Lt., this skilled pilot was killed when his C-46D landed short on an instrument flight plan, crashed and burned on return approach from Ledo to Myitkyina, transporting empty 55 gallon gas drums. He tried to let down below minimum altitude for instrument flight conditions, trying to fly contact and partial instruments. He lost radio contact and went down, tearing down communications lines, hitting railroad tracks, cartwheeling across rice fields and through bushes, about three miles from the airstrip. The crew of three perished.

Aside from the Purple Heart and the Air Medal, with 1 Oak Leaf Cluster, he was awarded the WWII Victory Medal, Asiatic-Pacific Campaign Medal and the Distinguished Flying Cross (Posthumously). John Mason was buried in Myitkyina, moved to the American Military Cemetery in Kalaikunda, India in 1947 and finally repatriated to the Honolulu Memorial National Cemetery of the Pacific in 1949 and buried in Section A, Grave 79. At death he was 24 years old.

S/Sgt. Charles Edmund McDermott, Jr.
12064102
337ᵗʰ Bomb Squadron
96ᵗʰ Bombardment Group, Heavy
8ᵗʰ Air Force

Mickey was born August 21, 1919 and lived with his father, who worked for the Travelers Insurance Co., at 332 Meadowbrook Ave. in Ridgewood. His mother died when he was young and his father remarried.

He attended the Harrison School and played basketball for Mount Carmel where he was on two championship basketball teams. He graduated from Ridgewood High School in 1937 where he continued to play basketball and added baseball. He was also an active golfer. He then went into the jewelry business before enlisting in the Army Air Corps in April 1942.

McDermott went overseas with the 96ᵗʰ Bombardment Group on April 1, 1943 and entered combat in May as an Assistant Armorer in a B-17 bomber flying out of Snetterton Heath, Norfolk, England.

The B-17 "Flying Fortress" was the successor to the XB-15 which had been developed in 1933 as a result of Project A, an endeavor to design and build a heavy bomber that could fly 5,000 miles at 200 mph – able to protect Hawaii and Alaska and also fly to Europe and back non-stop.

B-17

The B-17 was a four engine heavy bomber with a wingspan of 103' 9'. It was 74' 9" long and had a combat weight of 40,000 lbs. Its four 1,200 hp Wright engines could generate a maximum speed of 317 mph with a cruising speed of 183 mph over a range of up to 3,300 miles. Its crew of 8/10 was protected by a total of thirteen 0.5-inch Browning machine guns - twin guns in chin, ventral, dorsal and tail positions, two single guns in nose, two in waist and one in the radio compartment while carrying a bomb load of up to 6,000 lbs.

Their assignment was to attack shipyards, harbors, railroad yards, airdromes, oil refineries, aircraft factories and other industrial targets in Germany, Czechoslovakia, France, Holland, Belgium, Norway, Poland and Hungary.

On July 28, 1943 120 B-17s left on a mission to the Fieseler Works in Oschersleven, Germany in bad weather. 15 were lost including "Liberty Belle", McDermott's plane. The formation encountered continuous enemy fighter attacks and his plane was shot down over the North Sea near the German coast. His body washed ashore at Ballum, Denmark August 29. Originally buried in

Denmark among the unknown, he was identified by his ID tag and is buried in Plot A, Row 31, Grave 37 in the Ardennes American Cemetery, Neupre, Belgium. He was awarded the Air Medal with two Oak Leaf Clusters. At death he was 22 years old.

Maj. Thomas Buchannan McGuire, Jr.
O-437031
431st Fighter Squadron
475th Fighter Group

Ridgewood is the birthplace of the Congressional Medal of Honor winner for whom McGuire Air Force Base was named. With 38 kills, Tom McGuire was the second leading Air Ace of WWII, earning 6 Distinguished Flying Crosses, the Distinguished Service Cross with 3 Silver Stars and 15 Air Medals.

Tommy was born in Ridgewood Aug. 1, 1920 and attended the Willard School until age 10 when his parents separated. He spent the rest of his youth with his mother in Sebring, Florida. His father remained in Ridgewood to run his Packard automobile dealership.

In high school he played first chair clarinet in Sebring's nationally acclaimed marching band. At 5' 7¼" with brown hair and blue eyes, he was a bench-warmer on the football team, an avid sailor and a reasonable golfer. In his youth Tommy flew kites and model airplanes and later focused on aviation. He acquired a reputation as a hell-raiser by driving his car too fast through town, emulating his uncle who had been a fighter pilot in WWI. He attended Georgia Tech, played clarinet in the college band, joined ROTC and Beta Theta Pi and was an excellent scholar but left college in his third year to join the Army Air Corps in July 1941. His father later said that Tommy "blackmailed" him into letting him join Officer Training School after just two years of college.

His first assignment was flying patrols over the Aleutian Islands and Alaska and he married just before going overseas in August 1943 with the 49th Fighter Group. In August he joined the 431st Fighter Squadron "Satan's Angels", 475th Fighter Group. The first time he engaged the enemy he was flying cover for bombers attacking Wewak, New Guinea. Approaching the target, the fighters were attacked by Japanese aircraft. During the battle, McGuire had three kills. On the following day, again piloting his P-38 "Pudgy", he downed two more enemy aircraft.

With five kills, he established himself as an air ace after engaging the enemy only twice and immediately gained national renown. His exploits were followed closely in the press and earned him flights with Charles Lindberg. There were regular articles in the Ridgewood newspapers keeping tally of his kills and following his progress up the ranks of fighter pilot aces.

Medal of Honor Action:

On Christmas Day 1944, McGuire voluntarily led a squadron of fifteen P-38s to protect American bombers as they attacked the Japanese airfield at Mabalacat. Suddenly attacked by twenty Zeros, he had to protect his squadron from attack. Often outnumbered three-to-one, he fought off the enemy until his guns jammed but instead of fleeing the area, he lured the Japanese pilots into his wingman's line of fire and scored two more victories.

The next day McGuire volunteered to lead his squadron on another bomber escort mission over Clark Field. He described the action saying: "The bombers had completed their run and were heading away from the target when, at 10:35, I sighted one enemy aircraft at 8 o'clock high. There were about five Zekes coming down on the tail of the bomber formation from above, out of the overcast. We were about 2,000 feet above and behind the bombers.

P-38

"As I started down, I saw two enemy aircraft heading south below us. As I started my attack, the first Zeke had finished his pass and the second was driving up the last bomber flight's tail. This was at about 13,000 feet. As the enemy was pressing his attack, and I could see no return fire from the bomber, I opened fire from 45-degrees deflection from about 350- to 400-yards range, getting hits right in the cockpit.

"The Zeke started to burn, but as he was still on the B-24's tail, by then about 50 yards behind it, I closed to within 100 feet, firing another burst. The Zeke rolled over and burst into flames. Captain Edwin R. Weaver, my wingman, saw the Zeke burst into flames and explode. I shot at the third Zeke in the string, shooting in about 70-degrees deflection but observed no results. Turning to the left and down, I shot two bursts into another Zeke at about 60-degrees deflection. The enemy plane started burning, and Captain Weaver saw him crash in flames.

"About three more had come, so I turned on one, shooting a burst from 30-degrees deflection, then another good burst from about 45-degrees deflection and got hits around the cockpit. The enemy started down and crashed in a dry stream. Lieutenant Herman, my element leader, who had broken off to clear himself from another Japanese, saw him crash, going down from 5,000 feet.

"I was then by myself, as my wingman had lost me on that pass. I saw another Zeke heading down, so I turned on it and caught it at about 1,500 feet. I fired two bursts from about 40-to 60-degrees' deflection, getting hits around and behind the wing roots, and the Zeke started burning, then crashed near the dry stream. Lieutenant Herman saw the Zeke burn and crash.

"As I was on the deck, I started climbing, and at about 6,000 feet I saw an enemy aircraft diving down quite a distance in front of me. The enemy plane pulled up, so I gave chase, but another flight came down from above to attack him. As the Japanese started for the clouds, it was hit and burst into flames just before reaching the clouds. I saw Lieutenant Pierce, leader of the 8th Fighter Squadron flight, destroy this aircraft."

The following day he was hospitalized for three days, suffering from stress. On January 6 he was reinstated and on Jan. 7, 1945 he led a group of four P-38s out of Dulag Strip over a Japanese-held airstrip on Negros Islands in the Philippines. An enemy aircraft zeroed in on one of the P-38s who radioed for help. McGuire was quick to respond but died in his attempt to save his friend.

A Zero piloted by Japan's second leading air ace, Shoici Sugita, surprised them from out of the clouds. McGuire's group surrounded the Zero which then made sharp turns trying to escape the trap. The P-38s followed him, descending to 200 feet. They then scattered and the Zero maneuvered into position right on the tail of one of the Lightnings. The attacked pilot called for help and, as McGuire tried to respond, his plane fell off and crashed into the ground on Hacienda Progresso, Cadiz near Pinanamaan, Negros Island where he was buried by natives. His body was recovered in November 1947 and repatriated to the USA in June 1949 with great fanfare through Ridgewood to his burial May 17, 1950 in Section 11, Grave 426 at Arlington National Cemetery.

Medal of Honor Citation

"He fought with conspicuous gallantry and intrepidity over Luzon, Philippine Islands. Voluntarily, he led a squadron of 15 P-38s as top cover for heavy bombers striking Mabalacat Airdrome, where his formation was attacked by 20 aggressive Japanese fighters. In the ensuing action he repeatedly flew to the aid of embattled comrades, driving off enemy assaults while himself under attack and at times outnumbered 3 to 1, and even after his guns jammed, continuing the fight by forcing a hostile plane into his wingman's line of fire. Before he started back to his base he had shot down 3 Zeros. The next day he again volunteered to lead escort fighters on a mission to strongly defended Clark Field. During the resultant engagement he again exposed himself to attacks so that he might rescue a crippled bomber. In rapid succession he shot down 1 aircraft, parried the attack of 4 enemy fighters, 1 of which he shot down, single-handedly engaged 3 more Japanese, destroying 1, and then shot down still another, his 38th victory in aerial combat. On 7 January 1945, while leading a voluntary fighter sweep over Los Negros Island, he risked an extremely hazardous maneuver at low altitude in an attempt to save a fellow flyer from attack, crashed, and was reported missing in action. With gallant initiative, deep and unselfish concern for the safety of others, and heroic determination to destroy the enemy at all costs, Maj. McGuire set an inspiring example in keeping with the highest traditions of the military service."

His 38 kills made him the second leading American air ace of WWII (the leading Japanese air ace had 102 kills; the leading German air ace had 352 kills; the leading Russian ace had 62). Although he never attended Ridgewood High School, RHS offers an annual memorial scholarship for "academic achievement, service to the school and the potential to uphold the high ideals embraced by Major McGuire". At death he was 24 years old.

Gunner's Mate/2 Charles Victor McHenry
07100291
USS Twiggs DD-591

Japanese Admiral Takijiro Onishi created Special Attack Groups of suicide dive-bombing pilots known as "kamikazes". The idea was first proposed in the summer of 1943. Initially refused, Prime Minister Tojo relented and ordered the first official kamikaze attack in the spring of 1944. A kamikaze pilot would aim his plane at the Achilles heal of a ship, the central elevator of enemy aircraft carriers or the bridge of enemy warships.

Education was key in shaping kamikaze pilots. Throughout the 20th century, the Japanese had been taught to die for the emperor. During WWII, slogans like "sacrifice life" were drilled into soldiers. These pilots wanted to die for their country. Training took barely a week.

Looking at results, it is unclear that the kamikaze missions were successful, given the cost in Japanese lives. Japanese forces flew 2,314 sorties, of which 1,086 returned. Kamikaze operations sank thirty-four ships and damaged 288 more. One of the U.S. ships hit was the *U.S.S. Twiggs* with Charles McHenry aboard.

USS Twiggs – DD 591

"Mac" was born in Glen Rock November 2, 1920. After early schooling in Glen Rock, he graduated from Ridgewood High School in 1939 where he was the star miler on the track team for three years and played intramural basketball. He was a Boy Scout and active at the Community Church of Glen Rock. He then spent a year at Duke University and later worked for the Wright Aeronautical Company in Woodridge. He enlisted in the Navy in 1943 and was assigned to the *Twigs* as a gunner's mate.

As the battle for Okinawa drew to an end in late June 1945, with US ground and Navy forces closing in on what remained of the 32nd Japanese Army. Kamikaze flyers were increasingly active as the *Twiggs* was on radar picket duty off Senaga Shima.

At about 8:30 in the evening of June 16, a *Nakajima B6N Tenzan – "Jill"* Torpedo bomber struck the *Twiggs,* stationed off Okinawa. It came out of the sky like a bolt of lightning. When it was less than 1,000 yards from the *Twiggs* it unleashed a torpedo that tore into the No. 2 ammunition magazine. Then the Jill circled and completed its kamikaze mission as it crashed into the ship between guns 3 and 4.

The combination of the torpedo's explosion, the magazine's explosion and the plane's explosion ruptured the destroyer's frame and sent fire throughout the ship while ammunition sprayed everywhere. Sailors scrambled topside only to find the deck engulfed in flames.

Half an hour after the Kamikaze hit, the ship's after magazine blew up and the ship sank immediately, taking with her 18 of her 22 officers and 165 men. Among them was Charles McHenry. He is listed on the Tablets of the Missing at the Honolulu Memorial. At death he was 24 years old.

Sgt. Albert Montick
32597713
790th Bomb Squad
467th Bomb Group
8th AAF

In WWII, 407,000 Americans died. Of those deaths, 115,000 were accidental. Albert Montick was one of them.

Montick was born in Ridgewood March 2. 1916 and lived at 266 Edward St. with his parents and three brothers. His father worked at the Village Water Department. At Ridgewood High School he participated in intramural football and basketball and played on the high school baseball team and graduated in 1935. For awhile he worked at Wright Aeronautical Corp. in Paterson and married Marion Kiefer on June 6, 1942. They lived in Fair Lawn until he entered the service on December 7, 1942.

He did his basic training at Harvey Parks Airport, 9 months training at Coffeyville, Kansas and went overseas November 1, 1944 as a radio operator in the 8th AAF, 467th Bomb Group, 790th Bomb Squad.

On departure for a December 29, 1944 mission targeting a communications center in Prum, Germany he was one of 10 members of crew 53 killed when his B-24 crashed in dense fog on take-off from Wroxham, England. The mission was scrubbed.

His body was repatriated in July 1948 and buried in Plot 1549 at Valleau Cemetery. Bethlehem Lutheran Church dedicated the Altar Vases to him. At death he was 28 years old.

Crew 53
Joseph Fearon, Edward Materewicz, Karl Koller,
Lewis Byers, Albert Montick, Robert Williams,
Clem Plaskiewicz, Richard Hagist, Kurt Schellhas,
Clifford Pheneger

Lt. Jack Neil Moore
AO 2227742
435th Fighter Day Squadron
U.S. Air Corps

Neil was born in Lima, Ohio October 11, 1930 and moved to Ridgewood with his brother and parents to live on Upper Bd. when he was 8 years old. He went through the entire Ridgewood school system and graduated from Ridgewood High School in 1948. In high school, he was a member of the Booster Club, cafeteria committee, was active in drama presentations, played football and ran track.

He then attended the University of Alabama and his family moved to Oakland, Ca. He followed them and spent 3 years at the University of California, Berkley.

Moore enlisted in the Air Force in 1951 and got his wings in early 1953. Carefree, he was hit with an Article 15 as punishment for having been caught buzzing the nearby town of Selma, Alabama.

He then did advance flying training at Nellis Air Force Base. His fellow pilots considered him a "tiger" and a good pilot but he took some chances.

Neil died May 28, 1954 in an air crash at the Yakima firing range in Washington State during the 6th Army's air to ground maneuvers entitled "Operation Hilltop". While piloting an F-86F out of George Air Force Base, Victoriaville, Ca., he was flying very low making simulated napalm passes and strafing runs while diving on artillery positions. Traveling at 500 mph, he did not have enough time to pull up and hit the top of a hill belly first.

He is buried in plot R 3680 at the Golden State National Cemetery, San Bruno, CA. At death he was 23 years old.

F-86F

Pfc. Robert La Roy Morris
32925709
Company K
351st Infantry Regiment
88th Infantry Division

Of the 98 names on the original WWII, Korea and Vietnam memorial plaque at Van Neste Square, 17 had misspelled names. One such inaccuracy concerns Bob Morris.

Bob was born July 7, 1923 and lived in Ridgewood as an only child at 202 Walnut Street. He attended the New York Military Academy and then returned home to graduate from Ridgewood High School in 1941 where he was in the International Club and worked on the senior play. He was an avid outdoorsman and hunter. He was a member of the Paramus Reformed Church and became engaged to his RHS classmate Ruth Board.

After high school Morris attended the University of Virginia but was called to the service June 2, 1943, going overseas in February 1944 as a combat infantryman with the 88th Infantry Division.

The 88th arrived in Naples February 6, 1944, staged in the Piedmont d'Alife area and relieved the 36th Infantry Division on Monte Castellone February 28.

On May 11 Morris and the 351st attacked toward Rome against strong opposition. They came under heavy fire May 18 while attempting to take Monte Grande but succeeded and, on June 2, they overran S. Cesareo and pressed through Rome on June 4. Later in this push, Morris died of shrapnel wounds to the head and left leg received at Gesso Ridge, Italy October 8, 1944. As was often the case with combat casualties, he was listed as missing for a month.

For his efforts he was awarded the Combat Infantryman Badge.

For his sacrifice he was awarded the Purple Heart (posthumously). His body was returned to the USA in December 1948 just in time for a joint funeral service with his mother who died shortly after his repatriation. He is buried in the Morris Mausoleum at Valleau, Lots 1369 and 1370. His name was incorrectly listed as Robert Leroy Morris on the memorial plaques at Van Neste Square. At death he was 21 years old.

2 Lt. George Cotton Munroe, Jr.
O 2073194
600th Bomber Squadron
398th Bomber Group, Heavy
8th USAAF

Flight in the late 1930s and early 1940s was still in its early stages. FAA regulations as we know them today were unknown. Many WWII pilots dreamed of flying under the Golden Gate Bridge or the George Washington Bridge. Some managed to buzz their hometowns and even their old schools. One such lucky young man was Cotton Munroe of Glen Rock who was instructed to do a fly-over at his home town.

Cotton was born in Paterson January 12, 1922 and lived with his family at 28 Boulevard in Glen Rock. He received his elementary schooling in Glen Rock and graduated from Ridgewood High School in 1939 where he was in the band, Hi-Y, Dramatic Club, German Club, played Jayvee soccer and later was soccer manager. He performed in "Black Flamingo", was on the class play selection committee and the "Arrow Business Staff". Although an Episcopalian, he served as President of the Presbyterian Young People during his senior year. He then went on to graduate from Penn State in 1943 with a degree in Geology where he became a member of Triangle Fraternity.

He joined the Army Air Corps and was commissioned at Selma Field in Alabama in January 1945. Shortly before that, he was selected as one of a hand-picked crew chosen from all over the USA to fly to West Point for graduation ceremonies. The formation flew over Glen Rock and Ridgewood.

He announced his engagement to his high school classmate Barbara Croll just before going overseas in February 1945 as a precision navigator in a B-17. Based in Nuthampstead, Hertfordshire, England he was lost near Stindal, Germany April 8, 1945 on his 12th mission. His crew of 10 was on a mission to Derben, Germany when, three minutes after bombs away, they were hit by anti-aircraft fire. The left wing was badly damaged and torn off causing the plane to go into a barrel roll. It then exploded before hitting the ground. Only one man managed to parachute out and survive.

Initially unidentified, he was buried with three others in a mass grave in Krusemark, Germany. His remains were identified and he is now buried in Plot D, Row, 35, Grave 12 in the Ardennes American Cemetery, Neupre, Belgium. Aside from his posthumous Purple Heart, he was awarded the Air Medal. At death he was 23 years old.

Pfc. Gustave W. Nadler
1209712
Company A,
107th Infantry
27th ("New York") Division

At different times throughout the 20th century, kids from other towns attended Ridgewood High School. During WWI, students came from Glen Rock and Allendale for their high school experience. One of these students was Gustave Nadler.

Nadler was born in August 1898 and lived with his parents and two sisters at 70 Franklin Turnpike in Allendale. Gustave attended Allendale schools until 1912 and graduated from Ridgewood High School in the class of 1916. The family attended the Episcopal Church in Allendale although Highlands Presbyterian Church now has a window dedicated to him.

Nadler enlisted in the army on May 9, 1917 in New York and, like almost everybody else from Bergen County, trained at Camp Wadsworth, Spartanburgh, SC. before going overseas May 9,

1918, sailing from Newport News, VA. During this time, his father was Mayor of Allendale from 1914 - 1918.

Because he valiantly fought in the trenches at Dickebush Mount Kemmel, Belgium, the Hindenburg Line, Schelat Canal, south of Vendhuil, Brisigny to Souplet Canal, he was promoted to Pfc. July 9, 1918.

Four months later, as the fighting seriously heated up, Nadler was killed October 13, 1918 in the battle of St. Souplet as the Germans retreated towards the homeland. He was the first WWI Allendale casualty and is buried in Plot 588 in Valleau Cemetery. At death he was 20 years old.

Pfc. Walter Jacob Neske
32762320
Co. C
26th Infantry Regiment

Manpower needs were great during WWII. It was not enough to draft teenagers, train them a bit and send them green into combat. The military also recycled its wounded personnel. One Purple Heart was often not enough to get an infantryman off the front lines. Not even a Purple Heart with Oak Leaf, indicating a second combat wound, would guarantee a reprieve. Some did not want a reprieve. Walter Neske was hit twice, patched up twice and run back into combat for a third and last time.

Walt was born in Ridgewood December 17, 1923 and lived at 323 East Glen Ave. with his three sisters, five brothers and parents. The family attended the Paramus Reformed Church. He attended the Harrison School and graduated from Ridgewood High School in the class of 1941 where he was on the track team. His high school quotation "I know him of a noble mind although a lion in the field" foretold his military career.

He left Ridgewood to enter the service February 3, 1943 and went overseas three months later to join the 26th Infantry Regiment, the "Blue Spaders" for North African operations. He received a Purple Heart for wounds received during the invasion of Sicily. The 26th returned to the UK November 5, 1943. After staying in the hospital for some time he was re-activated for the D-Day invasion of France where he was again wounded, receiving an Oak Leaf to add to his Purple Heart.

Neske died September 13, 1944 near Namur of shrapnel wounds to the shoulder and groin, four days after arriving in Belgium with the Blue Spaders. His ticket home finally came when his body was repatriated in April 1949 and buried in Section 10, Lot 127, Grave 1 at Laurel Grove Cemetery in Paterson. At death he was 20 years old

Apprentice Seaman Milton Ness
9081206

In WWII, because of the extreme pressure to produce quick results, the Navy's enlisted personnel procurement program included an element called specialized procurement (V7) by which the Navy recruited enlisted personnel between the ages of 18 and 37 who possessed special qualifications, experience or training which the average recruit could not be expected to possess. This was generally done by direct recruitment or voluntary induction. Often the incentive offered was the rank of Petty Officer but, because of inadequate standards to measure qualifications, there was a danger in passing over non-rated or lower rated men already in the service who might have been as well or better qualified. These special volunteers were given intensive training after their initial recruit training. One such selected volunteer was Milton Ness.

Born and raised in Brooklyn, he and his wife moved to Ridgewood to live at 79 South Maple

Ave. while his parents, one sister and four brothers remained in Brooklyn. After attending New Utrecht from 1922 to 1926 he received a Bachelor's of Social Science Degree from the College of the City of New York in 1934. He then went on to get a Master of Arts Degree from Columbia in 1938. He was also a swimming champion and a member of the Coast Guard Auxiliary, fire department auxiliary, a Red Cross Life Saving examiner and a Red Cross First Aid instructor. He had been actively interested in the consumer cooperative movement and the State, County and Municipal Workers of America. Prior to enlisting in the Navy he was a Supervisor with the Welfare Department of the City of New York.

Ness participated in the selected volunteer program in the Navy, enlisting on March 28, 1944 after having completed five and one-half months in the Army. Because of the need for sailors, boot camp had been reduced from 10 weeks to four. As a 36-year old recruit, he was assigned to the Naval Training Station at Samson, New York where the average age of the recruits was 17. He died suddenly a month later on April 23, 1944 of intercranial injuries, a brain hemorrhage.

Ness, the only Jew among Ridgewood's 113 Honored Dead, is buried Section I, Grave 12332 at Long Island National Cemetery at Farmingdale. At death he was 36 years old.

Capt. William Ward Nichols, Jr.
O86484
3rd Battalion, 40th Regiment
22nd Infantry Division
US Military Assistance Command

In 1955 President Eisenhower sent the first military advisors to Saigon to help the South Vietnamese government in its war against the Vietcong guerrillas. In late 1961 President Kennedy raised the number of military advisors from 685 to several thousand. Over the next few years U.S. military personnel continued to serve in advisory positions as the U.S. presence crescendoed into full involvement. By the time Ward Nichols joined them in 1965, the U.S. Military Assistance Command counted 16,000 advisors, a number dwarfed by the 185,000 American troops in country as the U.S. commitment transitioned from advisory to hands-on, catching Ward Nichols in its crossfire.

Ward was born March 17, 1937 in Hackensack, raised in Rutherford and moved to

Ridgewood with his brother and parents to live at 287 Woodside Ave. after the 9th grade. He graduated from Ridgewood High School in 1955 where he was active in the Spanish Club, Booster Club, junior and senior Play committees and the Arrow art staff. He ran track his senior year and served as Treasurer of the youth group of Emmanuel Baptist Church.

While at Penn State he was active in ROTC, was part of the Pershing rifle drill team, a member of Phi Kappa Tau fraternity and was singles and doubles handball champion. He married Warrene Shreve.

He entered the service in August 1959, did Ranger training and finished first in his Airborne training class at Fort Benning. He then served 3.5 years in Germany.

Ward was then assigned to Fort Ord in California and went to Fort Bragg for refresher training before being sent to Vietnam in February 1965 with the US Military Assistance Command in the often-frustrating role of adviser. Before leaving he was able to spend time with his infant son David. He was a big and cheerful man, diplomatic but determined. Dedicated to his task, he wrote "whatever will be, will be so we must put our faith in God and use our abilities to the utmost to accomplish the goals we have prescribed as a nation".

On the morning of October 4, 1965 he was an advisor to the 22nd Infantry Division of the Army of the Republic of Vietnam trying to establish a perimeter defense to protect engineers who were working on the Phu Lay bridge in Ninh Dinh Province, 250 miles north of Saigon. At about 5:00 in the morning the unit came under intensive fire. Disregarding his own safety, he left the comparative safety of his command post to personally feel out the strength of the opposing force. Despite heavy mortar and small arms fire, he remained in the front line with his men until mortally wounded.

Ward Nichols was Ridgewood's first casualty of the Vietnam War and was awarded the Silver Star, Bronze Star and two similar awards from the Vietnamese government – the Gallantry Cross with Palm and the National Order, fifth class. The award cited him for "disregarding personal safety to move through intense hostile small arms and mortar fire to insure weapons being served to the friendly force and to see that they were properly emplaced. While advising them on the effective use of suppressive fire against the enemy Captain Nichols was mortally wounded by a communist mortar round." He is buried in Block X, Lot 98, Section B, Grave 4 in George Washington Memorial Park in Paramus. A stained glass window at Emmanuel Baptist Church is dedicated to his memory. At death he was 28 years old.

Lt. Heather O'Mara
U.S. Army Judge Advocate General

Most vocations have targeted markets that they serve, be they geographic or related to a specific population. There are very few fields which serve everybody throughout the entire nation. Military service is such a field so the death of a person who has dedicated their life, or a portion of it, to all of us through military service has a special meaning. Ridgewoood's 113 Honored Dead went down with their ship, died in front line combat or aerial dogfights in time of war. Yet some of them died of illness or accidents – sometimes far from the front lines. These 113 are remembered and honored at least once a year. But what about those who dedicate a part of their life to their country outside an official period of war and die doing so, regardless of where, when or how? Is their death any less honorable? Is their sacrifice any less meaningful? Is their loss unworthy of being memorialized? I think not. One such casualty was Heather O'Mara who died in the crash of a commercial airliner while she was serving on active duty in the Army.

Her high school quote spoke directly to her approach to life: "We are limitless for we believe in our dreams. So don't dream it, be it." Heather realized her dreams only to have them disastrously and prematurely cut short in a tragic accident.

Heather O'Mara was born July 22, 1964 in Evanston, Ill. and moved to Ridgewood with her parents in 1967 to live at 325 Mastin Place. She graduated with high honors from Ridgewood High School in the class of 1982 where she played the tuba in the band, was in the New Players and was Business Editor for the yearbook.

Upon graduation from RHS, she attended the University of New Hampshire where she was again in the marching band, graduating in three years. She then attended Tulane Law School. Admitted to the Bar in New Jersey, and having done a summer internship with the Army, she joined the Army and graduated in the 118th Basic Course of the Judge Advocate General School in March 1989 to become a prosecuting attorney at Fort Carson in Colorado Springs.

It was on a commercial flight from Denver to Chicago that she died. Heather was on her way to the funeral of her 25-year old cousin who had died while climbing a glacier. Just after three in the afternoon of July 19, 1989 she was aboard United Airlines Flight 232, a McDonnell Douglas DC-10-10 cruising at 37,000 feet when the aircraft suffered a catastrophic engine failure. The disintegration of the fan rotor in the number two engine caused the loss of all three of the aircraft's redundant hydraulic flight control systems and made the aircraft almost uncontrollable. After about 45 minutes of valiant efforts to control the plane, the Captain and his crew, assisted by a DC-10 instructor pilot who was aboard as a passenger, were able to reach the municipal airport at Sioux City, Iowa where the plane crash-landed. Of the 285 passengers and 11 crew members aboard, 174 passengers and 10 crew members survived. Heather, who was scheduled to be promoted to Captain August 1, was not one of them.

Her mother and grandmother had seen her get on the plane and themselves had taken another flight. When they arrived at O'Hare the news of an air accident was circulating but no specifics were available for hours; however, a mother's intuition, plus the fact that Heather had not called, convinced her mother that Heather had not survived.

Heather O'Mara is buried in Queen of Heaven Cemetery, Hillside, Ill. At death, she was 24 years old - three days short of her 25th birthday.

S/1 Harold Bacon Parks
07102368
USS *HAZELWOOD*

His nickname was "Hap", short for Happy. He was born July 9, 1923 and lived with his brother and parents at 116 Lake Ave. in Ridgewood, was confirmed at West Side Presbyterian Church, went through the entire Ridgewood public school system and graduated from the high school in 1942. He was a cut-up with a natural wit, a bit of a ham and was exceptionally good at dramatics. He was in the Christmas and Easter plays, Junior and Senior plays and on the make-up committee. He served on the art staff of the high school's yearbook, *The Arrow,* participated in boxing and bowling and was a member of the boosters club. He also was one of the younger members of the Civilian Defense group and a loyal member of the Ridgewood Military Training Unit which drilled regularly on the school field. He went to Pratt Institute after graduation and majored in

Illustration but was called to service in the Navy December 11, 1942.

After three months of basic training at the Great Lakes Naval Training Center he shipped out to Treasure Island off San Francisco, Ca. and was piped aboard the Fletcher Class destroyer U.S.S. *Hazelwood* with the rank of Seaman Second Class. They departed the West Coast September 5, 1943 and reached Pearl Harbor September 9th. In his first month at sea they participated in carrier-based air strikes against Tarawa and Wake Island. In November 1943 they joined Task Force 53 in the New Hebrides to take part in the invasion of the Gilbert Islands on November 20th. They returned to Pearl Harbor in December 1943 to prepare for the next operation.

A month later they sailed from Pearl as part of Task Force 52 for the invasion of the Marshall Islands. The *Hazelwood* was involved in the invasion of the Palaus, hammering enemy shore positions with gunfire to weaken the Japanese opposition as the 1st Marine Division landed on Peleliu on September 15th, 1944. They patrolled off Peleliu until early October when they sailed for Manus Islands where they participated in the invasion and liberation of the Philippine Islands.

Easter Sunday April 1, 1945 was D-Day for Okinawa. The *Hazelwood* was operating off Okinawa on radar picket and escorting patrols through intense Japanese air attacks. Kamikazes made 1,500 attacks, sank 34 naval craft and damaged 358 others. On April 29th the carrier group they were escorting was attacked by kamikazes that dove out of low cloud cover. As a Quartermaster, Hap was on the bridge. The *Hazelwood*, all guns blazing, maneuvered to avoid three of the "Zekes". A third screamed out of the clouds from astern. Although hit by the *Hazelwood's* fire, the bomb-laden zero careened past the superstructure, hit the #2 stack on the port side, smashed into the bridge and exploded.

The *Hazelwood* was decapitated with an astonishing explosion so strong that the outlines of men thrown into the bulkheads were easily recognized. Flaming gasoline spilled over the decks and bulkheads as the mast toppled and the forward guns were put out of action.

USS Hazelwood after the attack

77 men, including the Captain, were killed and 35 men were reported missing in action, including Hap Parks.

He is listed on the World War II Tablets of the Missing in the Honolulu National Cemetery and Memorial. In October 1945 the Ridgewood Art Association hosted an exhibition of artwork done by local GIs. Hap was one of two Ridgewood war casualties whose work was displayed. At death, he was 21 years old.

MM 2/c Franklin Moore Patterson, Jr.
USNR, Sub Chaser 209

Ridgewood's first Naval casualty of the great war was Frank Patterson, a victim of friendly fire.

Frank lived at 85 Lincoln Ave., Ridgewood with his brother and parents. The family eventually moved to Pitman (Gloster) NJ. He enlisted in the Navy in New York May 28, 1917 and was lost at sea when his 110' Sub chaser 209 was sunk off Long Island by friendly fire at 3:15 Tuesday morning August 27, 1918 – the first such incident resulting in the loss of life. Coincidentally, the flagship of the special U-boat hunting squadron of destroyers that sank Sub Chaser 209 was the *Patterson*.

Sailing in the same direction 200 feet away in foggy weather, the supply transport *Felix Taussig,* en route from Bordeaux to New York, mistook SC 209 for a U-boat trying to submerge and shelled the sub-chaser when it did not show its lights or signal its identity. According to the "Rules of War" at the time, it was normal for vessels to run without lights. The nervous crew of the *Taussig,* aware of the presence of enemy submarines, had already been spooked by two unidentified vessels earlier that night.

The *Taussig* had an armed guard aboard but the Captain of the *Taussig* claims to not have given an order to fire. An apparent miscommunication between the Chief Gunners Mate and a S/2 allowed for five shots to be fired, two of which struck SC 209, most likely hitting a depth charge. Only then did SC 209 show its lights but it sank in three minutes. 17 members of the crew, including Patterson, the commander and the executive officer, were lost.

As early as 1920, Sub Chaser 209 became a popular destination for divers off Long Island. In remembrance of the officers and men who lost their lives on SC 209, the first vessel of the sub-chaser class to distinguish itself in action, a memorial trophy was donated to the Navy in 1942. At death he was 20 years old.

WWI Sub Chasers

Pfc. William Robert Petsche
33841678
23rd Infantry Regiment
2nd Infantry Division

America has always been a mobile society. Even in time of war families were on the move. Sometimes that could mean that a favorite son who moved out of town and later died in combat while officially registered in another state went unnoticed in his original hometown. Fortunately, I have not found any instances where a combat casualty slipped between the chairs and was not – or will not be - mentioned on any town's memorial plaques. On the contrary, several of Ridgewood's casualties are listed on memorial plaques in more than one town. Better too many than too few. William Petsche is such a case.

He was born May 12, 1925 in Yonkers but moved with his sister and parents to Glen Rock and then to Ridgewood to live at 41 Garfield Place. He graduated from Charles E. Gorton High School in Yonkers and immediately entered Chicago University in September 1943 where he majored in science and math. His family spent summers in Bloomsburg, PA where he registered for the draft. Although he was eligible for deferment because of the type of work he was doing, he enlisted just before Christmas break, 1943 and entered the service February 22, 1944.

Petsche trained at Camp Wheeler in Georgia and, despite the specialized work he had been doing in civilian life, went to France August 22, 1944 as a combat infantryman with the 23rd Infantry Regiment, 2nd Infantry Division. He arrived in France September 1, went into combat September 2 during the battle for the port city of Brest, which was liberated on Sept. 18, 1944. It was this action that was fatal to Petsche who died September 19, 1944 in Brest.

William Petsche is buried in Plot H, Row 2, Grave 13 in the Brittany American Cemetery, St. James, France. In addition to Ridgewood, he is also listed on the memorial plaques in Yonkers. At death he was 19 years old.

Pvt. George Hobart Rae
Company A
Battalion Engineers
U.S. Army

My friend and supporter, Ridgewood local historian Joe Suplicki, came across a notice in the January 18, 1901 issue of the *Ridgewood News* which states that "Mr. Frank B. Rae of this village has received notice from the War Department of the death of his son, George H. Rae ... killed at Luzon, Philippine Islands on December 30, 1900". This makes him Ridgewood's first service casualty since incorporation of the village in 1894 although it is very possible that he, like several casualties among Ridgewood's 112 Honored Dead, never set foot in Ridgewood. Nonetheless, a Ridgewood family lost a son on that day. Private Rae is not listed on Ridgewood's memorial plaques and his sacrifice has apparently gone unacknowledged all these years. How he got to the Philippines is an interesting story.

George Rae was born in the late spring of 1873 in Syracuse, NY. Known as Bert, he lived in Chicago with his family until leaving home. The family subsequently moved east in 1900 and built a house on West End Avenue, Cantrell Park in Ridgewood. Like his father, who was an electrical engineer, he was an electrician and draftsman. His brother Frank Jr., an artist and designer of books and printed matter, was the first tenant of the Pioneer Building at the corner of Chestnut and Ridgewood Avenue and later became a fireman with Protection Hook and Ladder.

Slight at 5'6" tall with blue eyes and light brown hair, George left home and was employed on the Transport *Port Arthur* in the South Pacific before he enlisted for a three-year hitch in the Army in Manila on December 24, 1899 during the Spanish-American War. Fearing his mother would worry, he did not tell her.

351

As background, in the waning years of the 19th Century, the USA was concerned for its citizens living in Cuba where bloodshed, starvation and general devastation at the hands of the Spanish authorities had become rampant. It was a harbinger of the Spanish American War.

After many tries at appeasement, American involvement officially began in the spring of 1898, shortly after the infamous sinking of the Battleship *Maine* in Havana harbor. At the same time, President McKinley ordered Commodore Dewey to destroy the Spanish fleet in Manila. The fighting did not last long and the Treaty of Paris was signed between Spanish and American representatives on December 10, 1898. Among its conditions was the yielding of the Philippines, Guam, and Puerto Rico to the United States. At the same time, the US annexed the Hawaiian Islands and Cuba was granted its independence.

However, the Filipinos had been fighting the Spanish colonialists since 1896 and wanted independence. A native army had been organized and had taken control of several islands, including most of Luzon. They condemned seizure by the US and threatened war. The Philippine Insurrection, a.k.a. the Philippine-American War, began after two American soldiers killed three Filipino soldiers in a suburb of Manila on February 4, 1899, setting off a coda to the Spanish American war that would last for more than three years. Some veterans of the Spanish-American War served in the Philippines but the War Department considered them to be different conflicts, listing the official dates for the Spanish-American War as 1898 and for the Philippine Insurrection as 1899-1902.

The Philippine Insurrection was a highly controversial involvement from which the U.S. could not withdraw without suffering "dishonor". This inspired Mark Twain to state that "An inglorious peace is better than a dishonorable war." In 1901, convinced of the futility of further resistance, the insurgents swore allegiance to the United States and lay down their arms. In 1902 President Roosevelt declared the Philippines pacified.

In the Philippine Insurrection, only 17 enlisted US army soldiers were killed - one of whom was Private Rae who was killed by insurgents December 30, 1900 near Quiom, Ilocos Norte of gunshot wounds to the head and buttocks as well as bolo knife wounds. Private Rae was buried in Grave 3 Batac, Ilocos Norte in the Philippines. At death "Bert" was 27 years old.

Lt. jg Gerald Thomas Ramsdell
154-56-9440
USS *Barbey* (FF-1088)

Not every Ridgewood service casualty is listed on the memorial plaques at Van Neste Square. Gerald Ramsdell did not die in an "official period of war" and therefore is not listed with Ridgewood's 112 honored war dead. That in no way diminishes his contribution to his country, and his death in 1988 was as great a loss to his family and community as any other premature death.

He was born April 7, 1963 in New York City and moved with his family to live at 111 South Van Dien. He had three sisters and two brothers. The family attended Mount Carmel Catholic Church in the Village.

Ramsdell graduated from Ridgewood High School in 1981 where he served as class president for 2 years. While in high school he was captain of the track team, played soccer, was in the marching band and was a member of the National Honor Society. He was a single-digit handicap golfer.

He continued his studies at Lafayette, was on the varsity cross-country team in the fall of 1981 in his freshman year and was a middle-distance

354

runner on the indoor track and field team in the winter sports season that same year. His fraternity was Zeta Psi and received his degree in chemical engineering in June 1986.

After working briefly at Paine Webber, he decided he wanted to fly so he joined the Navy in 1986. After finishing Officer Candidate School, he was assigned to the USS *Barbey* during the time the Navy was protecting commercial shipping in the North Arabian Sea.

While aboard he was DJ on the ship and broadcast the evening news. His duty was as a copilot in the Navy SH-2F Lamps Mark I helicopter "Seasnake 17" on routine flight recovery operations.

SH-2F

All three crew members of his aircraft died in a pre-dawn crash November 11, 1988 in the North Arabian Sea while trying to land on the frigate *Barbey*. Halfway through a planned 90 mission the #1 engine began to lose power so the crew headed back to the *Barbey*. While attempting to land, the chopper was waived off. On the second attempt the chopper came amidships, rose suddenly to about 125 feet, began to spin clockwise and then pitched into the sea nose down and sank immediately.

No bodies were ever recovered. There is a marker in his memory at Arlington National Cemetery. Ridgewood High School offers an annual memorial trust scholarship fund in his memory, sponsored by his family

Flight Sgt. Charles Derek Redgrave
R/159999
463rd Squadron
Royal Canadian Air Force

Before the attack on Pearl Harbor, approximately 15,000 Americans joined the Royal Air Force and Royal Canadian Air Force in order to participate in the war before the USA got involved. Several young men from Ridgewood were among them. Derek Redgrave, the only non-US citizen among Ridgewood's 112 Honored Dead, probably felt he could get to defend his homeland faster by going through Canada.

Born December 24, 1921 in London, England, his father worked for the Liverpool and London Globe Insurance Company and was assigned to the New York office when his son Derek was quite young. The family first lived on Long Island but moved to Ridgewood and lived at 419 Alpine Terrace. They attended Christ Church.

Young Redgrave attended the Harrison Avenue school through the eighth grade and then spent four years at the Augusta Military Academy in Virginia where he was on the swimming team and was a member of the Monogram Club. He enjoyed all sports and graduated in 1940 after which he clerked with his father for the Insurance Company of Great Britain before joining the Royal Canadian Air Force in Montreal on April 17, 1942.

He went to England in March 1943 and as of November was based in Waddington, Lincolnshire as a bombardier with the newly-formed 463rd Squadron, a unit of the Royal Australian Air Force, flying the RAF" main bomber, the Avro Lancaster. Although considered vulnerable to fighter attack, it was fast, had a high ceiling and could carry enormous loads for its size. The "Lanc" was a four engine heavy bomber that stood 20' 4" high, was 69' 6" long with a wingspan of 102' and a gross weight of 65,000 lbs.

Avro Lancaster

Powered by four 1,620 hp, 12 cylinder Rolls-Royce engines, its crew of 7 could cruise at 200 mph or accelerate to 272 mph at a ceiling of 24,700' over a range of 1,660 miles. It was armed with 8 machine guns and could carry a bomb load of up to 14,000 lbs.

Redgrave was reported missing and presumed dead over Berlin January 2, 1944. On that date, Hitler's Chancellery was 75% destroyed, trapping many in the underground shelters after a direct hit during an RAF raid on Berlin. Redgrave's 7-man crew had taken off in an Avro Lancaster to attack Berlin but all contact was lost after takeoff. An extensive search failed to find the aircraft and the crew.

He was awarded the Air Bombers Badge in August 1943 and the 1939-45 Star, Air Crew Europe Star, Defense Medal, Canadian Volunteer Service Medal with Clasp and the War Medal 1939-45. He is enrolled on the Runnymede Memorial of the Missing, Surrey (Panel 255). At death he was 22 years old.

Pharmacist Mate 3rd Class Joanne Daisy Redyke U.S.M.C.

In WWII, more than 265,000 women served in the U.S. Army, Navy, Coast Guard, and Marines. Although the intent was for women to "free a man to fight", women had to fight for that right. Politicians early in WWII were inventive in devising means to keep women out of the military. Two strong women, Congresswoman Edith Nourse Rogers of Massachusetts and Eleanor Roosevelt, felt otherwise. Congresswoman Rogers introduced a bill in 1941 to establish a Women's Army Auxiliary Corps. (WAACS). The bill was stalled and all but thrown out until General George C. Marshall took an interest and literally ordered the War Department to create a women's corps. Finally on May 14, 1942 the bill to "Establish a Women's Army Auxiliary Corps" became law and the "Women Accepted for Volunteer Emergency Service" (WAVES) were created. The initial degree of general acceptance of the WAVES is indicated by the suggestion that WAVES meant "Women Are Very Essential Sometimes". Before the WAVES, neither the women who served in WWI nor Navy nurses were permitted to become officers.

At that time, the Marine Corps Commandant was against creating a Women's Reserve for the Marine Corps. Regardless, the Marine Corps Women's Reserve was established in February 1943. Acceptance was slow, with early comments from their Director that WAVES would be allowed to wear enough makeup "to look human". Defying this mentality, over the next year the Marine Corps Women's Reserve grew from four women to 15,000. Before the end of WWII, 23,145 officers and enlisted women reservists served in the Corps. and there were 8,000 WAVE officers and 76,000 enlisted WAVES. Women Marines in World War II assumed over 200 assignments, from clerical work to parachute riggers, mechanics, radio operators, map makers, motor transport support and welders. By June 1944, women reservists made up 85% of the enlisted personnel on duty at Marine Corps Headquarters and almost two-thirds of the personnel "manning" all major posts and stations in the United States and Hawaii. They had indeed freed up the men to fight.

The call for women recruits was amplified in 1944 as the U.S. prepared for the invasion of Europe. One of the U.S.M.C. women reservists to answer the call was Joanne Redyke, the only woman listed among Ridgewood's 112 Honored Dead. Born November 5, 1921 in Maywood, her family lived in Rochelle Park and moved to 207 Pershing Ave in Ridgewood in 1940 where she lived with her three sisters, two brothers and parents. Before coming to Ridgewood, she graduated from East Side High School in Paterson and was associated with the Hawthorne Gospel Church.

She joined the WAVES in December 1943. After training at Hunter College, St. Alban's School and Saint Alban's Naval Hospital on Long Island, she was assigned to Bainbridge Training School in Maryland. She was engaged to be married. Shortly thereafter she came down with appendicitis but was treated too late and died November 23, 1945 in the Marine hospital, Baltimore of peritonitis, more than three months after the end of the war. She is included on the plaque for Women in Military Service Memorial at Arlington. She is buried in Section 7 433, grave 2 at Fair Lawn Cemetery. At death she was 24 years old.

2 Lt. Richard Kinsley Robb
O-71222
584ᵗʰ Bomber Squadron
394ᵗʰ Bomb Group Medium
9ᵗʰ AAF

    A few of Ridgewood's 113 Honored Dead have been memorialized by friends and family so that even to this day we recognize their gifts and their sacrifice. One such memorial was created in the name of Richard Robb.

    Sometimes known as Roscoe, he lived at 12 East Ridgewood Ave. and 334 Prospect Street. His only brother died in 1934. He attended elementary school in Ridgewood, was a Boy Scout and was active in the High School League at West Side Presbyterian Church. He also worked an afternoon job at a local Texaco Station. Before graduating from Ridgewood High School in 1941 he was in the Willow Club, played the trumpet in the swing band, acted in the Junior Play and was on the music committee for the Senior Prom. A lineman on the football team, his football coach later said "Richie was the epitome of all good virtues. He was an aggressive football player who ran like a deer".

He went to Virginia Tech and later to Lafayette College to study engineering. While there he was a member of Phi Delta Theta fraternity. He joined the service and received his aerial gunner's wings at Ellington Field in Laredo, Texas in October 1943 and his commission at the Bombardier Quadrangle School in Childress, Texas on February 26, 1944. He was then assigned to Barksdale Field in Shreveport, La. Two months later on April 15, 1944 he married June Gorham, his RHS classmate, in the Post Chapel at Barksdale Field. Three months later he was best man at the marriage of another eventual Ridgewood casualty, Ronnie Helps.

As a member of the 584th Bomber Squadron, 394th Bomb Group Medium (9th AAF) his B-26 Marauder was engaged in low level bombing of railroad bridges and yards in the Rhine River Valley. He was killed in eastern France October 8, 1944 when his B-26 collided with another plane while landing upon return from a mission in Ahrweiler.

In 1983 friends created the Robb Football Trophy at RHS which is still presented to the outstanding varsity lineman upon the player's graduation in June. Robb is buried in Plot B, Row 20, Grave 71 at Epinal American Cemetery, Epinal, France. At death he was 21 years old.

2 Lt. Theodore Donahue Robb, III
O-722798
513ᵗʰ Bomb Squadron
376ᵗʰ Bomb Group
47ᵗʰ Wing
15ᵗʰ Air Force

In 1947 the Quartermaster General of the Army instituted a repatriation program addressed to the next of kin of war dead entitled "Disposition of World War II Armed Forces Dead" through which the bodies of American service personnel killed overseas could be brought back to the United States for re-interment. The remains of 49 of Ridgewood's Honored 112 Dead have been repatriated from overseas. It was a cumbersome, bureaucratic and impersonal exercise. One mother wrote back "Please try not to write to other mothers as if a shipment of merchandise was involved." A frustrated father wrote "The government was very quick in taking our boys and sending them out to the combat zones with very little or no training, and the least they can do is to exert every effort to bring back the boys who gave their lives, instead of making arrangements to transport foreign war brides and permitting refugees to utilize space on ships for traveling and entering our country."

All the memorial services conducted upon receipt of the remains were closed casket, mainly because of the ravages of time but also because often there was not much in the casket.

Ted Robb was born in Ridgewood May 24, 1921 and lived at 311 Marshall St. He was an only child. His father, a Signal Corps. veteran of WWI, was on the technical staff of Bell Laboratories for 38 years and belonged to the Telephone Pioneers of America. Ted graduated from Ridgewood High School in the class of 1938 where he was a member of the boys' Glee Club and the A Cappella Choir. He was the manager of the baseball team, a bowler and a basketball player and belonged to Hi-Y.

He went to Bowdoin College and graduated January 25, 1943 with a B.S. degree in history and government. In college he was in the Glee Club, ran track and played football, participated in inter-fraternity athletics and was on the Dean's list. He was a member of Alpha Tau Omega fraternity. He was also in the Enlisted Army Reserve and was sworn in immediately after graduation as an aviation cadet in Portland, Maine, entering the service February 17, 1943. His training took him to Boca Raton, Akron and San Antonio where he was classified as a Navigator. He received his wings and commission at Ellington Field, Houston on April 22, 1944.

As his parents saw him off in New York City for overseas assignment, he said "mother, when the big emergency comes, keep your head and you'll be quite perfect". She replied "Teddy, dear, happy flying and safe landings and I'll be seeing you". On August 9 he buzzed the Bowdoin campus on his way overseas in a B-24 with the 513th Bomb Squadron, 376th Bomb Group, 47th Wing, 15th Air Force. The 376th was based in San Pancrazio, Italy where it participated in bombing raids against Axis targets in southern Europe, the Balkans and as far as Vienna, Austria and Regensburg, Germany.

He was one of five crew members killed two weeks later in an aircraft crash during a test flight August 31, 1944. The crew was testing a new engine on a B-24 that had previously suffered flack damage. Their mission was to fly the newly installed engine at sufficiently low power to enable the engine to become properly broken in before continuing scheduled missions. Flying at 2,000 feet near Pomigliano, excessive engine noise was heard as parts of the plane broke off and fell to earth, causing the plane to go into a steep dive. They made no call to the control tower and there was not enough altitude to bail out so the entire crew went down as the plane crashed, exploded and burned. It is possible the left elevator was worn loose and broke off because of hidden internal flack damage. All that could be found of any remains of the entire crew were ten fingers, five of which matched the prints of Lt. Robb.

Christ Church in Ridgewood recently named its Education Building in his memory. There is a small chapel dedicated to him in the sanctuary and the Celtic Cross on top of Christ Church was given in his memory. His remains were repatriated in 1949 and is buried in Plot 1186 at Valleau Cemetery. At death he was 22 years old.

Ens. Frank Joseph Roehrenbeck, Jr.
USS *Midway*

Military personnel who die while in the service, but not during an official period of service such as WWII or Korea, are not listed on any of the monuments. Those who die under such circumstances and whose body is not recovered are neither on the monuments nor listed with the MIAs. It is wrong that a person should give their life for their country but remain fully anonymous, simply an overlooked statistic in the government's personnel files. Frank Roehrenbeck of Ridgewood is such a case.

Frankie was born September 21, 1925 in Jersey City and moved to Ridgewood with his brother and parents to live at 130 Unadilla Road. His father was general manager of the radio station WMGM in New York City. Frank graduated in the class of 1943 at Ridgewood High School where he ran track, participated in Hi-Y, captained the Hi-Y bowling team, was on the cafeteria committee, student council cabinet, grounds committee and the war stamp committee.

Upon graduation he was immediately called to Officers Training School with the Marines and

367

assigned to the Marine V-12 group at Princeton. In July 1944 he was transferred to Yale where he remained until March 1945. He also studied Japanese at the University of Colorado and at Oklahoma A&M.

With such academic credentials he was assigned as a Staff Sergeant to the Office of Strategic Services (OSS) at Camp Elliot and was later based at the Brooklyn Navy Yard until January 1946 when he was released to inactive duty as a 2nd Lt.

He returned to Yale in March. While there, he played football and belonged to Stillman College, York Hall and Chi Phi. He graduated in the class of 1947 with a degree in Mechanical Engineering. He went to work for Monsanto Chemical Corp. in Oak Ridge. He was a member of the Society of Automotive Engineers and the American Society of Mechanical Engineers. By this time his family had moved to Suffern and maintained a summer home on Greenwood Lake.

Also known as "Slipstick", he re-enlisted in the Navy in 1948 under the Direct Procurement Program to attend flight training at Pratt & Whitney. In 1948-49 he trained at Corpus Christi, Texas, spending most of the next two years at the Quonset Point, R.I. Naval Air Station. He got his Gold Wings in early 1950.

As a jet fighter pilot based on the U.S.S. *Midway* he died July 18, 1950 when he overshot the deck, missed the tail hook and went off the side of the carrier. His body was not recovered. At death he was 24 years old.

Staff Sgt. Steven Roos
32243763
400th Bomber Squadron
90th Bomber Group, Heavy
5th Bomber Command

On Tuesday October 12, 1943 Allied Air Forces in the South Pacific began a sustained bombing campaign in the Bismarck Archipelago with the first big daylight bombing mission against Rabaul on New Britain Island. Nearly 350 heavy bombers and RAAF airplanes pounded the town, the harbor, and the airfields. Over 120 Japanese aircraft were destroyed. 3 enemy ships were sunk and several ships and small harbor craft were damaged. Among the American planes lost was the B-24 "Pregnant Polecat" with Steven Roos of Ridgewood aboard.

Roos, whose name is misspelled as Ross on the memorial plaques at Van Neste Square, was born November 25, 1905 which makes him the second oldest WWII Ridgewood casualty. He came to Ridgewood as a young boy and lived with his parents, two sisters and brother, who died in 1942,

on E. Ridgewood Ave. – first at number 345 and
later at number 965. He graduated from Ridgewood
High School with the class of 1924, participating in
class soccer and baseball, varsity soccer and the
glee club. He then took classes at NYU and Cooper
Union. He had brown hair and gray eyes, was 5'
9¾" tall, was an outdoors man and loved the rigors
of hiking, mountain climbing and hunting.

He first worked on Wall Street and later for
the Sperry Gyroscope Company in Garden City
before entering the service March 2, 1942, reporting
to Camp Dix. He trained at Keesler Field in
Mississippi and was in Armory Gunnery School at
Harlinder Field in Texas when he received his
wings. After training at Pocatello, Idaho he was
assigned to the South Pacific in July 1943 as an
aerial gunner in the "Mission Belle", a B-24
Liberator of the 400th Bomber Squadron ("Black
Pirates"), 90th Bomber Group, Heavy ("Jolly
Rogers"), 5th Air Force. Their main obstacle was the
Japanese "Zero", a highly maneuverable single-
engine, single-seat naval fighter with a top speed of
336 mph and armed with two 20mm cannon and 2
machine guns.

Based at Ward's Airfield in Port Moresby,
the "Mission Belle" participated in the Allied-
bombing mission over Rabaul and Wewak, scoring
seven enemy kills on October 12, 1943 and
returning safely to base. But Roos flew that day
with the crew of the "Pregnant Polecat", one of six
American planes lost in that action.

Their assignment was to bomb the Simpson
Harbor shipping. Amid heavy flak and under attack
by 40 to 50 Zeros, they released their payload
sinking a destroyer and three other ships, badly
damaging two tenders and two merchant ships.
Although severely shot up, the plane was last seen
flying at low altitude but in no apparent danger. It
is presumed to have run out of fuel and ditched at
sea, about 60 miles southeast of Wide Bay. Search
and rescue efforts were fruitless.

Sgt. Roos was awarded the Air Medal and is listed on the Tablets of the Missing at Manila American Cemetery in the Philippines. There is a stained glass window in his memory at First Presbyterian Church in Ridgewood. At death, he was 37 years old, just one year short of the age limit for this sort of service.

Crew of the Mission Belle:
Lester B. Danks, Lucien B. Gray,
William K. Murray, Donald K. McNeff,
John E. Gormley, John L. Ford,
Walter E. Kuchta, Steven K. Roos, John A. Smith,
Francis E. Walker

Pfc. Donald Hector Rose
42084033
I Company, 255ᵗʰ Infantry Regiment
63ʳᵈ Infantry Division
7ᵗʰ Army

Don was born November 18, 1925 in New York City and moved to Ridgewood from Great Neck in 1930 when he was five. The family eventually lived at 745 Hillcrest Road. He had a sister and a brother and was an accomplished cartoon artist. He graduated from Ridgewood High School in 1943. While in high school, he was active in the camera club, dramatics, was class treasurer and on the student council his junior year. He worked for awhile at AT&T and joined the service February 22, 1944.

He went overseas at Thanksgiving 1944 with advance elements of the 63ʳᵈ Infantry Division and landed in Marseilles on December 8. While at sea, he was confirmed in the Lutheran Church to follow the faith of his fiancée. He was assigned to I Company, 255ᵗʰ Infantry Regiment, 63ʳᵈ Infantry Division, 7ᵗʰ Army. The 63ʳᵈ defended the Vosges and Maginot Line area from December 22 to December 30 and fought south of Bitche from January 1 to 10.

The 225th was in heavy combat around Saarguemnes and later attacked the Bois de Blies Brucken in mid-February. St.Ingbert and Hassel fell to the 255th on March 20. After frontal assaults on Hardenhauser Forest failed, the division had enveloped the woods by April 8. Rose was killed that day.

That morning his company set out on their mission in the vicinity of Widdern. Don was leading the second platoon, flanked on each side by the first and third platoons. They advanced toward a small woods when Don's platoon took heavy gunfire from the edge of the woods. His platoon was ordered to withdraw under cover from the first platoon. Don held his lead post and provided rifle cover for his men until they all had safely withdrawn. As he attempted to withdraw himself he was hit and killed instantly by shrapnel fragments to the back of the head. Because of his heroic feat, his comrades recommended him for the Medal of Honor but instead he was awarded the Silver Star Medal award, posthumously. The citation states that "after securing a bridgehead on the Jagst River, the Second Platoon was attacked by SS troops. When bazooka fire was directed at his squad from a distance of 15 yards and machine gun and rifle fire increased in intensity, Private First Class Rose signaled his men to withdraw while he moved in to the open for a better field of fire to cover their withdrawal. Gallantly and single-handedly, against a numerically superior force, he continued to fire fight until all men had successfully withdrawn. While attempting to withdraw himself, Private First Class Rose was fatally wounded. The bold and determined action of Private First Class Rose enabled his squad to withdraw without further casualties."

He had previously been awarded the Bronze Star. His comrades in I Company later dedicated a memorial field to him in Morlach, Germany, 15 miles from where he fell. Bethlehem Lutheran Church dedicated the Altar Vases to him.

In October 1945 the Ridgewood Art Association hosted an exhibition of artwork done by local GIs. Don was one of two Ridgewood war casualties whose work was displayed. He is buried in S 185B #1 in George Washington Memorial Park in Paramus. At death he was 19 years old.

Donald Rose and his band of brothers

Lt. Peter Fransson Russell
656966
Light Attack Squadron VAL-4
United States Naval Forces, Vietnam

Another ship that passed in the night was Peter Russell who spent his late teens in Glen Rock and studied at Ridgewood High School before leaving the area.

Pete was born March 12, 1940 in Hartford, Ct. He moved to Glen Rock with his two brothers and parents where he lived for four years. During that time he attended and graduated from Ridgewood High School in 1958 where he played football and was on the swimming team. He later moved to Dover and enlisted in Wharton, NJ.

Pete graduated from Columbia University in 1962 with a major in International Relations. He spoke fluent Russian and Mandarin. A career Navy man, he enlisted June 5, 1962, was commissioned and went directly into flight training, receiving his wings in 1963 as a Navy Aviator.

On October 19, 1966 while flying an A-1H off the U.S.S. *Intrepid* on Yankee Station in the Tonkin Gulf as section leader of a flight of four VA-176 A1H's, Pete was credited with a MIG kill when four MIGs jumped first one section and then another section of A-1Hs. The final score was one confirmed kill, one probable and one possible MIG kill.

His second tour began March 15, 1969 with VAL-4. Light Attack Squadron Four "Black Ponies" was commissioned in January 1969 and moved to Vietnam three months later with detachments at Binh Thuy and Vung Tau. They were equipped with the North American Rockwell OV10A "Bronco", a twin-turboprop short takeoff and landing aircraft, which competently fulfilled their duties of close-in air support for Naval riverine forces.

While flying his Bronco out of Binh Thuy, he was killed May 23, 1969 over Kien Giang Province when he came under small arms fire and crashed at Kien Giang south of Saigon while providing air cover to a riverine patrol. During a strafing run, a single shot struck him and his OV-10A. He was the first aviator lost in VAL-4.

Pete was awarded the Distinguished Flying Cross with gold star, Purple Heart (posthumous), Air Medal with numeral 9, Navy Commendation Medal with combat V, National Defense Service Medal with gold star, Viet Nam Service Medal with 4 bronze stars, Republic of Viet Nam Campaign Medal with 1960 device and Republic of Viet Nam MUC Gallantry Cross.

Pete is buried in Evergreen Cemetery in Boothbay, ME. At death he was 29 years old.

Lt. Col. Seaton Sailer M.D.
O-438399
25th General Hospital Unit

Not everybody that died in war died in combat. Not everybody who died in the war knew how to fire a gun. Of the 407,316 Americans who died in WW II, 115,185 (28%) did not die in combat. Most died in accidents or of illness. Some were non-combatants who made up the support infrastructure that greatly outnumbered the combatants. They included clerks who recorded combat action every day in Morning Reports to skilled medical personnel who put the physically or spiritually wounded back together. One such medical specialist was Dr. Seaton Sailer of Ridgewood, known to his friends as Mike.

He was born in New York City October 9, 1905 and moved to Ridgewood with his family when he was nine years old to live at 334 Heights Road. His father was Chairman of the Board of the Commercial National Bank of Paterson. Young Sailer won the Junior Tennis Championship (12 to 14 year olds) at the Y.M.C.A. in 1919 – the same year his brother won the Intermediate championship (15 to 18 years old) in the same tournament.

He was also an artist and enjoyed painting and sketching. He attended Trinity Episcopal School and Parson's Prep and was in the graduating class of 1927 at Cornell University. Because his mother had died while he was still young, he decided to go to medical school and studied at the Long Island College of Medicine and later worked in the Pathology Department at St. Luke's Hospital in New York City for four years. He then studied abroad for a year and a half in Hamburg, Paris and the Far East and was considered brilliant in his field, authoring many authoritative articles. He was also a consulting Pathologist at the University of Cincinnati before enlistment. A gourmand, he was a member of the Salamagundy Club in New York City.

Dr. Sailer entered the Medical Corps as a Major on June 24, 1942 and became engaged before going overseas as a Pathologist in the 25th General Hospital Unit. He was soon promoted and put in charge of pathological work. He died of a fractured skull when he was hit by an Army truck during a black out in Lison, Calvados, France November 24, 1944. His body was repatriated in February 1948 and buried in Lot Southeast 16648, Section 149/148 Plot Clover in Woodlawn Cemetery in the Bronx, New York. At death he was 39 years old.

Yeoman 2nd Class Karl Lother Sandmann
04026290
USS SHARK SS-174

Imagine knowing there are people outside your house trying to get in. Imagine no moon, 2:00 in the morning; suddenly, all the lights go out and you can't see your hand in front of your face. Then you feel something enveloping you and you have nowhere to go. No escape, no way out. It must be a horrible way to die - knowing you are facing imminent death but not being able to do anything about it. Such is death in a submarine.

"Sandy" was born June 8, 1916, lived at 1101 Linwood Ave. and was in Ridgewood High School's class of 1932 where he participated in the physical Training Exhibition, the New Jersey State Art Exhibition on World Friendship, the Book Week contest, was on the pyramid team, played intramural football and won an award for 4 years of perfect attendance. He then worked for a time at the Hayden Planetarium in New York City before joining the submarine service and being piped aboard the *USS Shark*, a P-3 Type submarine.

The *Shark* was launched in 1935 and commissioned in 1936. After shakedown in the

North Atlantic and Caribbean she arrived in San Diego in March 1937 to spend the next 18 months in training. She sailed for Pearl Harbor in December 1940 and eventually joined the Pacific Fleet in Manila. Three days after the attach on Pearl Harbor the Japanese attacked Manila but the *Shark* was at sea, patrolling Tayabas Bay until she returned to port on the 19th to embark Admiral Thomas Hart, Commander in Chief of the U.S. Asiatic Fleet. The *Shark* then departed on its second war patrol in January 1942, avoided an enemy torpedo and continued to Surabaya to contact Dutch submarines in the harbor of Ambon. In anticipation of an enemy landing the *Shark* patrolled to the east of Lifoematola and the area to Bangka Passage where she survived a torpedo attack and being depth charged.

The *Shark* was instructed on February 8 to proceed to Makassar Strait via the north coast of Celebes and later was asked to report information. Nothing further was heard from her and she was reported as presumed lost, probably in an enemy depth charge attack, making it the first US submarine lost in WWII. Sandmann was lost with the crew of the *Shark* east of Menado, Celebes February 11, 1942 and is listed on the Tablets of the Missing at Manila American Cemetery, Manila, Philippines. At death he was 25 years old.

SS Shark I SS-174

Pfc. Chester J. Sawicki
32771969
28th Infantry Regiment
8th Infantry Division

  If there ever could be a doubt about the role of Willie and Joe or Private Ryan, 34 of Ridgewood's 113 casualties had the rank of Pfc. or under. Their average age was 22 years old. One wonders therefore what a Pfc. half as much older than the others is doing on the front line.

  Chester Sawicki was born July 20, 1911, attended East Side High School in Paterson for two years and later moved to Ridgewood to live with his mother Anastasia Fetkowitz, his brother and his half-sister at 365 Goffle Road. His brother, Stanley Sawicki lived at 218 East 16th Street in Paterson. Chester married and he and his wife Ina eventually moved to Paterson and lived at 118 Pine Street. Prior to entering the service, he worked for the Ming Toy Silk Dyeing company of Paterson for six years.

  "Chet" entered the service on March 3, 1943. He joined the 28th Infantry Regiment, 8th

Infantry Division and trained at Camp Laguna, Arizona and Camp Forest in Tennessee and sailed to Belfast for more training. During this time, the 28th was honored with a regimental review from the Supreme Commander, General Eisenhower.

The 28th sailed from Belfast on July 1, landed on Utah Beach July 4, 1944 and saw their first action in late July as they established a bridgehead over the Ay River to allow armored divisions to breakout and attack into Brittany and Northern France. This marked the start of the mass retreat of the German Seventh Army. Sawicki died of head injuries in France during the subsequent battle for Brest August 27, 1944.

He is buried in Plot L, Row 15, Grave 1 in the Brittany American Cemetery, St. James, France. At death he was 33 year

1 Lt. Charles William Schlenz
O30885
Marine Fighting Squadron 324
Marine Aircraft Group 23
3rd Marine Aircraft Wing

He was born October 15, 1923 and was named after his father so they called him Bill. He lived with his brother, sister and parents at 218 Wyckoff Ave. in Wyckoff, N.J.

In the late 1930s, West Side Presbyterian Church had a mission outreach to East Wyckoff and would offer worship services there. The Schlenz family came to West Side because of this outreach mission. He was confirmed at West Side April 20, 1941 and graduated from Ramsey High School in 1942, the same year as his brother graduated, although he was held back a year in high school so he could get his grades up.

He joined the service on July 30, 1943. His father and brother were also in the service. His first assignment was to Naval Air Training Center in Pensacola where he was commissioned a Naval

Aviator October 22, 1943. He then attended preflight school in Miami until February 1944 when he was detached to the U.S. Marine Corps Air Station in Edenton, N.C. It was there that he met Marine Pfc. Florina (Bunny) Beall of Alexandria, Va. whom he married May 29, 1944 in South Mills, North Carolina near where they both were stationed.

He became a flight instructor using the Vought Corsair FU4, the distinctive 'cranked wing' monoplane fighter. Being an instructor gave him the chance to fly a lot, even to fly north to visit his family and friends in New Jersey. In September 1944 he flew a torpedo bomber up to New Jersey and buzzed Ramsey High School on the second floor level. He then flew over the nearby Ramapo Mountains and came back at roof top level over the town of Ramsey and flew between the gym and the three story High School. All the papers wrote about it but nobody knew who had done it.

In April 1945 he was promoted to Second Lt. and was transferred to Columbia, S.C. where he joined the Corsair Squadron for a refresher course. By the time the war in Europe ended he wrote home that he was "leaving S.C. sometime this month for California". Bunny was pregnant but in July she had a miscarriage. Just before the war ended in August he went overseas to Midway Island, later moving to Hawaii as Assistant Wing Police and Billeting Officer.

Bill Schlenz survived the war but did not survive a mid-air collision with another aircraft off Oahu on October 1, 1945 - two weeks short of his 22nd birthday. He was originally buried in the Hawaii Naval Cemetery but his body was repatriated and buried in the cemetery at the Wyckoff Reformed Church in August, 1947. The town of Wyckoff paid honor to its fallen son by naming Schlenz Court, located near the Wild Life Center, for him. At death he was 21 years old.

Sgt. Jay Julius Schmid
51981194
Company D, 2nd Battalion
27th Infantry Regiment
25th Infantry Division

1968 must be considered one of the most momentous years of recent history. In our living rooms we witnessed in living color the assassination of Martin Luther King, Jr. and Bobby Kennedy, watched as Soviet troops invaded Czechoslovakia and listened to a despairing Lyndon Johnson refuse to run for reelection. There were riots at the Democratic Convention in Chicago as protesters nominated a live pig for president. Students rioted on 100 campuses and seized control of Columbia University; they rioted in Mexico as the French produced "mai '68". Tommie Smith and John Carlos raised a defiant fist as the Star Spangled Banner was played to honor their victories at the Mexico City Olympics. 10,000 sanitation workers struck in New York City, just four months before the city introduced the 911 emergency number, and a "Magical Mystery Tour" hit number one.

Certainly not unnoticed amid this global turmoil, it was the year of the Tet Offensive and the My Lai Massacre in Vietnam. With over half a million GIs in 'Nam at year's end, it was also the bloodiest year of the Vietnam War. Headquarters U.S. Military Assistance Command Vietnam estimated that 181,150 North Vietnamese and Viet Cong had been killed. On the other side, 14,584 Americans, nearly 28,000 South Vietnamese and 1,000 allies had been killed. One of the U.S. casualties was Jay Julius Schmid of Ridgewood.

Jay was born January 22, 1943 in Ridgewood and lived with his widowed mother and sister at 523 Lotus Road. He was in Ridgewood High School's class of 1960; while there he played soccer, bowled, was in the Spanish Club and played intramural volleyball and basketball. He participated in Sunday School at the First Church of Christ, Scientists. He went on to Gettysburg College where he majored in engineering. When he was drafted in September 1967 he was majoring in industrial management at Fairleigh Dickinson University. While at FDU he worked at Julius Schmid, Inc in Little Falls.

5' 7" tall with brown hair, Jay entered active duty October 20, 1967 and trained at Fort Polk, La. and Fort Benning before being sent to Vietnam October 7, 1968 with the 27th Infantry Battalion (Wolfhounds), 25th Division. Two months after his arrival in Vietnam he died of extensive chest and abdomen wounds received in ground combat in the Cu Chi area late in the afternoon of December 7, 1968. On that day, enemy shelling of populated areas hit six towns, including Haunghia where Schmid was in action. Before his death he was awarded the National Defense Service Medal, Vietnam Service Medal, Vietnam Campaign Ribbon, Expert Rifle Bar and the Sharpshooter Badge with machine gun bar. Sgt. Schmid was awarded posthumously the Silver Star for gallantry in action, Bronze Star, Purple Heart, Good Conduct Medal and the Combat Infantryman Badge. He is buried in Section C, Plot 1 in the New Paltz Rural Cemetery, New Paltz, NY. At death he was 25 years old.

Private Lansing P. Shield, Jr.
AF 57127045
3075 Basic Training Wing

Another Ridgewood man who gave his life in the service of his country, and whose name is not listed on our memorial plaques, is Lansing Shield who was killed outside and official period of service.

"Lanse" was born in Hackensack October 25, 1929 and moved with his sister and parents to live at 320 North Murray in Ridgewood. He was received into membership at West Side Presbyterian January 2, 1944 and was active in the youth groups. He attended Ridgewood elementary schools, went to the Kent School and then entered Ridgewood High School and graduated in 1947. His mother, President of the George Washington PTA for the school year 1938-1939, died in April of that year. His father was President of the Grand Union Company, based in New York City. In high school Lanse played varsity tennis, was active in Hi-Y, the Booster Club, the Co-Y and played in the band. He also organized his own amateur orchestra.

After attending Rutgers and the University of North Carolina, he entered the Army Air Force in August 1948. He was killed near Muldrow in eastern Oklahoma at 11:00 in the morning of November 1, 1948 in the crash of a C-47 while returning to Ridgewood to visit his father, ailing from pneumonia in Doctors' Hospital in New York City. The plane, based at Sheppard Air Force Base in Wichita Falls, Texas was bound for Washington, D.C. An hour fifteen minutes in to the flight they encountered bad weather. Flying low in a driving lightning and rainstorm the plane broke into three pieces and was scattered over nearly four miles of cornfields. The cause can most likely be traced to turbulence which had thrown the plane into an unusual position. While attempting to recover, it disintegrated in midair due to excessive speed and stress. Eleven airmen lost their lives. His father heard the news of the crash on the radio before being notified as next of kin.

In memory of Lanse and his mother, his family donated a Hammond Organ to Ridgewood High School in March 1949. Lanse is buried in Grave 8, Lot 1332 at Valleau Cemetery. At death he was 19 years old.

Capt. Howard Anthony Smith, Jr.
O-413109
Cannon Company
168th Infantry Regiment
34th Infantry Division

Known as Howie, he was born in Brooklyn May 14, 1918 and moved to Ridgewood in 1923 to live at 180 West End Ave. and later at 316 Mountain Ave. with his sister, 2 brothers his parents. His father was President of the Ridgewood Country Club and Executive Vice President and Treasurer of American Express.

Howie graduated from Ridgewood High School in 1936 where he was Junior Class President, captain and star of the football team, ran track, played golf, intramural basketball, was a member of the school's polo team and was on the Student Council. He was a teacher on Senior Day and attended Mount Carmel Church. After graduation he attended Lawrenceville School for the 1937 school year and then went on to graduate with honors from Princeton in 1941 with a degree

390

in Economics. At Princeton he was a member of the Cap and Gown, captained the freshman football team and played one year of varsity for the tigers before an injury forced him to quit. He then served as line coach for the 150-pound football team.

He entered the service as an artilleryman in the summer of the year he graduated. After spending some time in Ireland and Scotland, he took part in the landing at Algiers in November 1942. His unit was the first to meet German ground forces, on November 19, 1942 at Medjez-el-Bar, later capturing Hill 609 in Algeria. As Executive Officer of Battery B and temporarily in command he gave the orders to fire the first shells at the Germans. His unit was attached to the British First Army during the Tunisian Winter Campaign and when the Americans were brought together in the spring he was transferred to Cannon Company, 168th Infantry and took part in most of the major battles of the Tunisian campaign. Landing at Salerno after the beachhead was established, the 168th was active in the Italian campaign and took part in the battles that pushed the Germans back through Naples towards Casino.

He was awarded the Silver Star "for gallantry in action in October 1943 in the vicinity of Italy. When the attack of this 2nd Battalion, Infantry was stopped on low ground, observation upon enemy positions was nil except in places covered by enemy automatic weapons fire. In the absence of an artillery observer, Captain Smith, with utter disregard for his own safety and on his own initiative went forward and established an observation post. He exposed himself to enemy machine-gun fire to secure the much-needed observation and brought the fire of his Cannon Company to bear on the enemy position, neutralizing their fire. Later, when one platoon was making an attack upon enemy positions, Captain Smith went forward through intense enemy machine gun, small arms and mortar fire to gain better observation. By doing this, he was able to locate several enemy machine gun emplacements, direct the fire of his Cannon Company on them and destroy them. Captain Smith's initiative, courage and devotion to duty were exemplary and are a credit to the Armed Forces of the United States".

On November 1, 1943, in the Naples-Foggia Campaign, observation was very limited and his infantry regiment was halted under heavy enemy automatic weapon fire. Howie went forward from his command post at Prata near Ailano to establish an observation post and was killed by a bomb fragment during an air raid. His body was repatriated in September 1948 and buried at Maryrest Cemetery in Darlington. His name is inscribed in Nassau Hall with all the Princetonians killed in the war. The Ridgewood Country Club sponsored a Member/Guest Memorial Tournament for several years. At death Howie was 25 years old.

2 Lt. William March Smyser
O743117
345th Bomb Squadron
98th Bomb Group

Normally, aircrews were formed and trained together in the US, went overseas together, bunked together, flew missions together and sometimes died together. Occasionally, a man from one crew would fill in for a crewmember from another plane who could not fly that day. This was the case of William Smyser of Ridgewood who had fulfilled his quota of 50 missions but volunteered to help another crew out. His adopted crew took the "togetherness" scenario one step further. They were buried together.

His friends called him Bill and he was born in New York City February 18, 1919 and moved to Ridgewood when he was 6 weeks old to live at 302 Prospect Ave. with his parents and brother. During his elementary school days he was a delivery boy for the *Ridgewood Herald*. He went through the entire Ridgewood school system, graduating from Ridgewood High School in 1937. While in high school, at 5' 7", 157 lbs, he was active in intramural sports, played football, speedball and basketball, was on the varsity soccer team and pitched for the baseball team. With brown hair and brown eyes he was voted "Most Vivacious" and "Wittiest" in his class.

He attended Pace University for one year before enlisting in October 1940 as a member of the Old Seventh Regiment, later known as the 307th Coast Artillery. He was stationed at Camp Stewart before the war was declared. He then trained in California, was commissioned in the spring of 1943 and went overseas April 12, 1943 with the 345th Bomb Squadron, 98th Bomb Group, "The Pyramidiers".

Based in Libya as of July 1943 he was a co-pilot on a B-24 called the "Bengazi Express" flying low-level bombing missions on the Ploesti oil fields in Romania. Probably their most famous mission was the low-level raid on the Ploesti oil refineries on August 1, 1943 in Operation Tidal Wave (initially known as Operation Soapsuds). The Ploesti oil fields covered 19 square miles and supplied 1/3rd of the fuel needed by the Germans. On this raid, of 47 B-24s launched by the 98th, only 21 returned safely. One crashed on takeoff with the loss of all but two crewmembers, six aborted before reaching the target, seventeen went down in enemy held territory and two went down at sea.

His unit was transferred to Italy in November and based in Brindisi. He had flown 50 missions when he volunteered to replace a buddy as co-pilot on a B-24 mission to Germany. His plane "The Sandman" was seen leaving the target area over Augsburg, Germany just before noon on December 19, 1943. The flak was moderate and inaccurate and, although attacked by about forty enemy aircraft, they did not appear to be in trouble. Nonetheless, his B-24 never returned, having crashed on a mountain near Corvara Badia, Italy.

The bodies of the crew were buried in a mass grave in a local civilian cemetery.

They remained listed as missing until the wreckage along with all the crew was found in 1947. Only three of the ten crewmembers could be positively identified. As individual identification could not be determined, the remains of the entire crew were repatriated and buried together in common Grave 224 in Section B, Zachary Taylor National Cemetery, Louisville, Kentucky, a location central to all surviving families of the victims. There is a marker for Bill Smyser at the family plot in Union Lloyds Cemetery, Lloyds, Ulster County, New York. He was awarded the European-African-Middle Eastern Campaign Medal, the American Campaign Medal and the World War II Victory Medal. At death he was 24 years old.

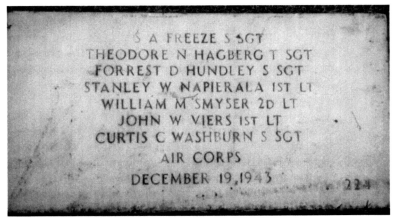

Zachary Taylor National Cemetery
Louisville, KY

Lt. William Howard Sprague, Jr.

Several young Ridgewoodites performed gallantly during a war only to die after the fighting had stopped as a result of injuries or illnesses received during their combat service. In most cases, they are not listed on the memorial plaques at Van Neste Square.

Lt. William Sprague was born in Milton, Pa. but moved to Ridgewood to live with his parents and sister at 118 John Street. He graduated from Ridgewood High School in 1938 where he played varsity football and intramural basketball. He also ran track and was in the band. He then attended Rutgers and Texas A&M where he was a member of Delta Upsilon and continued to play football, run track while adding lacrosse to his activities. Upon graduation he married and went to work as a sales engineer for John Manville Sales Corp. After his father died in 1941 he considered the care and protection of his mother his chief responsibility.

Then came the war and Bill enlisted in the service in April 1942 and was appointed Aviation Cadet Captain and Group Commander in the Cadet Corps. He was commissioned August 30, 1943. He soon went overseas as a P-47 Thunderbolt pilot where he flew 19 combat missions and was awarded the Air Medal. While based in England to escort medium and heavy bombers and to provide ground support for advancing forces, Bill was shot down shortly after D-Day in June 1944 in the vicinity of Les Pieux, Avranches and Domfront, France and seriously injured. He spent most of the next two years in and out of hospitals in England, Tennessee and New Jersey and died of kidney failure after an operation for bleeding ulcers in Hackensack Hospital on July 18, 1946 shortly after being retired to inactive duty.

Normally husky and healthy, but intent on protecting his mother from distress, his widow feels he never admitted to his family the true nature of his injuries, constantly saying he was in great shape, listing his medical problems only as broken ear drums and deafness from dive bombing and an injury to his ankle from flack and a broken nose from the crash, none of which would seem to require 24 months of hospitalization. At his death, the attending doctor told Sprague's mother "Your son died as a result of kidney failure, but what killed him was guilt – your son was a patriot, but he was no killer". Bill was refused a Purple Heart for "lack of evidence".

The Office of the Actuary at the Department of Veterans Affairs in Washington gives December 7, 1941 to December 31, 1946 as the dates for Periods of Service for World War II. It seems clear that Bill died as a result of injuries sustained in combat. He died within the period of service for WWII, although he was discharged shortly before his death. There is one other of Ridgewood's 112 Honored Dead listed on the memorial plaques who died in 1946 shortly after having been discharged. William Sprague should therefore be listed on our memorial plaques. Regardless, he is not forgotten. He is buried in lot 1437 at Valleau Cemetery. At death he was 25 years old.

1 Lt. Arthur William Stanley
O-215106
57th Base HQ

Arthur Stanley was born February 24, 1904, raised in Morris County and moved to Ridgewood in the mid-1930s to live at 281 Gardner Road. He was married and had two daughters. The family was active in the Christian Science Church.

He was commissioned on September 17, 1942. While assigned to the 57th Base HQ Craig Field, Selma, Alabama, he was put on detached duty recruiting cadets with the 1st Service Command in Augusta, Maine as a recruiting officer.

Apparently taking a hop to visit his family, he died with 11 members of the 1st Radar Calibration Detachment, 1st AAF stationed at Fort Dix in the afternoon of February 22, 1944 on a training flight from Dow Field, Bangor, Maine to Fort Dix. Their B-17F crashed in a Boy Scout camp in the Kittatinny Mountains, 7 miles northwest of Blairstown, NJ while flying on instruments in heavy fog and bad weather. The crash site was considerably off-course and local residents reported that the plane was flying low, back and forth. It exploded upon crashing and the motor became embedded in soft soil. Two propellers were found to be feathered, indicating mechanical problems, and one engine was burned, implying it may have been on fire while in flight.

The plane was first found by local residents who guided the State Police to the accident site. Stanley's body was cremated and buried in the Stanley Tworger Mausoleum at Valleau Cemetery. At death he was 38 years old.

Major George T. Starck
O-272914
5ᵗʰ Air Force Service Command Depot #2
HQ & HQ Squadron
4ᵗʰ A.D.G.

War chooses its victims indiscriminately. The passage of time often seals their fate. Even a very popular kid in school, a very successful professional and a happily married man can soon be forgotten.

George Starck was born in Brooklyn March 10, 1907 and moved to Ridgewood as a young lad and lived with his parents, brother and sister at 153 S. Van Dien Ave. He graduated from Ridgewood High School in 1925 where he was class president his junior and senior years. He also ran track three years, played football two years and captained the basketball team. He then attended Union College and graduated from the Guggenheim School of Aeronautics at NYU in 1929. He was a member of Christ Church, married Louise Neisken (RHS '27) of

Glen Rock in 1935 and lived with his her in Glen Rock. He was 6' tall and weighed 165 lbs.

He entered the service as a reserve officer in August 1940 and served as chief inspector and assistant engineering officer of the maintenance division with the 5th Air Force Service Command, Advanced Echelon at Patterson Field where he spent most of his three-year military career. He went to the South Pacific in July 1943 and was stationed with the 5th Air Force Service Command at the base of Mount Louisa, Townsville, Australia. The versatile twin engine B-25 "Mitchell", a 6-seat medium bomber made famous when used in the celebrated Doolittle Raid over Japan in April 1942, was based there.

B-25 "Mitchell"

Armed with up to eighteen .50 cal machine guns and able to carry up to 3,000 lbs. of bombs, the B-25 was 52' 11" long, 15' 9" high, weighed 28,460 lbs and had a wing span of 67' 7". It was powered by two 1,700 hp Wright engines, has a range of 1,200 miles with a maximum speed of 275 mph at a ceiling of 25,000 feet.

He and two other Majors were killed in the crash of a B-25G early in the afternoon of September 23, 1943 near Townsville during a gunnery test flight. They were testing field modifications to install extra machine guns to the nose of a B-25. The unsatisfactory condition of the external fuselage package guns caused a fire in the navigator's compartment and the plane crashed in 50 feet of water, three miles off Rattlesnake Island. He was awarded the Legion of Merit, posthumously, for "conspicuous efficiency as chief of maintenance and engineering for the advanced echelon, Fifth Air Service Command", further stating that his work was "marked by extraordinary fidelity and a most unusual measure of technical skill. In particular, his efforts were untiring in bringing to satisfactory completion, a modification for increased armament of aircraft, which later contributed to the successful operation of combat units."

His body was repatriated in March 1948 and lies alone in a four grave plot in Section 20, Plot 265, Grave 2 in Hackensack Cemetery. At death he was 36 years old.

Pvt. Floyd Alonzo Stevens
10,442
United States Army Ambulance Service
Section 648

When war broke out in Europe in 1914, the American Hospital in Neuilly-sur-Seine near Paris was the headquarters for Americans in France who wanted to help care for the increasingly numerous war wounded. It quickly became evident that larger quarters were needed so a newly built school was transformed into a hospital and was named the American Ambulance Hospital in the Lycée Pasteur, capable of holding 600 casualties. Shortly thereafter, a second American Ambulance Hospital – the Collège de Juilly – became operable 30 miles east of Paris with American surgeons in attendance. In September 1914 a dozen automobiles donated by Americans were put into service, driven by American volunteers, giving birth to the American

Ambulance Field Service. Eventually, many more vehicles were donated and many more Americans volunteered, moving ever closer to the front. Often unofficially attached to various French armies, they served dressing stations and army hospitals in the combat zone. One of those American volunteers was a distinguished scholar from Columbia University and Ridgewood, NJ., Floyd Stevens.

Floyd was born November 4, 1889 in Jersey City and moved to Ridgewood in 1908 to live with his sister, two brothers and father at 97 Prospect Street. His mother died when he was very young. He was a member of Ridgewood Methodist Church and graduated from Ridgewood High School in 1910, continued his studies at Wesleyan, where his poetry was published, and graduated in 1914. He got a master's degree from Columbia and nearly completed work for his Doctorate in preparation for a teaching career. On June 7, 1917 he enlisted in the Columbia University Ambulance Unit, trained on campus and in Tobyhanna, Pa. and sailed for France in December. He wrote home about his convoy's transatlantic crossing during which he served as a lookout in the crow's nest unmoved, unlike many of his shipmates, by the turbulent seas.

In May 1918 he again wrote home from France saying "No time for worry over here, and really no cause. So there should be no anxiety back home. It isn't as bad as it sounds, after one gets used to it. It hardly seems possible that I am actually in historic France. But some day things will change, and instead of traveling farther and farther away from the home hearth and the homeland, I will right about face and then I will make a grand retreat from cannon, airplanes, ambulances, hospitals and submarines and then Westward Ho!"

While serving with the French Army in the United States Army Ambulance Service Section 648, his daily "commute" took him from peaceful and picturesque country villages to the front line and even behind enemy lines to pick up casualties. On June 11, while looking down the long, straight Mouchy road near Compiègne, with shells dropping all along it, he drove into the chaos and brought five wounded men to the base hospital. While on his way back to the trenches for another load he was helping a comrade to his ambulance when shrapnel burst over his head and hit him in the chest and around the neck. The next day, June 12, 1918 he died of those wounds. He was Ridgewood's first combat casualty of WWI. He was also the first casualty to be repatriated in 1921 and is buried in Plot 1015 in Valleau Cemetery. At death he was 27 years old.

American Hospital, Paris
with ambulances

Lt. jg Clement Olin Stevenson, Jr.
681235
Naval Air Transport Wing
Pacific Squadron VR-7

It is difficult to find a clear definition of the term "Missing In Action". Having asked historians at the National Archives in College Park and the Pentagon in Washington, D.C., the key word seems to be "Action". It seems that MIA applies only to casualties resulting from hostile action but not to an active serviceman who died when his plane slipped off the side of an aircraft carrier or exploded in mid-air. The latter are listed as casualties but are not included among the MIAs. Despite the fact that MIAs have their own flag, ask a grieving family if they care about such an innocuous distinction. There is no closure – the key word certainly is "Missing". The bodies of 23 Ridgewood men who died in the service have never been found. One of them was Clement O. Stevenson whose plane exploded in mid-air - but he is not listed among the Vietnam MIAs.

Known as C.O., he was born March 11, 1942 and raised in Charlotte, NC. After graduating from Georgia Military Academy, where he was the starting quarterback on the football team, he attended and graduated from the University of North Carolina, Chapel Hill where he was in the Navy ROTC. He moved with his brother and parents to Ridgewood and lived at 236 Richards Road.

He loved flying and earned his wings in October 1965. While stationed with the Naval Air Transport Wing, Pacific Squadron VR-7 at Moffett Field, Ca. he was returning from a mission to Vietnam as copilot of a C-130 Hercules Naval Air Transport plane.

C-130 Hercules

The C-130 had a crew of 5, was powered by four 4,300 horsepower Allison turboprops. The plane was 97 feet, 9 inches long, 38 feet, 3 inches high, had a wingspan of 132 feet, 7, a top speed of 374 mph at 20,000 feet but could reach 33,000 feet with a 100,000. Its maximum takeoff weight was 155,000 pounds. With a maximum range of 5,200 miles with no cargo, it could carry up to 92 troops or 64 paratroops or 74 litter patients, or five standard freight pallets.

They had taken off from Cam Ranh Bay bound for Okinawa and Moffet Field on June 17, 1966 when the plane exploded in mid air and crashed 20 minutes after take off, witnessed by boat crews in the area. Officially listed as a non-hostile casualty, it is believed a Viet Cong altimeter bomb caused the accident. All eight airmen and six passengers on board were lost. At death he was 24 years old.

2 Lt. Robert Donahue Stockbower
O-50881
44th Bomb Squadron
40th Bomb Group
2nd Air Force

he code under which many police forces operate requires that a policeman defend public safety, protect the innocent, only reply with equal force in combat and follow the law in all things. Robert Stockbower learned these tenets when he joined the Ridgewood Police force. He later applied them to his duties in the Army Air Corps.

Known to some as Stocky, he was born in New York City April 14, 1916 and lived at 136 Pershing Ave. with his brother and his father. He attended local schools and graduated from Ridgewood High School in 1935 where he starred on the football team, played golf, soccer, ran track, wrestled and participated in many intramural sports. Unable to afford college, he went to work for Wright Aeronautics and then became a Ridgewood policeman in July 1940.

He was the first patrolman to enter the police force via a Civil Service examination even though civil service had not yet been established for Village employees. After a one-year probationary period he was accepted as a full-fledged member of the Ridgewood Police Force. At that same time, his father was clerk for the Village police, the police court and the Board of Health.

Stockbower was drafted into the military in September 1941 as a Private in the Signal Corps, rose to Technical Sergeant, was approved as an Air Cadet and earned his wings as a pilot of multiengine bombers at Stockton Field, California July 28, 1943. He then completed the Pilot Transition Four-Engine course at Hobbs Army Air Field in New Mexico.

As a member of the 40th Bomb Group, 44th Bomb Squadron, 2nd Air Force he was lost November 18, 1943 when the B-26 he was copiloting failed to return from a cruising trip from Salt Lake City to its home base at Pratt, Kansas.

The last message received from it was 30 minutes out of Salt Lake City. Heavy snowfall high in the Rockies forced search parties to interrupt their task on December 18. Seven months later the crew was found with the wreckage in the vicinity of Adams Lake, 12 miles Northwest of Glenwood Springs, Col.

On July 18 a shepherd who was riding though the country on horseback noticed burned tree stumps and scorched earth which he thought was the result of lightning. He then found a wheel from the plane. As the plane had crashed at the base of a cliff, parts of the bomber were found scattered over hundreds of yards.

Stockbower was the only Ridgewood police officer to die in WWII. He is buried in Section 10, Grave 10834 at Arlington National Cemetery. At death he was 27 years old.

Pfc. Max F. Stoessel
32919825
Company D
38ᵗʰ Infantry Regiment
2ⁿᵈ Infantry Division

On December 16, 1944 the Germans began a major counterattack in the Ardennes Forest of Belgium, hoping to surprise and stop the advancing Allies. As the center of the Allied line retreated, a bulge was created, giving birth to the name - the Battle of the Bulge. By the end of December, after strong Allied resistance combined with supply problems, the German's were forced to slow their attack and by January 21 they had been pushed back to their original line with the loss of 120,000 men. The Allies suffered 81,000 casualties, 77,000 of whom were Americans. Winston Churchill said the Battle of the Bulge was the greatest American battle of the war. Among the American casualties was a seasoned soldier from Ridgewood, Max Stoessel.

Max was born October 27, 1918 and lived with his sister and parents at 252 Lakview Drive in Ridgewood. He graduated from Ridgewood High School in 1937 and went on to New York University and Columbia before entering active service on May 3, 1943.

After training at Camp Shelby in Mississippi and in Maryland, he went overseas with the 2nd Infantry Division and landed on Omaha Beach June 7, 1944. He went on to participate in the Brest Offensive and fought in the Rheinland. As a member of Company D, 38th Infantry Regiment, he was initially reported missing in the ferocious fighting December 17, 1944 during the Battle of the Bulge at Rocherath, Belgium in the Ardennes. It was on that same day a short distance away that the Germans captured and executed at least 80 Americans southeast of the town of Malmedy. Evidence sufficient to establish his death on that date from a gun shot wound to the head was determined in February 1945.

Stoessel was awarded the Combat Infantryman Badge for superior performance of duty in action against the enemy in France and Germany. Bethlehem Lutheran Church dedicated the Altar Vases to him, although his name is misspelled on their memorial plaque. He is buried in Plot G, Row 8, Grave 51 at Henri-Chapelle American Cemetery, Henri-Chapelle, Belgium. At death he was 26 years old.

Chief Mate Richard Campbell Stowell
SS Daniel Morgan

In the early 1940s, many young Americans rushed to join the service. Some who could not pass the Army or Navy physical examination, or were too old for those services, served their country by joining the Merchant Marine. Before the war the Merchant Marine counted 55,000 experienced mariners. This figure grew to over 215,000. But as in all services, these recruits were trained and led by veterans. Ridgewood's Richard Stowell was such a veteran. He was also one of the 9,349 Merchant Mariners who died in WWII, giving the Merchant Marine the highest casualty rate of any US service.

Dick was born in November 1914 but his mother died in the influenza epidemic of 1918. He then lived with his stepmother, four brothers and sister on Paramus Road and later on Dayton Street. The family attended Christ Church. His father Clarence was an educator and was chosen for the

412

lead role in the March of Time movie, *The Ramparts We Watch*, a rousing propaganda saga that premiered at Radio City Music Hall in August 1940. Dick attended the Merchant Marine Academy, graduating in September 1937, married and moved to Brooklyn with his wife Ariadne.

Over 500 Merchant Marine vessels were lost in 1942 – the most of any year of the war. Chief Stowell survived his first torpedoing when his ship *The City of New York* was torpedoed by U-160 and sank in 15 minutes on Palm Sunday March 29, 1942. He and other survivors were picked up after being adrift in a lifeboat for some days and put ashore at Lewes, De. Three months later, while on the return leg of a trip from Baltimore to Archangel, Russia aboard the Liberty Ship *SS Daniel Morgan* with a cargo of steel, food, explosives, tanks and cars, he was one of three casualties when the *Morgan* was sunk in the Barents Sea July 5, 1942. She was part of Convoy PQ-17, disbursed by the British Admiralty and carried a complement of 41 crew members and 28 Naval Armed Guard.

At noon July 5, a German aircraft attacked the ship, bombing in the vicinity of #4 and #5 holds. Due to the heavy bomb damage and flooding of the holds, it was necessary to slow down the ship. At 4:00 in the afternoon, a torpedo from U-88 struck on the starboard side at the #3 hold, putting the main and steering engines out of commission. The ship went down shortly afterwards, stern first and all hands abandoned ship. Three crew members were lost when their lifeboat capsized. Stowell was trying to help another man into one of the boats that had been launched when another lifeboat dropped and struck him on the head. He sank immediately and was never seen again. The survivors were picked up from the lifeboats by the Russian tanker *Donbass* the following morning. Initially listed as missing, his family finally received definitive word of his loss in October from the

Morgan's Chief Engineer who had witnessed his death.

Chief Stowell was awarded the Atlantic War Zone Bar, Combat Bar, Mariner's Medal, Victory Medal, Merchant Marine Service Emblem, Honorable Service Button and a Presidential Testimonial Letter. At death he was 28 years old.

**Pfc. George Alexander Tatosian
32597667
I Company
513th Quartermaster Corps**

Of the 16,260,000 Americans who served in WWII, 407,000 died: 292,131 died in battle, leaving 115,187 who died of other causes. Aside from accidents, illness took many service personnel, including George Tatosian of Ridgewood.

Tatosian was born March 20, 1923 and lived with his mother, sister and two brothers at 42 Pershing Ave. "Tat" graduated from Ridgewood High School in 1940 where he played football, participated Hi-Y and in intramural boxing, wrote for the *Spectator* and *High Times* and was on the scenery committee for the Junior Play.

He worked at the Grand Union, which used him as a poster boy in their salute to local servicemen, and was a member of Christ Church. He enlisted in the service December 7, 1942 and served in I Company, 513th Quartermaster Corps at Camp Phillips, Kansas – the combat service support

415

branch in the Army that provides quarters, provisions, storage, clothing, fuel, stationery, and transportation for troops.

After being ill for several months, he died November 19, 1943 at Winters General Hospital in Topeka, Kansas of subacute bacterial endocarditis. He is buried in Plot 1393 at Valleau Cemetery. At death he was 21 years old.

**1 Lt. Edward Alven Taylor
01292089
22nd Infantry Regiment
4th Infantry Division
3rd Army**

The 22nd Infantry Regiment distinguished itself from the time it landed on Utah Beach June 6, 1944 through the St. Lô breakthrough and the liberation of Paris. They sent the first American patrol to set foot on German soil, fought the battle of the Hurtgen Forest and helped liberate Luxembourg during the Battle of the Bulge. It was the only Regiment to earn two Presidential Unit Citations in the European/African theaters.

An average rifle company went into action with 162 soldiers; a week later they averaged eighty-seven men of which 42% were replacements who had arrived during the battle. By the end of a battle, losses could reach 151% of the original strength. The practice of replacing casualties while units were still in combat kept them from ever falling below 75% of original strength. One of those replacements was a Ridgewood lad who joined the 22nd for Christmas 1944 in the middle of the Battle of the Bulge.

Born October 22, 1918, Eddie Taylor moved to Ridgewood in 1928 and lived at 143 South Maple and later at 111 E. Ridgewood Ave. as the only child of his mother, May Pflieger. Known to some as Knotty, he attended Christ Episcopal Church where he was active in the Cottage Club. He graduated from Ridgewood High School in 1936 where he was voted "best natured", helped on various committees, ran track, played basketball, JV football and intramural basketball. He then went to work for the Chemical Bank in New York City, attending NYU at night.

He was one of Ridgewood's earliest draftees and joined the service on January 7, 1941, entering active duty August 29, 1942 with the 174th Infantry, Medical Department at Camp Dix. He became a second sergeant in the supply department before going overseas for more than two years on special assignments, stationed in England. He was also the first Ridgewood draftee to be made an officer. While in England he married and English woman. They divorced in November 1944 while she was pregnant with their son who was born four days after his father's death.

Taylor went into combat Christmas Day 1944, joining veterans of the D-Day landing, the 22nd Infantry Regiment, 4th Infantry Division, in General Patton's 3rd Army. On June 6, 1944 the 4th Infantry Division was the first allied unit to assault German forces on the Normandy beaches. Landing on Utah Beach, the 4th pushed forward for 26 days at the cost of 5,000 killed in action.

During the Battle of the Bulge Taylor's 22nd Regiment stopped the German advance December 27 and liberated Echternach, Luxembourg - receiving a Presidential Unit Citation and the Belgian Fourragère. Resuming the offensive in Germany, Taylor suffered a head wound and was killed February 7, 1945 in Prum. Initially listed as missing in action, his body lay unclaimed and unidentified for a month before evidence sufficient to establish the fact of death was determined on March 5. He is buried in Plot A, Row 3, Grave 10 in Luxembourg American Cemetery, Luxembourg. At death he was 26 years old.

Arthur Warren Travell

Among Ridgewood's 113 Honored Dead and Ridgewood High School service casualties, four died of the Spanish flu during WWI; 2 were graduates of Ridgewood High School and two are included among Ridgewood's 113 Honored Dead.

In a few early autumn weeks in 1918 an epidemic of Spanish Influenza ravaged the United States. It was called the Spanish Flu because it was believed to have been carried to the USA on a Coast Guard Cutter from Spain. You would be working with someone one day, they would go home because they didn't feel well and within days they were gone. The death toll around the world was 21 million of which 548,452 were in the USA – ten times more than the 53,513 American lives lost in WWI. Remote Eskimo villages in inaccessible Alaskan regions were completely wiped out. The flu began with a high fever and aching bones. After about four days, many cases developed pneumonia. The lungs of the victims would fill with fluid, causing death. Highly contagious, "open face sneezing" in public was subject to fines and imprisonment. The Spanish Flu killed its millions and then mysteriously disappeared.

It circulated in the military, striking first at Fort Riley, Kansas in March 1918 but remaining relatively dormant until the fall. Eventually a call-up of 140,000 draftees was canceled because camp hospitals were full. It also circulated on college campuses and two of these casualties died of the flu while at college.

One was Arthur Travell, Ridgewood High School class of 1916 who lived with his family on Ethelbert Avenue. He was the nephew of Ira Travell, Superintendent of Ridgewood schools from 1912 until 1930 and for whom the Travell School is named. It was while Arthur was at Cornell University that Spanish Influenza caught up to young Arthur who died October 20, 1918.

He is not listed on our memorial plaques because his family had moved to New York. At death he was 20 years old.

2 Lt. Edward Leonard Vanderbeck
O-682407
405th Bomb Squadron
38th Bomb Group

Born in Newark July 11, 1918 he moved with his sister and parents to Ridgewood in 1926 to live at 34 Walthery. He graduated from Ridgewood High School in 1936 where he participated in various intramural sports and varsity soccer, was assistant manager of the baseball team and was class treasurer his sophomore year. He was 5' 7", 155 lbs with brown hair and gray eyes.

He was working for William C. Atwater Co. in Radio City when he was inducted into the service on June 2, 1941 on Governors Island. He transferred to the Army Air Corps October 1, 1942, got his wings June 3, 1943 and was commissioned at San Angelo, Texas July 17, 1943, receiving a "Dead Reckoning Navigation Certificate" at Carlsbad, New Mexico, the only one of its kind, which qualified him as a "double-threat man" – a highly skilled air crew officer able to direct a plane to its objective, drop the bombs and plot the course homeward.

He went overseas in March 1944 as a Bombardier/Navigator with the Green Dragons, 405th Bomb Squadron, 38th Bomb Group. Flying out of Nadzab, New Guinea, he and four crewmates were killed on Wakde Island, New Guinea May 14, 1944 when their plane went down. After a second strafing attack on an enemy airstrip, the aircraft hit a tree, cartwheeled, crashed and exploded.

When the 155th and 167th Regiments, 31st Infantry Division invaded the island June 3 they discovered the bodies of the crew in a cave nearby. The pilot had been decapitated. The fate of the other members of the crew is uncertain. They were initially listed as unknown casualties but subsequent reports indicate the bodies, "or parts thereof" were burned and mangled. Vanderbeck's body was only definitively identified later using dental records, fingerprints and shoe size, was repatriated in June 1948 and buried in 12 Park, Plot 1474 at Valleau Cemetery. At death he was 25 years old.

Capt. Allan H. Vanderyerk
78th Fighter-Interceptor Group
84th Fighter-Interceptor Squadron
Air Defense Command

During the period of the Korean War, 5,764,143 U.S. personnel served in the armed forces worldwide. Approximately 20% of them had also served in WWII. One of them was Allan Vanderyerk of Saddle River and Ridgewood.

Often the irony of the way a serviceman dies is stranger than the double life of a family man/warrior. Vanderyerk was a highly experienced, respected and decorated career pilot, a seasoned combat veteran from WWII and Korea as well as a family man when he died in an accident in 1951. 18 of Ridgewood's 112 Honored Dead (15%) died in accidents.

Vanderyerk was born April 25, 1915 and lived with his brother and parents in Saddle River. He graduated from Ramsey High School in 1933 where he was in the Glee Club, Tau Gamma Gamma and was on the senior play committee. His family later moved to 243 Van Emburgh Ave. in Ridgewood.

He originally entered the Army Air Force in 1942 and by May 1943 was flying solo at Chickosha, Oklahoma. He received his wings on October 1, 1943 at Eagle Pass, Texas before assignment to Dale Mabry Field in Tallahassee. He went on to spend 18 months in Calcutta and Burma to pilot a Thunderbolt fighter plane in 78 missions over the Hump in the China/Burma/India Theater until Army regulations forbade him from flying more missions. He was decorated with the Distinguished Flying Cross and two Air Medals.

He returned to the USA in 1946 and worked for a commercial airline in California before re-enlisting in the Air Force. He was stationed at Hamilton Air Base for about a year before taking jet plane training in Nevada in preparation for an assignment in October 1950 in Korea with the 6th Air Force. He attracted nationwide attention on March 12, 1951 when, while piloting an F-51, he crash landed near Chunchon, ten miles south of the 38th parallel and was rescued by a Third Air Rescue Squadron helicopter from behind enemy lines. Six Australian mustangs and eight American fighters provided air cover and held off communist troops with machine guns and dropped fire bombs on a nearby hill from which the Red troops fired 1,500 rounds of ammunition at him while the helicopter picked him up. He escaped unhurt.

He returned to the USA in May 1951 with the 78th Fighter-Interceptor Group, 84th Fighter-Interceptor Squadron, Air Defense Command as a pilot of a twin-engine Northrop F-89 twin jet Scorpion fighter plane "Nora Blue" based at Hamilton Air Force Base in California. The F-89 was a fighter-interceptor built to locate, intercept, and destroy enemy aircraft by day or night under any weather conditions. It carried a pilot in the forward cockpit and a radar operator in the rear who guided the pilot into the proper attack position.

It was 53' 8" long, 17' 6" high, weighed 47,700 lbs. and had a wing span of 59" 10" and was armed with two air-to-air rockets with nuclear warheads plus four Falcon missiles.

F-89

On December 16, 1951 Vanderyerk was scrambled during a red alert on an intercept mission in instrument weather conditions. He intercepted and identified the aircraft and was returning to base when he missed the approach and crashed into the mud in San Pablo Bay, 2.5 miles from base. Captain Vanderyerk left a widow.

Many think the F-89B was rushed into squadron service too rapidly. There were not enough trained pilots or radar operators and there were not enough maintenance personnel who knew the intricacies of the complex and troublesome Hughes E-1 fire control system. The in-service rating of the F-89B was terribly poor and crashes were frequent. On September 22, 1952, the entire F-89 fleet was grounded and remained grounded for 7 months.

Vanderyerk is also listed on the memorial plaques in Saddle River. At death he was 35 years old.

Sgt. Kenneth Maxwell Walter
12009097
Company K
16th Infantry Regiment
1st Infantry Division

Ken Walter was from Newark. Nonetheless, we should all be proud of, and thankful for, this highly decorated veteran of more than two years of front line combat. His story is the stuff war movies are made of.

He was born August 22, 1920 in Newark and lived there with his parents, two sisters and two brothers. His mother died when he was 16 and his sister Grace Abel moved to Ridgewood to live at 105 John Street. Ken attended Roseville Presbyterian Church in Newark, graduated from Sussex Avenue Boys' Vocational High School, also

427

in Newark and worked at the White Tower
hamburger restaurant in Hackensack after
graduation.

He joined the service October 8, 1940 at
Fort Jay, Governor's Island, trained at Fort Devans,
Mass. and took amphibious operations training at
Edgewood Arsenal, Md. and in Puerto Rico. Then,
as a member of the 16th Infantry Regiment, 1st
Infantry Division, he sailed on the *Queen Mary* for
England in the first week of August 1942. The next
26 months would mostly be spent in front line
combat.

In November the 16th participated in the
invasion of North Africa where he earned a Purple
Heart for wounds received. He mailed the Purple
Heart home to his sister with a letter but the Purple
Heart arrived two weeks before the letter, causing
temporary distress to his sister. In his letter he said
"Everything here is going along fine and it won't be
long now before it will be all over".

In April 1943 the 16th landed in Sicily where
they fought until August, returning to Liverpool in
October for seven months training in preparation
for the invasion of Europe. It was at this time that
he married Eileen Bourke from Dublin on March
21, 1944. They shared the same birthday and birth
year.

On D-Day the 16th landed on Omaha Beach
at 7:05 and was immediately pinned down but
succeeded in fighting on to Hameau by late
afternoon. As a Private, he was awarded the Bronze
Star (posthumously) "for heroic achievement in
connection with military operations against the
enemy in Normandy, France 6 June, 1944." By
mid-August they were south of Paris and by mid-
September they had breached the Sigfried Line on
their way to Aachen. He had now been promoted to
Sergeant.

Walter died after being hit by shrapnel in
the head during a bombardment near Buschmuh.
It was during this action that he was awarded the

Silver Star "for gallantry in action in the vicinity of Stollberg, Germany, October 3, 1944. When his squad was captured during a fierce engagement with the enemy, Sgt. Walter made a daring break from his captors and despite coverless terrain and intense hostile fire, fearlessly attempted to reach his command and furnish them with important information. In the performance of his gallant deed, Sgt. Walter was mortally wounded."

Ken Walter is buried in Plot E, Row 12, Grave 62 at the Henri-Chapelle American Cemetery, Henri-Chapelle, Belgium. At death he was 24 years old.

Ulmont White

In a few early autumn weeks in 1918 an epidemic of Spanish Influenza ravaged the United States. It was called the Spanish Flu because it was believed to have been carried to the USA on a Coast Guard Cutter from Spain. You would be working with someone one day, they would go home because they didn't feel well and within days they were gone. The death toll around the world was 21 million of which 548,452 were in the USA – ten times more than the 53,513 American lives lost in WWI. Remote Eskimo villages in inaccessible Alaskan regions were completely wiped out. The flu began with a high fever and aching bones. After about four days, many cases developed pneumonia. The lungs of the victims would fill with fluid, causing death. Highly contagious, "open face sneezing" in public was subject to fines and imprisonment. The Spanish Flu killed its millions and then mysteriously disappeared.

It also circulated in the military, striking first at Fort Riley, Kansas in March 1918 but remaining relatively dormant until the fall. Eventually a call-up of 140,000 draftees was canceled because camp hospitals were full. Two of Ridgewood's 112 Honored Dead died within a week or each other, victims of the flu.

Ridgewood's first service victim of Spanish Influenza was Ulmont White who lived at 296 Prospect St. He went to Ridgewood Preparatory School and graduated from Ridgewood High School in 1917 where he was a star running back on the football team, manager of the basketball team, member of the dramatic club, the glee club and the mandolin club. He was also a member of the rifle club, on the athletic campaign committee, business manager of the Shakespearean play in 1916 and business manager of the *Arrow* in 1917. He was a parishioner at Mt. Carmel and was a member of the Ridgewood Battalion Home Guard. His mother procured the first ever "Gold Star" and attached it to the service flag in honor of Lindley DeGarmo. His father was President of the Board of Health.

On September 17 he went to Lafayette College in Easton, Pa. with the intention to join the recently established Lafayette Student's Army Training Corps in preparation for assignment with the American Expeditionary Forces in France. He immediately developed a severe cold, was hospitalized on Sunday and died of Spanish Influenza at 3:30 the following Saturday afternoon, September 28, 1918. He was buried October 1, 1918 in Plot 1150, grave 4 in Valleau Cemetery. At death he was 20 years old.

Lt. jg. John Christopher Williams
592563
Fighter Squadron 14
Naval Aviation Safety Center

The most difficult casualty to research was John Christopher Williams. I could find no link to Ridgewood; no official or unofficial documents – county, state, federal or school - gave his home of record as Ridgewood, NJ and I found no mention of his death in our local newspapers. First, he did not attend Ridgewood public schools; second his death was not considered as having occurred during a period of combat and third there is no burial site because his body was not recovered. The clue that gave it away was the unconfirmed story of an elderly yet elegant lady arriving by taxi to Ridgewood's Memorial Day ceremonies saying that her son was the last name listed on the plaque. That name was John C. Williams. The woman was Lillian Williams, his mother. She lobbied hard and long to get his name on Ridgewood's War Memorial but Williams seemed to have fallen off the radar screens of the bureaucrats who decide on who should or should not be included on Vietnam War Memorials.

Despite the fact that the first official death in the Viet-Nam War was an Air Force Technical Sergeant who was killed by another U.S. airman June 8, 1956 and the last casualties were recorded on May 15, 1975 when 18 marines were killed in a rescue mission, because of disagreement and confusion over the official start and end dates for the Vietnam War, John C. Williams of Ridgewood, NJ, who died December 27, 1962, has not been considered a Vietnam War casualty.

There is as much dissent about the official dates for the Vietnam War as there was about the conflict itself. Based on enactment of Title 38 US Code, Section 4212, the Office of the Actuary at the Department of Veterans Affairs in Washington gives August 5, 1964 to May 7, 1975 as the dates for Periods of Service for the Vietnam War. The U.S. Army Center of Military History in Washington states "Prior to the enactment of Title 38 US Code, Section 4212, Federal agencies differed on the inclusive dates for the Vietnam conflict, and there is a lack of uniformity even within the Department of the Army." However, based upon current Veterans' preferences in force in the U.S. Government, the dates have apparently been changed to 28 February 1961 - 7 May 1975. These are the dates used for membership in the American Legion. Other dates used are:
1. Office, Chief of Public Affairs, Department of the Army: 1 Jan 1961 - 28 Jan 1973;
2. Military Awards Branch, Military Personnel Center, Department of the Army: 1 July 1958 - 29 Mar 1973;
3. Center of Military History, Department of the Army: 11 Dec 1961 - 29 Mar 1973;
4. Veterans Administration: 5 Aug 1964 - 7 May 1975.

The bottom line is what the official web site of the Vietnam Veterans Memorial Wall in Washington D.C. states: "During and after the Vietnam War, the Department of Defense compiled a list of combat zone casualties according to criteria in a 1965 Presidential Executive Order. The Executive Order specified Vietnam, Laos, Cambodia and coastal areas as a combat zone. If the Department of Defense, acting in accordance with these directives, considered an individual to be a Vietnam conflict fatality or to be missing, his/her name would be included." There are three exceptions to these conditions:

1) there are 68 Marines on the wall who were killed when their R&R flight crashed in Hong Kong. This exception to the criteria was ordered by President Ronald Reagan;

2) the geographic criteria were enlarged to include 95 servicemen killed outside the war zone while on or in support of direct combat missions;

3) 15 servicemen who had subsequently died of wounds received in Vietnam.

As a result, to this day our John C. Williams is not included on the New Jersey Vietnam Veterans Memorial or on the Vietnam Veterans Memorial Wall in Washington D.C.

John was born December 16, 1937 in Riverside, CT, but grew up with his parents and sister at 146 Melrose Place in Ridgewood. His father was Director at Lederle Laboratories in Pearl River. An Eagle Scout, John graduated from St. Peter's Prep School in Jersey City in 1955 where he won the Honor Pin and was active in a classical literature club while playing football three years, basketball two years and track two years. He was also class secretary. He then attended Holy Cross College before receiving a Senatorial appointment to the U.S. Naval Academy, entering June 25, 1956. Known as Bear, J.C. or Big City, he played lacrosse for three years and was on the 1960 United States Intercollegiate Lacrosse Association national championship team. There is a seat dedicated to him at the Navy Marine Corps Memorial Stadium

His favorite hobby was driving sports cars and he was president of the Automotive Engineering Club. His varied interests included skin diving and Coleman Hawkins. He graduated in 1960 with the ambition of flying the fastest airplanes and the goal of becoming a test pilot in the new space age. He earned his "Wings of Gold" in October 1961 after training at Pensacola, FL and Kingsville, TX. His first plane was a McDonnell F3B Demon jet fighter with Fighter Squadron 14 at Cecil Field Naval Station near Jacksonville.

The Demon, a Navy carrier-based jet fighter, entered service in 1956. With a crew of 1, it was 59 ft. long, had a wingspan of 35 ft., was 14 ft. 7 in. high and weighed 21,287 lbs empty. It was powered by 1 Westinghouse J40-WE-22 turbojet, had a maximum speed of 716 mph, a range of 1,800 miles and could reach a ceiling of 42,650 feet. Armed with four 20 mm Colt Mk 12 cannons and two AIM-9 Sidewinder missiles, it carried 6,000 lbs of bombs. After several fatal accidents and mechanical problems, the Demon was retired in 1964. Not soon enough.

One of those fatal accidents took John Williams' life. He was lost at 9:35 in the evening of December 27, 1962 when the Demon he was piloting off the USS Franklin D. Roosevelt, a Midway class aircraft carrier, plunged into the Mediterranean and exploded 30 seconds after takeoff on a night intercept training mission. Three other planes in the exercise had been withdrawn prior to take off. Visibility was seven miles in scattered skies and slight sea but there was no visible horizon, a key element in judging altitude. His Demon began a shallow climb until approximately a half mile off the ship and then began to descend, hitting the water a mile from the ship with the afterburner still operating. The plane disintegrated upon impact and sank in 1,600 fathoms of water. Search and rescue operations, including a motor whale boat, scoured the debris area. Only his helmet was recovered.

Williams had a pet monkey named Tamango AKA the "bloody monkey". Upon John's death, the elderly yet elegant lady who arrived by taxi to Ridgewood's Memorial Day ceremonies adopted the monkey who then had the run of her home. John's first child was born the day before the accident. At death, John Williams was 25 years old.

1 Lt. Sydney Ransom Windham
O-18284
Second Marine Division
Fleet Marine Force

Several of Ridgewood's 112 Honored Dead were not from Ridgewood – some perhaps rarely set foot here. They were from all around the country. Some enlisted here, some had one parent living here, some gave their home of record as Ridgewood because their family had moved here or, most often, because they married one of Ridgewood's ladies. Such an adopted Ridgewoodite was Sydney Windham.

His family moved from Syracuse, NY to Aberdeen, North Carolina in 1929 where he grew up with his parents and two sisters. His father was Manager of the Mountain Ice Company which provided ice for the refrigerated railroad cars of the Seaboard Airline Railway Co. for shipping local produce. Sydney was President of Aberdeen High School's 15-student class of 1936. A very popular and handsome young man, he was active in the Glee club and was very sports minded. With Pinehurst just a chip shot away, he became an avid golfer.

"Syd" continued his education at Mars Hill College and then returned to Syracuse to attend Syracuse University where he met Priscilla Stewart, Ridgewood High School class of 1938. They announced their engagement in their senior year at the 1942 spring formal of her sorority, Kappa Alpha Theta and were married January 30, 1943 in the Marine Chapel at Quantico, Va. They called home 144 Avondale in Ridgewood, NJ.

He joined the Marines in March 1942 but was allowed to finish his studies and was only called to service in September. He trained at Quantico, Va. and Camp Lejeune, receiving his commission December 3, 1942 before going overseas with the Second Marine Division. At that time his wife was in Washington, D.C. receiving overseas training for the American Red Cross.

The 2nd Marine Division won a Presidential Unit Citation "For outstanding performance in combat during the seizure and occupation of the Japanese-held Atoll of Tarawa, Gilbert Islands November 20 to 24, 1943." In that battle, more than 3,000 Marines were killed or wounded in seventy-six hours of heavy combat. Windham was one of them, receiving the Purple Heart for a wound to his hand in what was one of the bloodiest battles in Marine Corps history.

He was put back together in a Pearl Harbor Hospital and rejoined the 2nd on Saipan Island in the Marianas. The island was needed for use as a B-29 airbase to bomb Japan. The 2nd Marine Division fought 3 weeks non-stop to take the Island. That is where Windham was killed in action June 17, 1944. He is buried in Section 34, Grave 4167 at Arlington National Cemetery. At death he was 25 years old.

Lt. jg Paul Thornton Wines
USS TANG SS-306

Some think it is cheaper to conduct on-the-job testing than to waste time and expensive equipment conducting experiments. Particularly during the rush into war, time is an unavailable luxury. Unfortunately, the associated cost in human lives is incalculable, particularly when one considers the lost potential of brilliant and talented young men, such as Paul Wines of Ridgewood.

Paul lived at 144 John Street with his two brothers and his parents and was President of the Student Council, Ridgewood High School class of 1938 where he was prominent in dramatic and musical activities. He was in the county band, county orchestra, the state orchestra and was a member of the A Cappella choir, winning the Orpheas Club prize for music in both his junior and senior years. He won the coveted Thayer Award for good citizenship at graduation. With experience as drum major for the high school band behind him, and while a sophomore at Carnegie Tech, where he was also drum major, in August 1939 he won the

Senior Division in a nationwide baton twirling contest, sometimes twirling three batons at the same time, sponsored by the American Drummers Association in New York City, defeating 47 contestants. His gold trophy was awarded to him in the Court of Peace at the New York World's Fair. He also performed at Carnegie Hall. A future leader if there ever was one.

After graduating from Carnegie Tech, Lt. Wines joined the Navy submarine service and sailed on what became one of the war's most celebrated subs, the *USS Tang,* a Balao Class submarine. For the early part of 1944 the *Tang* was on lifeguard duty, picking up downed airmen. They claimed to have picked up every flyer downed on their watch. Moving to the attack, the *Tang* sank 24 major ships – the highest toll of the war. But the *Tang* is perhaps best remembered for its loss. Paul Wines died October 25, 1944 aboard the *TANG* on its 5th war patrol as a result of the circular return of its own torpedo.

USS Tang SS 306

The *Tang* launched a night surface attack at the north end of the Formosa Strait near Turnabout Island on October 24 against a Japanese transport. A first torpedo was fired and when it was observed to be running true, a second was launched. It curved sharply to port and circled back toward the *TANG*. Emergency evasion measures could not prevent the torpedo from striking the stern of *TANG*. The boat went down and settled in 180' of water.

Four men on the bridge were able to swim through the night until being picked up eight hours later. Of the thirteen men who escaped from the forward room, only eight reached the surface, and of these only five were able to swim until rescued. The nine survivors were picked up by a Japanese destroyer escort that had on board victims of *TANG'S* previous sinkings. The men from the *TANG* were tortured and then retained in prison camps until the end of the war.

The *TANG'S* commanding officer Richard H. O'Kane received the Congressional Medal of Honor for *TANG'S* final action. Specifically because of the way the *TANG* was lost, modern torpedoes are now designed to deactivate and go inert if they turn 180 degrees. Lt. Wines is listed on the Tablets of the Missing at Manila American Cemetery. At death, Paul Wines was 24 years old.

Elec. M/1 John Baptist Wohlrab
7119190
USS *Nestor (ARB 6)*

One of the best-kept secrets of the late war in the Pacific was the tiny western Pacific Ocean atoll of Ulithi. For only several months in late 1944 and 1945, it was the world's largest naval base and one of the U.S. military's most closely guarded secrets. It was from Ulithi in March 1945 that 15 battleships, 29 aircraft carriers, 23 cruisers, 106 destroyers and a seemingly endless caravan of oilers and supply ships sailed to undertake and support the U.S. invasion of Japan.

Japanese territory since 1920, the atoll was abandoned by the Japanese in 1944. The beneficiary was the US Navy whose Seabees quickly converted it to a forward base that eliminated the need to return to Pearl Harbor or other distant safe areas for repairs, maintenance or R&R. Among the thousands of Navy and Coast Guardsmen at Ulithi was Ridgewood's John Wohlrab.

Wohlrab was born in Brooklyn November 26, 1903, which makes him the oldest of Ridgewood's 112 Honored Dead. He moved to Ridgewood in 1920 to live at 374 Van Emburgh Ave. with his parents and four brothers. He married Augusta DePauw with whom he had four children over 17 years. An electrician by trade, he worked for Hasbrouck Electricians of Hackensack before starting his own business in New York, eventually working for two years as an electrician in the Staten Island Navy Yard. The Wohlrab family made superior contributions and sacrifices to our war effort as two of his brothers, his brother-in-law and his son were also in WWII. One brother was a prisoner of war and his brother-in-law lost a foot.

He joined the service November 17, 1943, was assigned to Boston Navy Yard and served on the USS *Nestor (ARB 6)*, a repair ship in the Pacific. Designed to make emergency repairs in forward areas to battle-damaged ships, the *Nestor* was commissioned June 24, 1944, left Norfolk August 4, 1944 for Guantanamo Bay, the Panama Canal, and Ulithi, arriving October 21 to take up her primary mission.

Ulithi, formerly a Japanese seaplane base only 1,300 miles from Tokyo, was the biggest safe anchorage in the entire Pacific, a natural harbor that could accommodate hundreds of ships at one time. In the months of preparation for the invasion of Iwo Jima and Okinawa, Ulithi became the hub of most naval operations in the Pacific. During the next five and a half months, as US forces recaptured the Philippines, the *Nestor* acted as tender to small craft and repaired all types of naval vessels from battleships to landing craft, some damaged by kamikazes, suicide boats, and even suicide swimmers.

On February 26, 1945 Wohlrab drowned while going ashore in Ulithi Atoll, Asor Island. The landing craft in which he was riding was hit by a large wave and he was thrown overboard and drowned. He was initially buried on Guam but was moved to Row N, Grave 896 in the National Memorial Cemetery of the Pacific, Honolulu in 1948. At death he was 42 years old.

Gunnery Sgt. Charles Wolfhegel
20th Company
5th Marine Corps Regiment
2nd Infantry Division

Established April 8, 1915, the French *Croix de Guerre* is awarded for bravery to military personnel mentioned in dispatches by a General or Commanding Officer. During WWI, it was also awarded to U.S. Army units and to individuals. One such individual was Charles Wolfhegel of Ridgewood.

Wolfhegel was born and raised at 15 Ellison in Paterson but his mother died in 1900. He worked for awhile for his brother-in-law W.C. Banta until enlisting in the Marines in 1906, serving eight years. His father was a pork dealer and died in August 1907 so he used his sister's address at 76 Walnut Street in Ridgewood during his first tour of duty.

When it appeared that America would enter the great war he re-enlisted and was one of Uncle Sam's first men to arrive in France with 20th Company, 5th Marine Corps Regiment, 2nd Infantry Division. The 5th gained worldwide fame when they turned back the Germans at Belleau Wood and Blanc Mont Ridge as the war wound down in the fall of 1918.

Blanc Mont Ridge dominated the Champagne region, providing a view from Reims to the Argonne Forest and was a highly fortified position the Germans had held for three years. The Second Division chased what was left of the defenders as they retreated to the Aisne River. An adage says that a retreating enemy is probably just falling back and regrouping. After participating in some of the fiercest fighting of the war, it was after 9 days of heavy combat in this battle that Sgt. Wolfhegel suffered wounds on October 12, 1918 that caused his death a month later on November 14 – three days after the armistice was signed.

For his gallantry, he received the French Croix de Guerre. The citation, signed by General Pétain, stated that Sgt. Wolfhegel "gave a high example in performing one's duty by continuing to advance in spite of his wounds and by giving encouragement to his men". His Commanding Officer added his expression of "appreciation of the splendid service rendered ... in France, where his conspicuous gallantry in the face of the enemy won the admiration of the French commanders and caused to be conferred upon him the Cross and Citation." Wolfhegel is buried in St. Mihiel American Cemetery, Thiaucourt, France. At death he was 37 years old.

Wagoner Daniel S. Yeomans
156049
Co. E, 1st Regiment
U.S. Engineers

Ridgewood families have been spared the trauma of losing more than one child in combat. Among our casualties are brothers in law who died during the Korean War, an uncle who was killed in WWI and his nephew who was lost in WWII and two cousins - Daniel Yeomans was killed three weeks before his cousin Jacob in WWI.

Born June 23, 1892 in Arcola, Daniel was the only son of Mr. and Mrs. Jacob A. Yeomans of Arcola and later of Hohokus. His sister, Mrs. Charles S. Zabriskie, lived at 67 West Ridgewood Ave. He was baptized October 31, 1897 in the True Reformed Church and later became a member of Arcola Methodist Church.

Yeomans entered the service May 8, 1917 in the Engineer Corps., did basic training at Fort Slocum, NY and sailed for France August 7. For the first few months he was a cook for his mess and afterwards became a wagoner, responsible for getting supplies and maintaining the wagons.

He was on the front for a year with Co. E, 1st Regiment, U.S. Engineers and was killed by a bomb at Baulney (Meuse) October 8, 1918, the first war casualty from the Fair Lawn Grange. He was awarded two service stars "for bravery under fire".

His body was repatriated in 1921 and is buried in Plot 1105 at Valleau Cemetery. In addition to Ridgewood, he is also listed on the memorial plaques in Paramus and Fair Lawn. At death he was 26 years old.

Pvt. Jacob Albert Yeomans
1280005
Co. C, 114th Infantry Regiment
57th Infantry Brigade
29th Infantry Division

Jacob Yeomans was born in Ridgewood and lived at 141 West Glen Ave. He joined West Side Presbyterian Church October 10, 1915 and initially enlisted in the service at Sea Girt June 26, 1916 and was among the first Ridgewood men mustered into the service on March 25, 1917. On September 6, 1917 he went to Camp McClellan in Anniston, Ala. before being transferred from home camps to the American Expeditionary Forces with Company C, 114th Infantry, 29th Division. The 29th was known as the "Blue and Gray" because it was formed from militia companies that had fought in the Civil War, putting sons of the Union and the Confederacy side by side. Its badge was the Korean symbol of good luck, a circle bisected by two half circles. One half of the circle was blue and the other gray.

They arrived in France on June 27, 1918 and assembled in St. Nazaire on the Bay of Biscay before moving on to the final training areas near Poitiers and Prauthoy. They moved to a "quiet area" in Alsace near Belfort in late July and were under French supervision until they moved to the Verdun area in late September. The 29th fought in the center sector of Haute Alsace and Grand Montagne, north of Verdun.

The 57th entered the offensive on October 9 as the only American division serving on the east bank of the Meuse River. Its initial objective was to cover the flanks of the main American effort. Using very sophisticated infiltration tactics rather than a full frontal assault, the division engaged in heavy fighting around such key terrain features as Malbrouck Hill, the Molleville Farm, the Grand Montagne and Etrayes Woods. Under the code name "Mocking Bird" the division advanced seven kilometers in three weeks, fighting elements of six enemy divisions. From October 12 to 25 Yeomans fought at Bois d'Ormont where he was wounded, dying of his wounds October 27, 1918. The division was relieved in the evening of October 29.

He was awarded the Purple Heart, World War I Victory Medal with Defensive Sector and the World War I Victory Button (Silver). His body was repatriated in 1921 and buried under the name Albert Yeomans in Lot 176 in Paramus Plains Cemetery in Ridgewood at the intersection of Ridgewood Avenue and Prospect. When the cemetery was removed in the late 1940s for the construction of the Sommerville School, his body was transferred to George Washington Memorial Park in Paramus and buried with many others in unmarked graves. His is Block J, Lot 39, Grave 4, Section A. As such, he is the only WWI casualty buried in George Washington Memorial Park. At death he was 20 years old.

Conclusion & Editorial

This book describes the lives and times of 147 young men and women – most of whom gave their lives in time of war – all of whom lost their lives while in the service of our country. Most of them have received public recognition in the form of a memorial plaque – somewhere.

However, Ridgewood does not publicly recognize those people who died in the service of our country outside an official period of military service (see page 49). On the other hand, we do publicly recognize the 12 civilians from Ridgewood who died in the attack on the World Trade Center on September 11, 2001 – and rightfully so. I believe we should extend this public manifestation of our gratitude to include all our fellow villagers who have died while on military service. An additional plaque in honor of those who died outside an "official period of service" is warranted.

Boys are the cash of war.
Whoever said we're not free-spenders
doesn't know our likes.
John Ciardi "New Years Eve"
This Strangest Everything 1966

Index   **Page**

Military Units

Official Period of Service:

Ships

Sources and Credits

My sources of information began with the reports of the person's death in the local newspapers - the *Ridgewood News,* its predecessor the *Ridgewood Herald News,* the *Sunday News* and sometimes the *Bergen Record.* There are many books in print about the units these men were in. Many veterans associations have Internet web sites, some of which are very detailed. Under the Freedom of Information Act the US government provided Aircraft Mishap Reports, Missing Air Crew Reports and Individual Deceased Personnel Files which allowed me to learn exactly what caused the death of our martyrs. I have also spoken to many of their siblings and friends. Thanks to everybody!

- American Legion Post 53, Ridgewood, NJ
- American Legion Post 5, Waterville, Me.
- The Ridgewood Public Library
- West Side Sun "Service Supplement", West Side Presbyterian Church, Ridgewood, N.J
- The History of West Side Presbyterian Church, Ridgewood, NJ
- First Presbyterian Church, Ridgewood, NJ
- Christ Episcopal Church, Ridgewood, NJ
- Bethlehem Lutheran Church, Ridgewood, NJ
- Department of the Army, U.S. Total Army Personnel Command, Alexandria, Va.
- Department of the Navy
- Department of Veterans Affairs, National Cemetery Administration
- Defense Prisoner of War/Missing Personnel Office
- Library of Congress
- National Archives, College Park, Md.
- National Archives of Canada, Ottawa
- National Personnel Records Center
- U.S. Army Center of Military History
- U.S. Air Force, Maxwell Air Force Base, Ala.

- U.S. Air Force Museum
- U.S. Navy Historical Society
- American Battle Monuments Commission, Arlington, Va.
- Commonwealth War Graves Commission
- Bergen County Police
- Genealogical Records at the New Jersey State Archives, Trenton
- Phil Eisenberg, Chief Actuary, MONY
- State Department of Health of New Jersey
- State Department of Health of Illinois
- State Department of Health of California
- James Hoffman, United States Merchant Marine Academy Admissions Field Representative
- Dr. Arthur M. Hughes: speech given at Ellington Air Field
- Yonkers Public Library

Newspapers

- *Ridgewood Herald, Ridgewood News* and the *Sunday News*, Ridgewood, N.J
- *Sunday News/Sunday Post*
- The *Bergen Record, Hackensack, NJ*
- The *Rutherford Republican and Rutherford American, Rutherford, NJ*
- The *Glenwood Springs Newspaper, Glenwood Springs, Col*
- *Rockford Morning Star, Rockford, Ill.*
- *Dayton Daily News, Dayton, Ohio*
- The *Kansas City Times, Kansas City, Ka.*
- *New England Journal of Medicine*
- *The News and Observer, Raleigh, NC*
- *Sandhill Citizen and Vass, Aberdeen, NC*

Books

- Assault Down the Spine
- Blood and Fire. Victory in Europe, 63d Infantry Division
- Combat History of the 8 Infantry Division in World War II. Lt. Marc F. Griesbach
- *"Duty, Honor, Privilege"* New York's Silk Stocking Regiment and the Breaking of the Hindenburg Line. Stephen L. Harris. Brassey's, Inc. 2001
- The History of Glen Rock
- The History of a Village, Ridgewood, NJ
- S.S. Leopoldville Disaster December 24, 1944. Allan Andrade
- The Naked Warriors. Commander Francis Douglas Fane, USNR. Appleton-Century-Crofts, Inc.
- Officers and Enlisted Men of the United States Navy who lost their lives during the world war, from April 6, 1917 to November 11, 1918: Government Printing Office
- Order of Battle U.S. Army World War II. Shelby L. Stanton
- Paths of Armor. Albert Love Enterprises
- Prep Charlie. Published by the Personnel of the USS Wasp and Air Group 81.
- The Rohna Disaster, WWII's Secret Tregedy. Dr. James G. Bennett. High Point Publishing
- The Tuskegee Airmen: the men who changed a nation. Charles E. Francis. Branden Publishing 1993
- Warpath Across the Pacific. Lawrence J. Hickey. International Research and Publishing Corp.
- Soldiers of the Great War. Soldiers Record Publishing Association, Washington, DC
- Here is your War: Ernie Pyle
- Duty, Honor, Victory: Gary Bloonfield
- Flyboys – A true Story of Courage: James Bradley

- World War II – 4,139 Strange and Fascinating Facts: Don McCombs & Fred L. Worth

Internet Web Sites

http://www.worldwar1.com
http://metalab.unc.edu/hyperwar
http://www.redraiders22bg.com
http://www.erols.com
http://www.csp.navy.mil
http://www.harwood.plus.com
http://www.plettenberg.de/75th
http://glycine.ncsa.uiuc.edu
http://www.subnet.com
http://www.ussrowan.com
http://www.rrking.com
http://www.geocitics.com
http://www.nautilus571.com
http://www.grunts.net
http://www.armoredforces.com
http://www.kwanah.com
http://www.yuma.usmc.mil
http://www.usmm.org
http://www.historychannel.com
http://www.10thmtndivdesc.org
http://www.usaaf.com
http://www.daileyint.com
http://www.au.af.mil
http://www.b24.net
http://www.webbergroup.com
http://www2.army.mil
http://www.pyker.dircon.co.uk
http://www.siscom.net
http://www.anesi.com
http://www.snycorva.cortland.edu
http://www.usshouston.org
http://www.ccia.com
http://www.104infdiv.org
http://www.coax.net
http://www.ritesofpassage.org
http://www.azstarnet.com

http://www.mcguire.af.mil
http://www.worldnet.net
http://www.nara.gov
http://www.militaria.com
http://www.home.st.net.au
http://www.22ndinfantry.org
http://www.16thinfantry-regiment.org
http://www.29thinfantrydivision.com
http://www.129th.net
http://www.no-quarter.org
http://www.taskforceomegainc.org
http://www.uploads.thevirtualwall.org
att.net/~newbooks/WWIIbooks.html
http://www.militaryhistoryonline.com/wwii

Schools

Augusta Military Academy, Fort Defiance, Va.
Columbia University
Cornell University
Eastside High School, Paterson, NJ
Evanston Township High School, Evanston, Ill.
Fort Lee High School, Fort Lee, NJ
Franklin & Marshall
Lehigh University
The Peddie School
The Pennington School, Pennington, NJ
Phillips Exeter Academy, Exeter, NH
Ramsey High School
Ridgewood High School, Ridgewood, N.J
Rutgers University
Rutherford High School
St. Luke's School, Hohokus, NJ
Shawnee Mission North High School
Solebury School, New Hope, Pa.
Syracuse University
Stevens Institute
The University of Akron
Yale University

Family & Friends

Robert Abel
Carol Harvey Barrows
Margaret Bracewell
Helen Brooks
Sally Sailer
    Caporlingua
Diana Casey
Robert Cella
Tom Chapman
Celine Cobb
Albert Condo
Bethany Holley Craig
Tom Crikelair
Martha Cummings
Joe Evans
Mary Fetkowitz
William G. Ford
Richard A. Freund
Cort Gorham
Veta Epps Gorman
Donald Graham
Brian Griffin
Robert Haldane
John Hargrove
Ruth Harvey
Walter Hayes
Robert Helps
Cora Himadi
Robert Hine
Henry Hird
Art Holter
Nancy Hughes
Warren Hurst
Mr. Robert Hyslop
Frank Iudica
Katie Jaeger
Suzanne Knapp
LeRoy E. Johannsen
Stan Kodey

Helen De Richmond
    Koechlein
Barbara Dempsey
    Kotora
Richard H. Leonard
C. M. Locke
Lonnie Nichols
    Macarthur
June Rose Marlow
James McGrath
Rick McGrath
Bruce H. Moore
Alfred Montick
Judith Trotta
Arthur Ramsdell
Victoria Jordan Reno
Robert E. Sandmann
Olivann Sebring
Mrs. Mary Shane
George Smyser
Eileen Redgrave Stage
Sue Connolly
    Stevenson
Elizabeth
    Stevenson
Samuel Stevenson
Charles Stribling
Harry E. Terrell, Jr.
Grace Gunster Tullio
Paul van Valkenburg
Hugh Walker
Victoria Weaver
Joan Shaw Helps
    White
George Withers
Leonard Wohlrab

About the Author

Born and raised in Pittsburgh, PA and Louisville, KY, Mr. Stout first moved to Ridgewood, NJ in 1967 where he now lives with his wife of 40 years. They have one daughter, born in Korea and adopted when 9 months old. A career banker by profession, having worked in New York City and overseas, he has always been concerned with local community interests and activities. He served on the Board of Directors of the Center for Food Action in New Jersey for 16 years. He and his wife are active blood donors, each having donated over 9 gallons to the Ridgewood Blood Donors Association. He is an ordained Elder in the Presbyterian Church USA, on the Mayor's Citizens Safety Committee and has been active in various youth recreation leagues, coaching baseball and softball for 17 years.

Mr. Stout has been associated with Rotary International, the Institute of International Bankers in New York City, the International Who's Who of Professionals and the New York Chapter of the French American Chamber of Commerce where he was on the Board of Directors.

As a radioman, he spent eight years in the U.S. Coast Guard Reserve, based in Louisville, N.O.B. Norfolk and sailing out of Boston Harbor on the USCGC *Duane*.

His interest in history and research dates to his school days. Educated at the University of Louisville, the Goethe Institut in Germany and the Université de Montpellier in France, Mr. Stout has written analytical pieces for the *American Banker* and the *Leasing and Financial Services Monitor*. Starting in June 2001, based on his own research, he wrote a column in the *Ridgewood News* entitled "Recalling First Line News" in which he described the lives and deaths of 20th Century service casualties from Ridgewood and the area, the foundation for this book.